SATSVARUPA DASA GOSWAMI

VOLUME 2

WITH INTRODUCTORY ESSAYS BY
REV. JOHN ENDLER

GNP 2019

# ALSO BY SATSVARUPA DASA GOSWAMI

Srila Prabhupada Lilamrita (vols.)

Handbook for Krishna Consciousness

Readings in Vedic Literature: The Tradition

Speaks for Itself

Here is Srila Prabhupada

Prabhupada Nectar (vols.)

Srila Prabhupada Smaranam

Japa Reform Notebook

Qualities of Sri Krishna

Vaisnava Behavior

The Twenty-Six Qualities of a Devotee

Japa Walks/Japa Talks

Japa Transformations

Story of My Life (vols.)

Looking Back (vols.)

Every Day Just Write (vols.)

SATSVARUPA DASA GOSWAMI

A RETROSPECTIVE 1997-1998

VOLUME 2

GNP 2019

ISBN-13: 978-1-942770-97-8

Cover artwork by Satsvarupa dasa Goswami
Cover design and book layout by Caitanya Candrodaya das

*To His Divine Grace*
*A.C. Bhaktivedanta Swami Prabhupada*
*who initiated me and thousands of young men*
*and women into spiritual life, and directed us into*
*devotional service*
*to Lord Krishna.*

*Without his blessings,*
*my life would have no meaning.*

**Retrospective:** (from Latin *retrospectare*, "look back") When an artist is using the format of a retrospective, revisiting the entirety of his prolific, dense output over many years, displaying the evolution of his body of work.

# CONTENTS

# ACKNOWLEDGMENTS

Thank you all who helped:
Saci Suta, Press manager and donation to print the book;
Caitanya Candrodaya, layout, design, covers, proofreader;
Krishna Kripa, proofreader;
Guru dasa, proofreader and donation.

# AUTHOR'S PREFACE

In this second volume of the *Poems* (as in the first volume), I declare that my Krishna conscious writing shall be *ars poetica* (a poetic art) rather than a dogmatic catechism. In the rough draft of *Volume One*, I even wrote the names of jazz musicians, but I later took them out when I made a vow in 2018 to not listen to jazz anymore. I retained, however, the spirit of improvisation and some "free writing."

The poems in these two volumes were written over twenty years ago. I rediscovered them in rereading, where I found them fresh and as good as anything I could write today. I continue the format of placing an introductory essay to each volume of *Every Day, Just Write* poetry by Rev. John Endler, clarifying the theme of the volume and inviting the audience to read the entire *EJW* series on my website.

John thinks that the poetry herein was written twenty years ahead of its time, and likens it to spoken word poems being performed by young writes before large audiences at events called poetry slams. I have seen and heard these poetry slam performances, and I like being included in their company.

Ultimately, I am simply trying to follow in the footsteps of my spiritual master, A. C. Bhaktivedanta Swami Prabhupada. I am presenting old wine in new bottles. I hope that the reader of this volume will find it accessible and entertaining, and that it will bring them closer to Krishna consciousness.

*Om tat sat*
Satsvarupa dasa Goswami

# INTRODUCTION

To enter the second volume of Satsvarupa dasa Goswami's *Poems: A Retrospective* is to leave home for a risky adventure across the vast terrain of the soul. Significantly, all but one of the *Every Day, Just Write* instalments collected here has been written in the solitude of Ireland. From Satsvarupa Maharaja's residence in Geaglum in the North to Wicklow in the South, these become the *bhajana kutirs* of an author pursuing life in devotion to Radha-Govinda, the Supreme Person and His eternal Consort, Herself the embodiment of love and beauty. Lest one assume that the solitary is one of stasis, beware: the reader will quickly discover that geographical stability never implies a provincialism of the heart and soul. On the contrary, one discovers that it is the case that the deepest wells of the spirit have been plumbed within the hidden environs of a cloister, a monastic cell or the *bhajana kutir* of Satsvarupa Maharaja. How true it is that the window of such a cell, or in the case of this author, the window within a tiny writing shed, will cast the writer's gaze upon a world far beyond that which can be seen by mundane vision. This volume of poetry will transport the reader to places far and wide, deep and hidden, as Satsvarupa Maharaja pursues his distinctive vocation as disciple of A. C. Bhaktivedanta Swami Prabhupada within the Gaudiya Vaisnava tradition.

I would suggest that in this volume of *Every Day, Just Write's* collected poetry, the twentieth-fifth instalment of this series itself, *The Ocean and the*

*Desert,* stands as both the theological and artistic centerpiece. Within *The Ocean and the Desert,* a singular contemplative mood arises, shaped by the *lectio divina* practice of meditative and contemplative reading. The volume further features Satsvarupa Maharaja's sustained meditation upon the *Nectar of Devotion,* Srila Prabhupada summary study of Rupa Goswami's definitive work devotional service, the *Bhakti-rasamrta-sindhu.* With the reading of this magisterial text, the author begins to poetically share his reflections upon the worship of his beloved Deities, Radha-Govinda. These meditations themselves become a significant feature of the unfolding *Every Day, Just Write* series.

For this reader, the *Nectar of Devotion* study and the emerging *puja* meditations become the connective tissue that unifies these *Every Day, Just* Write volumes. While this devotional reading may begin in *The Ocean and the Desert,* its presence will be felt throughout the writing of the *Every Day, Just Write* volumes gathered here. Undoubtedly, the geographical stability attained at this point in Satsvarupa Maharaja's life provides deeper clarity regarding his particular vocation, as one who pursues devotional service in solitude. With the first volume of these collected poems, the author embarked upon a challenging process of discernment to understand his place within a religious institution shaped by a commitment to preaching. At this time, in these volumes of this literary series, clarity is attained and a greater confidence is displayed.

What constitutes preaching? This is the question which animates the creative process at work within Satsvarupa Maharaja. Ultimately, a powerful conviction arises gently but definitively that his writing from solitude is a practice of surrender to Sri Krishna, and as such, the reader may understand that this is a truly sublime manner of preaching. As writing is a form of surrender, so too is the chanting, reading and *puja* – his worship of the Deity form of Radha-Govinda.

In this way, *Every Day, Just Write* may alternatively be titled, *Every Day, Just Surrender,* with the diverse artistic practices themselves demonstrating to the reader the *ars poetica* of surrender.

Satsvarupa dasa Goswami is a man of many voices. Certainly, in reading the poetry of these *Every Day, Just Write* volumes, one readily hears these voices, distinct yet complementary. At times contemplative, the poetry gathered here emerges from the spontaneity of the free-write, improvisational manner of expression, itself a hallmark of Satsvarupa Maharaja's writing. Crossing the customary boundaries between genres, his poetry moves with divergent rhythms. Ever playful with syntax and grammar, the author makes bold use of the page itself to configure and re-arrange the very structure of received poetry. Form and theme compliment one another as Satsvarupa Maharaja ranges from devotional meditations to autobiography and beyond, but always ultimately directing the reader to Radha-Govinda, who Themselves represent the spiritual and aesthetic foundation of this work. The reader will find these poems challenging and accessible as Satsvarupa Maharaja shapes a body of poetry spoken through his distinct voices, joined in a singular artistic pursuit to speak with authenticity and integrity of the beauty of Radha-Govinda.

As a *sannyasi,* Satsvarupa Maharaja has embraced the renounced order of life for over forty years. Within the Gaudiya Vaisnava tradition, the *sannyasi* is a traveling preacher, who moves from town to town spreading the *sankirtana* message of Sri Caitanya Mahaprabhu, in the footsteps of the great *acaryas*. But within the *sannyasa* tradition, there is also the *ksetra sannyasi,* one who remains in a particular place in this renounced order of life. Satsvarupa Maharaja is such a *sannyasi.* While dwelling in solitude, still he lends his voice to the preaching mission of his spiritual master through the beauty of his artistry. From Ireland, the breadth of Satsvarupa dasa Goswami's artistic vision challenges boundaries of every kind to lead his readers to new horizons of love and service. This volume of the *Collected Poems of Every Day, Just* is a remarkable gift to those who are seeking such love offered by the mercy of Radha-Govinda, and within these pages treasures are to be found.

Rev. John F. Endler

# CHAPTER ONE - THE LORD REIGNETH

Ireland, U.S., Caribbean, December 3–22, 1997

"The Lord reigneth..."
*Psalm 97:1*

Volume Twenty of Satsvarupa dasa Goswami's's literary project, *Every Day, Just Write*, entitled "*The Lord Reigneth*," will chronicle the author's journey from Ireland, to the United States, the island nation of Trinidad and Tobago, and the South American republic of Guyana. As in his prior trip to Europe, these extensive travels will provide disciples of Satsvarupa Maharaja an opportunity to visit with their beloved spiritual master. Similarly, Satsvarupa Maharaja undertakes this journey in the same mood as when he embarked for the European continent: to provide spiritual care to those for whom he provides spiritual guidance.

It goes without saying that such a journey is not simply one that traverses the vast geographical distance between Ireland and the Caribbean. This is a journey in which culture, climate, and politics will be significantly different; indeed Geaglum, Northern Ireland and Guyana are in many ways worlds apart, but as we shall see, possess a common bond as they are regions that have both seen political turmoil. The departure begins with the author's reflections upon an abiding reading companion, Thomas Merton, with whom the author has ongoing "conversations," if you will, regarding a shared monastic vocation as well as shared concerns and reflections about contemporary monastic reforms. Opening poetic offerings include two lovely pieces inspired by the African-American spirituals "Down by the Riverside" and "Swing Low, Sweet Chariot." With this, Satsvarupa Maharaja departs Ireland and begins the long trip to the Caribbean. Following an intermediary stop in the author's native New York, with an opportunity to visit disciples and friends alike, the reader is subsequently transported to Trinidad.

The pattern of life in Trinidad will perhaps call to mind for the reader the early volumes of *Every Day, Just Write's* poetry in which India is the setting. Satsvarupa Maharaja describes in detail the social setting of the temple, the taxing climate, and the austerities of being far from home. At the same time, there is joy to be discovered in reunions with disciples and the practice of Krishna consciousness in this setting. What becomes clear is that though global communities may possess a host of cultural particularities, still devotional service to the Lord is shaped by a standard of practice that transcends nation and culture, and holds all devotees as one within the worldwide household established by His Divine Grace A.C. Bhaktivedanta Swami Prabhupada. This entry confirms this very affirmation: "Loud music, reggae or whatever. I will chant my *japa* anyway." (*Part Two*, p. 19)

This reader has discovered that Satsvarupa Maharaja's time in Guyana serves as the centerpiece of this volume. A fascinating nation located on the northern coast of South America, Guyana is the home to predominantly two large communities, an Indian citizenry and Guyanese of African descent. As the author discovers after his arrival, the nation is in a precarious state in anticipation of an upcoming national election. This mood will provide a backdrop to Sastvarupa Maharaja's time in Guyana, but amazingly his prose and poetry possess a steadiness in the midst of uncertain days. The title to this volume is wonderfully inspired by a neighbor of the residence in which the author is residing, who owns a truck painted with the biblical verse, "The Lord reigneth". This vehicle is actually proclaiming a profound theological truth: at all times, everywhere, certainly in tumultuous Guyana, the Lord reigns. Certainly, this truck would daily bring a smile to our author's face.

Following the election, the situation becomes uncertain and dangerous for Hindu citizens, whose political party been victorious, triggering political violence toward this community. Under these circumstances, Satsvarupa Maharaja plans his departure. In the final section of the volume, the author creates in his writing the slowing of time, and the reader experiences this keen slowing of the pace of the narrative, which makes the uncertainty of the drive to the airport very palpable. Whether it be traffic jams, signs of violence, an irascible customs agent, or delays at the airport gate, each step proceeds ever so slowly. In the midst of this, Satsvarupa Maharaja spots a weathered "I Love Guyana" billboard which stands in great contrast to the political unrest in the capital city, Georgetown.

The volume concludes with a host of rapidly sketched drawings made by Satsvarupa Maharaja as he sits waiting for his flight to depart. The drawings themselves convey the restless energy caused by these terrible circumstances. At last, the flight does depart and with thoughts of the neighbor's biblically-themed truck, the author now peacefully departs for his next destination.

*God and The River*

There's a way out we all know –
don't let anyone hear this. It's loud I
know. You just be alone in your shed.
Those were good days all alone
you could even shout out there and
no one would bother. Woodshed.
Now you go to live among people in
crowded built up houses.

    I say okay I'll use secret
methods I'll live in inner
private...I'll write it and send it
    to you
    this way.

Old man river keeps rolling and
seeing the tragedy and wasted lives,
    he don't do nothing about it
he jes' keeps rolling along.

    The indifferent nature of the
big mighty
    who just keeps rolling
like Time itself,
    but the Lord in the heart is
not so indifferent.

    He's in each one, He...
    I don't know nuthin'.
And you wind up in jail.

Don't protest man's inhumanity to
man? I protest I speak by being a devotee
of Krishna and preaching among the ignorant
    starting with myself.
I don't know anything of –
please give me the right

to know You
I'm tired of these doubts
I want the blessed space –
But you've got to earn it.

Dear Krishna may I be one centered
in all I do
I too have some pains
but I like the way You limit me
cripple me
this body is no good
finally.
But for now let me
use it for You
in reading and writing
on this day I go forth
in Your service.

*pp. 2–4*

❧ ❧ ❧

*Down by The Riverside*
Let's go down by the riverside
It's a good time we all can have
Sing it's all right.
But I want to be religious
I want to see God in all things
in the company of His sincere
devotees.

Am I allowed
another day
to be Yours in this way
Let me try it and be true
in this world of false
well it's Yours too this world
Lord
I don't mock it as Nothing,
but You know what I mean.

There's another world,
*sanatana*, millions of them,
and I wish to go there
if I can kick off
all that clings to me here.
With Your help that's
possible.

Down at the river we'll
hold *kirtana, prasadam*
the Indian way in Slovenia
the transcendental way of Narada
in Ohio
    the triumph.

Down by the river of the
self I'll cry and dance
and play my horn I'll do the dance
and I'll sing
in the company of Your devotees
is all I've known for
all these years You've
protected me
    let me thank You
for that protection
that wall around my life
bullet proof is the
soul and even this body
of flesh You have allowed
to roam
    please take me home.
I'd love to be with You and Balarama
clean me up so I can
serve with bliss
and no complaints
menial servant
loving all duties
and persons.

Give me strength to finish
these days in this body
and the next and
right now I stand up and sing
my praise to You
    I always want to be
    a servant of Krishna
    and all others
down by the riverside...

*pp. 4–6*

⁂

*Looking Out A Frost-Melting Window*
(In Dublin at a desk, facing a frost-melting window...a busy town instead of the quiet lake)
So, you get in tune / will anyone stop me?
Take off your knit hat and
see. I am alone-master.
An angry man is nevertheless and artist
I don't know what you mean.
Well it's like this – everyone has to go
to work. But I don't.
Sign boards – guy who could kill
you, dissolute young beauty-
woman. They flash by so
fast I can't see, and don't look
anyway from back seat.

There's an ensemble, there are
millions of offices and schools and
people on the streets and dreamers
hard workers, swearers
priests too and people on the Dole
plenty of them
    in the pubs even this early?
Well, soon...
What about the priests and the
congregation? Are you one of them?

Are you an angel of mercy,
Our Lady, Sacred Heart or
the Vedic counterpart?
Yes I'm the
    sitting apart.

I'm the ancient one, rune, the
digestion pancake *muni*
the critic of all Godbrothers' lectures
the shorthand clerk and
short-order cook-poet.
What else? Wry master
pose novelist. Shivering
my boots...

So I say: Just put me on the
road pointing the direction of
American Airlines to Trinidad.
It's all within ISKCON. And what
we all do as a matter of fact.
It's a cold day. I am in
this body. Hey Hari Hari
Krishna. There is no lion here just
a toothless old hyena,
baby polecat, looks both
skinny and fat in belly like
the actor poorly cast who
played Gaurakisora dasa Babaji in
the film.

Why are you self-centered?
Because I can't see out the window.
Because I don't know anyone
else?

Why is he angry? Because he
said everyone screwed up his people.
Why am I blowing it? Am I?
Is this the police station? Do you

have my money? Can I be
safe from the fear of my
dreams – so they don't become
my flesh reality? Alfred
E. Newman? Prufrock,
Milquetoast, Mr. Magoo
Mr. Peepers, angry
Archie Shepp, James Dean,
Sonny Rollins, Tommy Oakland, me
treading on snow on my own
with four hundred in the bank 1964...
Take your choice
okay I'm on no subway, don't have to
be. Take it easy in a heated room. Don't
    talk to women
or anyone, kids, dogs, no
shed, no grass walk
just this place and one meal after
another it's called solitary
confinement.

Bitter trial
heavy storm could knock
out all lines
    drop from the sky
pray to God, that's it
now you're going. Tell your
readers to pin up their clothes
in curlers, Pray to God
kiss the Commander Good Night
pray to God.
I meant it
except I can't pay
attention. Grow
close. Ask no one
forget what you need to say.
This day your illusory
freedom you give to God
in heart

I will read the *sastra*
I do obey the cap'n
Because I want to
That's it man,
    from the wounded
lion and listen to
    affecting me influencing me
in the soul
    child cries...
(When the frost clears
you'll see row houses.)

*pp. 8–12*

⁂

*Swing Low*
(Alone at last, I hear a train horn, but otherwise, a lonely "spiritual" song in your head and blood.)
Swing low you do expect some
simple rescue at the end
Sweet chariot, sweet Jesus,
    Old Testament
            I don't know
            a guide will catch you up
it'll be unexpected just hang on
like the baby monkey.
But seriously. We got to work in
this life and be a man to accept what
comes. You cry to God almighty
God sweet Krishna
    for central secret of existence
no matter what the material
world deals.

It'll be / Hare Krishna Hare Krishna the
empty room and the empty heart
chanting his mantras
Don't know where he lost
it, somewhere

But he's got it too
old man you a laugh
I gotta say.

I looked over yonder and
what did I see? Not much –
the sun! So bright I couldn't
look at it, going down over row
houses in Dublin.

Coming for to carry me home
it's good
it's good
to have the time and not blow
it in the extreme, even to
have this peace
I blow low and thank You –
My spiritual master
is calling me that much
I know. Be grateful in
whatever form
that chariot appears.

*pp. 14–16*

❦ ❦ ❦

*Listening Alone*
I'm on my way wild Irish
rose, I'm taking you to where I'll go
listen in
this the time
short take.

Hey let me stay back I'll roam the rooms
saying God God quiet God
I didn't have to decide
it was decided for me.
Listen friends we can find peace
just check in with me
I've a trivial mind

and can't work courageously (he said
that before)
    now the window is clear enough –
    there is plenty out there
    but if you stay home
    there's plenty here too.

Hum Hare Krishna I'll be
listening to the bonk
    in my head.

If I could...he was
telling how the *gopis* and
cows and everyone heard
the flute
    best of my day
Krishna's flute,
    *I* didn't hear it
but heard him say it,
picked up *Krishna* book in my hand
Satsvarupa dasa Adhikari typed it

That I could read too,
Bhagavan
    it can come alive
you know
    it can come to you.
So Krishna Krishna I want to
stay on target.
There's a bare bones approach
Hare Krishna Hare Krishna.
When Krishna plays His flute
the calves stopped sucking,
the *gopis* and demigods' wives
feel conjugal attraction,
and I listen to *that*
    oh my
please include me.

*pp. 16–18*

*Alone in The House*

I don't have much time before
they come in on me
    and ask what were you doing?

I'll say
    it was fun I walking home
from school and saw a girl and guy
    You mean the Ajamila scene
        this is 1997.
He's on his own / doesn't need you
he's on his own / listen he wants to
be
an innovator but you must do it
with your own voice
    who are you?
        New York?
        Dublin?
        a devotee of your master?
But you seem to be something else
I don't know a monk
can do this.

Sure he can it's called dovetailing.
He's on his own
he's on his own
what I thought...
Don't think
just write your Krishna conscious ode to
your own spurious
    seed given
    restrained
actually don't want sex don't
want to see Xmas bells and lights
    want to be here
    workout.

You are the one he met
on his way home

It was you he met
I like it rough too
a rough sound but
I am ordinary
    solo
    so
    moan
the way he chants and chants
cuts a ravine down
    (no Grand Canyon)
but down the spires
    they said.

He's a do-nothing
he's a non-manager he's
this and that told someone
"You've got to die"
    I never said that.
So in the history of ISKCON
the ball of yarn falls
across the floor batten
by a kitten.
All alone for just two
minutes and then where were you?
Is talking in his head
    fifty guys and girls no
    question of ever being alone.
The question is if he can
capture God
capture God
    with *bhakti*
*vairagya*
    not me he says.
But I want you to
I say / dear mind you SOB /
rough broom stick points
mind! You are the
rascal
    ferret you

You are my only way if
God is to take over.

Little Way my only hope
turtle pace
split
No harm intended
so easily we get cut
bland – enigmatic – mysterious
silent got nothing to say
but some stuff
    wants out with his own stuff.
Okay Okay
    I don't know if you'll be
agreeable, but I smiled
    and shut up
    now I'll try again.
My mom's not home.

I didn't cut anyone's throat
or mess myself up.
I drank a little water
and looked out
    and in
    afraid to dive
is there really an abyss?
Like mystics say
or Krishna for preachers only.

*pp. 18–21*

❖ ❖ ❖

*Nobody Knows*
Nobody knows the troubles I've seen,
just because I'm one and each is one.
That's the way it is. Well brother
I don't mean to say I've had it so hard
    his yoke Jesus's

is easy if you take it
but again
    it's a Cross.
O it's a Bathos he said – almost
Who's to say?
I say it's individual threshold
of pain and sorrow you can't
say for me.

    Or the doctor or
shrink or priest or Hare Krishna man says
    You just got a case of
hepatitis lad,
    a little karma in
your row to hoe.
Don't bother us about it
pay at the desk.

We don't want to see you
even frown, why you
wear those baggy pants if you're
a *sannyasi* and that silly grin?
I just want my breakfast on time
hot porridge
    sorrow
don't talk you got none
at all.

But the dog cried and whined
at the front door.
Don't publish this just
get outta the way and
give us
    *Krishna* book and *Bhagavad-gita*
and Hare Krishna mantras.
Don't sob...And so they
talked back and forth in
the cold light front of
the house

Bathos or tragic
who's to say.

But I got my beads
and counting on my master
  for sure.

*pp.32–33*

⁂

*Life of a Devotee*
Now you please move along
Things and people are favorable is
your astrology
  if you go South it's disaster,
Be Freemins
  be mint tea.

Now go East to Krishna and it's
good go North, place a pic
of Radha-Govinda in your alcove,
and you'll be okay.
He's got hoarse voice.
The kids in this house are back
I heard they have chickenpox
  I want to tell you we yearned
to be free of the Navy and go it
  drank liquor sentimental.

Life of a devotee – busy you
don't know, you think we're a cult
There's nothing like that
Swamiji tried he's got his
own voice. The contributor-
poet said I sent three
poems and they only printed
two who the hell they think
they are s.o.b.
white men...
I said two out of three ain't bad

and maybe they were right calm
down. Stay under my wing
    Your wing?

Now waiting on meals. My Krishna
my Radha. I want out
screamed the man.
I take it a good way
they mean well
It's got to be a pleasing way
too remember...

What's free-writing? They're
talking back and forth. They
are bare elemental no nonsense,
(to put it mildly and politely)
"Honest to God" the reverend
says that maybe he doesn't even believe
in God. Call that honest?

Honest – I surrender
I know the way is thorny
I seek ease and the
kids need love and nourishment.
I'm selfish when she said she's
going to India I didn't even hear
it and said a little later something
polite as if I cared – all
you care is your own trip.
Such a selfish non-lover.

But Doc you does move
me to hear *your* anger and
hurt. I think it's unusual
a lion roars in the bush
we are running out of time – but
I'm scared of "bad" neighborhoods
me a white Hare Krishna
with a limp of left foot no money

sometimes naked sixty years old
in my – dreams.
Oh, those are just dreams.
Well call it what you will.
Bombs explosions he's
what? Unquenchingly brutal –
steal those words those
tires, slash with knife...
All right I'm here to calm
you down as long as I can
speak what Krishna says that's
the qualification of a speaker
really
he's got to just say what
the book says and have the guts
for that
    if he can *feel* the
truth the book speaks
    what Krishna speaks
then he's doing okay.
What hurts is when he
doesn't believe he's bored
he's out of joint and passes that
onto us –
I'm sorry / or he's so
blind autocrat dictator just
rams it down us.

Give us sweet Krishna speaking
from serious person not afraid
to repeat the same examples and
he's not bored and he's doing
okay with examples from his
own life.
    That'll be good for them.

Now I say this was fun
to be with you
veteran rovers / the high is claiming

you've got to eat and sleep and
pack your bags for Saint Thomas
stac-cat-o.
English and French and toe-tap
my own voice, dove
    crow
ant, mouse, scurrying
elephant /
the devotee in me says
okay I was happy to do it
for you, thank me, say hello to B'way
    in Amsterdam
        spare me from the
aches / and remind me of my master's
care for us
    protected I live in there
thanks.

*pp. 37–41*

*An Early Evening Prayer*
(A romantic mood...for a person about to travel, he knows not what will happen. He has to put his trust in airlines, but it really means trust in God within. If one could love.)
There's a way they tell it
so, I'm here to tell you.

I want to be with my spiritual master, and that's the inner way. It's scary sometimes
and I'm never the controller,
sometimes a weeper,
a whimper
    can't even reach up to
    hold His hand.

Now don't be blue about it. Tell
whoever you meet the universe

is happy. That's a Krishna conscious version.
Tell them as they look at you
smiling or frowning, there's a
truth in every Sanskrit word
of *Vedas* and we must believe
and here's why (briefly)
and here's what Swamiji
said.
Here is what I learned
"But what do you feel?"
That's not for you to know,
not required
it's my dark night
when those dreams come
and I'm helpless.

And those doubts – I'm more
aware of this fight that's
going on. Yeah you bastards.
This is the way. We're talking
on a Thursday night in row
houses in Dublin, this one
containing me, digit
digiter heart
    beat one of countless.
There's only one fish flapping
    you know...
So my prayer is for attention
and surrender to sweet will
sweet names
Radha and Krishna festival
far away like a star
I can so close when
I fold my hands and
pray pray
    *nama* heaven.

*pp. 44–46*

❖ ❖ ❖

*Swing Low (take two)*

(Want our chariot to swing not too low over the
Atlantic, but when it's time to go – as Krishna likes.
May He show me or not – may I hold onto His names –
sweet chariot.)
Swing-ing sweet Lord
I pray a fool I be
to carry me home.

You've sent trumpet call
ahead of You. You've sent
the messengers in many forms
sometimes a kick to
wake us
    like Indra as a
pig had to be.
On this day of December cold
I look over yonder and what
can I see without love anointed
eyes I see still Your
kindness in all You've given
especially the guidance of the
bona fide spiritual master.

Carry me. I'll ride –
but I'll work as You ask
work at it You said
to Arjuna bold – it's
already been done by Me
but you've got to take
some credit
    And he fought.

Hare Krishna is the carrier
for souls like me
Detached and knowledge in Your
*sastra* / I'm just repeating
ripe harvest

frozen grapes
words that come, and we
love this world too much I guess.

Can we see it as Yours, as
full of lessons...the bad
says, "Get out, not fit to live"
and the good says it's God's –
this is just a little sample.

As sun rises on a dirty town
as in myself chest in
head there is not only blood
confusion and congestion
    but a spirit of yearning
to go home to you
    my Lord.

*pp. 53–55*

*Something Sweet, Something Tender*
(What should you be doing? Chant?
Answer a letter? Can you write a poem...)
I saw a man in my mind he said
something sweet and tender
should be offered to God.
"Oh, why do you always talk of
Bhagavan?" I said I'm a
Prabhupada man.

He said you are true enough,
but I'm sad to be in New York
City, but you'll regret it. East
Side River, old roads, green point blacks.
The young woman is conducting traffic
in yellow raincoat – telling the
kids they could cross safely and
waving to the cars – to stop?

I like her very much. She
was a doing a good thing. Even
if she gets paid for it.
I didn't envy her.

Well tender doesn't mean
you have to be soupy you can
be soapy in Dr. Bronner's
but that's just the body.

Lord he's coming down with
hepatitis and gangrene and cancer,
he actually died, he was only
fifty-three years old – do you know
him? He's gone now. He
went to Vrndavana and left there.

I said, "Take me to Krishna-Balaram
Mandir at my end." Something
sweet and tender even in death
you better be that way to others.
Not just yourself.

Oh, I will, give me teeth and Tums
I saw the eight-week-old baby
sleeping peacefully in his bed,
he sighed and heaved little
breaths one after another while
Madhu played the accordion which
the baby liked and slept through.

Good life to you –
he mostly sleeps and feeds.
May he not have a sister who
beats him up every day or
an abusive father
    yea Lord it's a
tough life this here...
This is the day I

was born in 1939
I think the artists and devotees
who remembered to be loving
and that's the way.

*pp. 66–68*

⁂

*Day Time in Jackson Heights*
Here we were in New York
there's no subway in this
room, Ron Padget...
Mickey Mouse. Donald
was taking photos in
the sky screen theater
yesterday.

Now in New York
no mezzanine, jazz club
drink with ice cubes
no restaurant.
Then what? Shaven-headed
girl writes me she's
happy in temple, wants me
to initiate, but some days
the cookies burn.

There's the city I cringe,
and Madhu's going busking at
42nd Street subway!
with melodeon. He's
going got guts
    "You mad bastard!"
"Hare Krishna!"
Oh, and I'm not able to even
open the window,
and I've got my pinafore
stuck with safety pins and

my baby smile
my henry ho my
no TV
no football or eggs
mushroom.
How can we be blissful?
Lovey-dovey
no mushy but yes
happy
Having come to this
miserable and temporary
office

There's no way Krishna can
be attained but by
direct attack
direct action
    military assault
with love
    in *vaidhi* steps.
The night has a thousand
eyes
    "I's Nancy," said
the ugliest of three sisters
my mom was
    pretty?

She is dead?
Am I dead yet?
A skeleton can dance
a white man can
be a Haribol
    machete-bearing
Big guy says give me
your dough and your life
you mad bastard
    chopsticks
hen knows.

Don't be defensive.
Don't be in Maya.
Alone monk alone
joy
    stick with Krishna
ha ha it's just funny
old music and sad windup
toy
    no, it's good it's best
quality.

The night has
the has a gold
cat in backyard dead
gold leaves
    Jack's Heights
fenced in
    no flower pot on
window sill.
I can't write to heart's
content
it's true you love
me:
Black guy wearing
a beret hiring sky cap to
carry his electric guitar
blond white dark glasses
"wife" with him –
    I saw that
yesterday
epiphany.

*pp. 68–72*

⁂

*Early Morning Room*
(You want religious, you want straight, well
man...make it.)
There is the way to step into it

stars twinkling
there's no way I can con-
ceive.
I'm not blasphem' we're
seeing Krishna in many places
crips and licks and all
you see is also in it
    that's the exciting
prospect.

But you dear friend most
is Krishna pointing to His heart
with garland and *dhoti*
He's the one but not
    just in a form you
can contain
    His personal form
I don't know what I say
just recite.

Kitty cat black and white
nine mice he caught
let them out
bought me boots
we'll go to Trinidad
on Election Day of Guyana
I hope there's no trouble.
  But you can't expect all
smooth sailing. Just see
what Prema went through
to deliver her child. She
relaxed when she heard
her prayer had reached me.
  Life or death as long as
my guru knows it's me
it's a wild way out
how you agreed to be
a guru and you sit on the
floor.

It's the style in N.Y.C.
mode he said and
tell me where religion
fixed your hurts I
said I used to eat
only orange juice from Bodega
and pills for pep
no love (what's
that do you know)
no sex – and now
really NO
no trusted friend, reader
disciple,
    fun.

Well now it's getting late
indeed but we
are merry prepared to
go home
    to our route
please protect us even
in death hour so
we can remember
You.

Eventually we'll be soon
by Krishna's grace.
Hieroglyphic
Milosz Vietnam
now 1997 Bala and
others answering letters.
Geez
geez I thought you could do
better. Bring it together
it's nice with thee, and Monk I'm happy
in my seat
    that's all (for now).

*pp. 79–82*

*Don't Put Down This Music*

(Hurry get it in)
Music in any language...They put each
other...
I'm in charge of my own possessions. I
don't know the tune, do you?

Simple he was a lyrical and consummate player
get your own
a lyric a flower
I'm distracted man in a shirt
    and chest.
Just listen don't insist on your
own draw when words
collide.

Al fine tree ain't direct in
bird pad
oh it's pumpkin
Innisfree
despair.

He's a man from comfrey
to interrupt the genius
    Coleridge
he's an integer non-scientist
*burfy*-maker.
He's a thin lad from
Shropshire
    I can't spell
ink on my finger
he won't say
how it is
to others that's the thing
if you can.

Krishna consciousness is the joy fest
on the River Swanee

way down
it's transcendental to that
and I can't reach out
    above it.

To reach my Lord in
the temple on a Sunday
*kirtana* I prefer to be
here.

There the self he can
revolt
    Krishna consciousness.
Don't put down white men
black
    yellow
this dissonance
is body
skin disease.

My words are yours
trade force
trade horns, cars, and
hoards
    yo-yo Greek park
department supervisor
Moe's Mag's
escape the joint
he's afraid to
say what he was as
    a teenager.
The hiding heart
    Hare
    Krishna down in
the Swanee
    chest of Lord
Albert
Krishna is Lord of all
and I will read

you will see man
I promise to be good
one of these days get back to a
sonorous ridge.
Would you like me
that way?
Yes, I guess so just
be real.

*pp. 86–89*

⁂

*Ramblin'*

Yes, I know you
I remember you
you have no malice
I have not malice.
Let's make peace.
We may have warred
you too have been wronged
me too
But I know Krishna for
example.
I know Krishna and you
remind me
rambling is
okay permissible it can be
You got beat up
once by mean dudes and
you went to cops who
said, "Get out of town by tonight
or we'll kill you."

I wandered, he caused
so much trouble for others
forgive us God we will
tell the truth and
beauty of it despite
our woes

See good in others
rhythm and blues
new sounds *avant*
Krishna conscious *garde*
and good cheer (and you help)
I'll go down there to
primitive lands risking my
headaches
    to deliver Krishna consciousness
although sometimes doubt
the reality of all
    I don't know it
said it so many times
    seek a new way
(you help me of that too)
Old-time's sake, gray
haired, with paunches and
lines under eyes,
my disciples and dear
me with upper and
lower bridges still
I got
    chops
Oh, the language of Krishna
consciousness is
so nice
    synch, rise, be there
advocate Swami in '66
in '96 and say he taught and
they smile
    Krishna / no Mayavadis
keep going with your
rasslin' with your mind
wear your Nrsimhadeva medal
keep on giving to
others the benefit
of *harinama* and *prasadam*
with faith it'll do good.

See it in ISKCON as
helping all people
this movement
I'm yet another Swami
through the airport
arriving
    hey 'mon, look it's a white man
Haribol on his way
to Guyana on their
election day.

Go *by* Paramatma's house
all right place,
I'll carry you and look
for the best
and seek the sign
Seek the sign
Krishna's in the heart
keep away from Maya
ramblin' in the devotee's
backyard
and on *harinama*.

*pp. 93–96*

*Free*
(Hey man is this reggae hip hop rap or what and what is a perfect guru doing listening? We cleaned your room and found your dream tape under your pillow.)
Up and down the scales merry boys
you mean like the ones
    the short pants you can buy
black and white boys
    playing in water
buy in Carib tourists
buy in Carib tourist's bar
your own trip
    frees up the

adrenaline.
He's happy or not?
He's free
    he sez and we say
(they're all laughing at me
in my freedom.)
Make a tape
of this in the...
    me in field
    no shirt
white haired.

Old guy where is he?
My old disciple
    old flame.
Here's the key. Give it back
pastiche pasta
I saw it in your kitchen
your noodles hard and
button: "Mind your own business."
I saw scar face
doodled haired Negress
Trinidad talkin' captain of ship
Good view of Long Island.
    Cigar smoke ashes
M. broke spring on
melodeon
I know
those days sit on floor
and eat breakfast before
you take off.

No freedom from God
and limitations
toy trumpet
toy devotee
a pet cat.
Don't interrupt
he's in the bafroom

he's free of dat
the cat ate mouse
He's about a mouthwash
Gimme on my birfday
honors, towels a
straw ring
a couch I can carry
a toy trumpet
    wood recorder
free astrol
free of Brudders.
Give right to preach
rest on top of bed
fan
extra blanket.
Okay I'll give you all that you
don't be sad
    be wise to minimize.
I'm tired of this –
I lectured
as a good Bg. Servant
forgive me for all that.

And so Satsfer ate a big lunch
of boiled in *ghee* gobbers
of dipped in wax honey
ferns of local radish
and horse chestnuts
He ate in chompers?
and grinned
he was sorry
ran home to safety of
Father Bear
    Krishna
    and devotee
who knows better
can't *do* better (not
unless *makes* you free.)

*pp. 111–14*

*Bright Trinidad*

(Sunset. Cooler. Tanager and sparrow [I name them] and dog barking. Can you be true to your own? To whom do you belong?)
This way please the workers
comin' home
    to chicken no not in
this house
    non
    violent.
Beep bop beep bop
this way pleeze
you're takin' us...

Don't change the schedule on
me. We want it on time
please bright miss
    bright sun
the baby's name is
Jahnava
    I thought it was a boy
Chinese,
    forgive me.

My mistake I thought you
were a Hare Krishna monk
    I am.
Clever asinine
I today prepared
a *Gita* section
a humble speech
and ate chunks of *papaya*.

Squeak, squeak I want to
be alone
    they did the same
please leave this room
alone.

Please say
the train's comin'
the booze hound will
stay away
    the riff is the
same
    all the same.

Krishna is the cloud
is mercy
    jute field I'm all
alone in my ville
the book I eked
out
paeon
    to the Lord
    and guru
    Prabhupada.

I heard it wuz your birthday
I heard it was too late
we wanted to congregate to
see your dance
    sorry I danced
already on the wall
no reruns.

Bright T'dad
birds chirping in tropics
they've got good whistles
out the window
really
singing.

Like that whale in movie
black and white – I can
almost see this
insistent warbling yellow
tanager

He's joining got his own
song and beat.

All right this way / bright
day hazing out getting dimmer
and cooler under the mosquit
nets so I hope you can
digest your fruit.

We didn't expect you to dance with
a big girl just tell
us some Vedic truth behave
beehive. Trinkle trinkle
it's all right.

Now it's almost night
mosquits coming in
the open slats
greet their whine by
hiding out and keep moving
Bright Mis
bright knock on your door
Reunion of the best
players put his little
foot in thick socks
he's a happy
    but death bound
taking stealing a little
time before they say
That's it.
My man is out there straightening it out with the
temple president so we follow my way on the birthday.
Early as possible give the lecture in bright T'dad. Look
up and here *guru-tattva*.
It's a treat / there are
bad things happened there I know
but I am emphasize
    bright side
    train leaves and we are

on it to heaven Krishnaloka
It's a solid way *bhakti*
only. And we don't
get kicked out.
    Math Art Lit
    all allowed.

*pp. 120–24*

⁂

*His Footsteps in Sand of Juhu*
(He remembers a great one and I can do. Even while I hear the concert of dawn chickens in Trinidad.)

{Please don't interrupt or say this
isn't allowed / don't ring
my bell.}

Beard and hat – don't cross out
anything it's all allowed
we remember (bite mosquitoes)
we remember our guru walking on
sand of you know where
    Juhu
    yahu.
We were there with him.
I'm tired of proclo-
    mations
Lord Caitanya came with His and Srila Prabhupada
came with his
    – I prefer to say he
saved me.
And little ditty we accept
today. We like the toad
face horny eyebrows
the frog crawling up the
wall.
He sounded crazy they say
he used to be pretty

and orderly. We *like*
what happened to him
He improved as far
as we're concerned.

Yes students we are here
today on SDG's
    belly-button birth
Day
    freed
fried
    dumplings
puss puppies.
Fog horns they knew
what I like
    dumplings mixed
in cream
        deep
    *lassies –*
*lassies?*

The dog-faced whimper
the happy day
    we saved this for you,
junior.

    We know you like your
spiritual master quite a lot.
What's that?

A remnant of his tooth.
How do I know it's real?
How do *we* know *you are*
real?
Because I say so Look
into my mouth and see
all the worlds in
microcosm
    smell Aghasura.

Serious he came to NY and flew
out no one got to see
him.
    Here's an apron
    here's your mommy
    calm down
please.

Yes, we are happy son, that you attained guru-ship and survived so many years.

I told you we gave you a good frame to fill out and I watched you like a hawk.

(My dad said.)

Each one makes a tribute in his own way. Don't stop me. Let me say it. See how ink goes on page, and color and a bow saws,
    but some things bring pain
I know
cock-a-doodle-doo.

He was well known for funny
dissonant things and dropping the extra
step in the dark.
He was known for kindness
to all beings and not liking to go
out to preach. He did it by
writing (he hoped)
    he took a ride, he lay down in the back seat
    and dreamt
        of birds over Havana
        all whales happy and the
other creatures
    at least humans became
devotees / stopped bad.

Dream ISKCON at least let
him live his days.
O Prabhupada today we

honor you honest smart true
repeat your words best
of all we you alone
    are our master/take
us by hand/in your footsteps
in sand of Juhu I said
    repeat it best my own way.

*pp. 132–35*

✦ ✦ ✦

*Lonesome Road*

(Hurry. You went to *mangala-arati* and
*tulasi-puja* so you're entitled to this...)

& That lonesome road is long
and besot with fat frogs,
"Excuse me sir" – he wouldn't
budge and I would not step on him.

I am entitled to freedom – it's
not whimsical the ISKCON
preacher said Lord Krishna's *lilas*
are structured and complex
not whimsical.

Well I says to meself
what's wrong with whimsy –
    isn't is the same as
spontaneous?

Blow the wind breezes
clacking the bamboos
please tell us how Krishna
kidnapped Rukmini
What do you know of it?
From *Krishna* book here

in Trinidad.
I'll tell listen y'all
this is the great tale
He smiled so happy said,
"It's one of my favorite
stories."

Play it once a rendition
of the material make
it new. That
lonesome road...
Each has to trod
she said, "But isn't association (big word)
always needed
Is it the same as social
pressure?"

I was making good sense, and
that's okay too. So, I'll
tell you the road is loaded
with potholes
    chickens and dogs barking at
all sides
mayor and police
and drunken machetes.

But you got to make
it. I'll be with you
but speed up. Look
at your words. Breakfast
of fruits on the way.
Crown prince says don't
give me such a big pillow
to sit on.
"Here's a smaller"
No, I'm all right and
he wouldn't even sit
on the floor.

Because he's got a lonesome
road. Fat breasts of
the male *pujaris* – I
don't like to see
It's mine and his
each one on his/her – its own
seat
Froggy
a mismatch
a pap-aya
an elf
    rode
    tan
    tan
    it seems the same.
There's only one way he said to ride the only way is the
hometown back road, and you'll be in good company.

Good cheer, but the last
mile or so will be
    like Pandavas get tired
one by one fall
    a dog...
    you'll have to see hell...
you go back to Godhead
trying your best
and then it's up to Krishna to
see good in raise you
if He chooses.
Look down that road
maybe life after life
and beg the Lord Please take
me along it to Your
service. There is the *going*.

*pp. 146–49*

*Late Morning T'dad Mind*
Georgia on my mind
now's the day. Wind is playing

I was lying silent on my bed
and said instead
there's no way but the
day is goin' fast.

You're the nicest person I met.
The accordion sounds out
the slat windows of the
sun-beating-down temple
in Longdenville
white egret I see you
your yellow-orange bill
you suddenly walkin'
in the grass
temple backyard
trans state bored no
I can find a tune to like
the way we used to.

I am the only one
so, he sat back and said
no headache, the heat is such
you wear no T-shirt but
a lightweight *dhoti*
and I say...
money is hidden...
Sounds okay he said I'll be
there with you it
doesn't matter...
we sang despite the poorly
dressed Deity, and you asked
"Guru, sir, it was
only twenty-five percent my fault that
the woman and I broke up
and so, I ask your blessings..."
Another wrote – "I stopped
writing you letters 'cause
your replies were
direct and impersonal."

I said
here's another
No offense.
No fence broken down
glad I don't live here
cook dumplins and same old
excellent homegrown
bananas and melons.

I remember the old days
with tension between us
Don't recall.
Recall something nice
forget the rest
we're going home...

Chanting Hare Krishna chords
the same way I can
remember you were the
best guruji we wanted you
and you were sick with aches
but you came to us
aw, it didn't
amount to much remember
the old devotee died,
the one who called
himself
"Your toothless dog."
Now yours truly says
I love to be
save us
real Guru.

*pp. 151–54*

❋ ❋ ❋

*Risk for Krishna*

(First dimming of sunlight I noticed at 4:30 P.M. And so...)
We will go anyway to a
dangerous land
We will go with Krishna *nama*
They are simply after your
money
You have to face danger because that's
the nature of life,
and if you do it for Krishna
your spiritual master said at least they'll
see I risked my life
to preach
and said like Arjuna, "I
want to die on the battle
field"
well I say, "Hare Krishna Hare Krishna
is the way." They are right
but my Lord protect us
we're not this body
we should go meet our
friends, disciples who are
so eager for us to come
it's a sentimental thing to
risk your neck...

He should not interrupt when
    I'm...
    he's that way
    so, we'll go
    we'll chant
Nrisimhadeva
those artists who all
risked those book
distributors
Mayors shot down
they did it for Krishna

the devotees,
and Lord is pleased
what more could you
want? / that those days
you lectured with your time
running out.

There is a subject I
missed
a hundred more poems
Lord, beg the dacoit
Spare me I'm a writer
only fifty-eight
got a family
got a right
I'm a saint
no matter you just
white trash flesh to
them and my blessed
passport miraculous
medal Sacred Heart
needed
my errant soul
please
Lord the soul can't be
touched by them
    no way
you grasp it
Melvin Weeks knows in
the jail and the other
devotees chanting in cells
and the cancer, AIDS, liver
victims saw it and said
all right
I must accept – dear
Lord take me
    Not easy
we who remain say he
passed away and that's it

we have a feast on third day
after – get rid of these
morbid thoughts
fly while you can and tell
folks Krishna is God life
is for realizing Him God
in heart. They say no
we prove it by our media
*rasa*
    our faithful to the end
    lying in grave
chanting Hare Krishna Hare Krishna Hare Krishna
yes, going out of light
in that way
    they can at
least pass the word / he
died okay go on with your duties
your plan
still alive express chanters.

*pp. 162–66*

*Nervous Recalling the Soul*
Face of the bass
the face of the bass
The dark night is going
Lord Caitanya's movement is here too
in each little room.
We are doing exercises he said
yoga is not that
it's linking with Krishna
Don't forget
to smile like Lord Jagannatha even
if you are afraid. The
bass can talk in its own
way, a clumsy man
with a bad left ankle

I thought we'd have a little
show, a clown in limelight
hypnotize you while
if he goes for my wallet I
want my passport in
another place...and my mind
in heaven with Saint Francis
and Abhikrami jump over
that
  to Srila Prabhupada in earnest
then they can't hurt me
it's over as soon as
that. Just little boys playing
"I'm a bird" Don said
and slid over the ice puddle.

Remember the caseworker
you were –
just zip the film ahead
to 1966 summer that's
best. I've seen it before but
love it still
  Swami does save
me
  I become his disciple
Don Cherry plays on
via recordings and
I am not a caseworker
but a preacher
with shorn
and so, if I die in this
place I can remember that
Give us a paper and pen
even not the best
North American products
you'll get out you'll
remember your guru.

It goes both ways – you

learn from him and you
serve him back.
He accepts you and gives
your service to Krishna
that's the way I'm telling
you. Probably we'll get through
unscathed but if not
soul can't be cut or wetted
can't be twisted or robbed
Twelfth chapter very dear to
Krishna don't worry about such
things.
I'm telling you this is the
nervous hour of shout and
sing. We are the sober morn
face speaker with *Gita* under
arm. Give us a little time to
tell you.

I brought this pen and heart
shaped wafer to please
you
the juice of
dabs, the first light
in sky, that's the day while
it lasts it's called December
12 or something
now Lord the song I heard
the breakfast of predictable
papayas
Krishna name
rescue us.

*pp. 175–78*

❦ ❦ ❦

*Breeze on A Hot Day*
Going with my mind and wind
hope I'll be okay

yeah, but you could get a
headache you know
a twinge begins. A pill
M. playing his melod-
eon
        gone with the wind is the
old south gone
I'm hip to the
present
            we will eat and sleep
look at old face
reflected in glass
the big bug face
he's the only one I
know who runs like this
let go let go this way
is open and clear for a
squeak
now Krishna you pick
your take. I say many
splayed
      can't know Him
smile man you're
on
          Krishna serious
in all things
or reduce none but
*japa*
      in a *kutir*
he's on instant access
e-mail what about
you?

Crippled pen hand
Don't rob me sir
please let me go
'cause I've got a mission
to run a poem through
this pipe line

Krishna science is to
chant holy names
go up to folks and say
For religious reasons you
should let me
    enter your country
    tell the people
God is one
and they will see I say
Krishna with my last breath
advise them Look
buy land, get up early
in your house
and tell folks
    Krishna is supreme
                will
in this room
breeze open door
*sannyasa* top-piece hanging on it
as it goes
*subji* in pots
offered to Radha-Gopinatha
"He's independent" – t.p.
gave no recommendation
tell him: Move out of
the temple and come back
in back door as
congregation
so I'm gonna go tell
them I've got limits
    read the scriptures and
search your mind for
lecture themes
go to poor section
give offered offered
do it for Krishna
    raise children
cane
    *subji*

cats and dogs laugh
at the *mudhas*
invite *sadhus*
drive your taxi
and give money to print
books.

*pp. 180–83*

*(Part two numbering starts here)*

*Equinox at mangala-arati*
This is *mangala-arati*
They are singing in temple sounds
This man is singing to God
says I was born at the time
of Equinox.
I'm sad and worshiping
I'm trying my best.

They are singing to Radha-Gopinatha.
They are pious, they are pressured
they are who they are –
group and single souls,
shuffling block bare feet.
The Deities are *darshaning*
and outside the walls
dark the full moon.

Controlled by praying to God
please let the art roll out
to rescue the people or
not.
Some may be able to
listen.
How this is love of God
and why I am here and not

at the altar
rail performing guru.

Got a towel wrapped around
my neck and sweatshirt
hood up under
the cinquefoil, the
florescent tube,
under the weather.
Was weak yesterday,
Lord.

It's equal my being here or
there where Gaura-Nitai
are upraised arms.
The tender one,
in fear where I make the
journey
be thrown into the ditch,
more pain?

What adventures will You put
me through, and please allow my
love to grow.
The sonorous, the hypno-
tizing. The please we got
to give *our* love, he's trying,
the conditioned soul
each lives equally.
*Mangala-arati* is auspicious and
the frogs and weeds and
crumby people nondevotees
are wrong and deluded and
we are right.

  Obey
Be strict
Follow
Be at *mangala-arati*.

I am there, I am a privileged
guru like Srila Prabhupada – he didn't
go to the temple *m.a.*
but was upholding it.
In his room at low desk
finished his *Srimad-Bhagavatam* translation
and purport and began to chant
*japa*, about five A.M. in Juhu
he went out for a walk.
We'd hear them singing in
the distance and think they are
pious, they are upholding
the world. Someone has
to be there. It's them.

May God bless the
attenders of *m.a.*
Wherever they may be
equinox bless us I
don't know much.

But will make my own
way to the temple hall
If You let me
to speak –
If you have faith
you get supreme peace.

*pp. 7–10*

*Notes for Lecturing on "Tac chrnu"*
(Playing this in Trinidad while Madhu plays melodeon
in temple and the music drifts over here, Patita
accompanying
him 'n' cardboard box drums.)
Now we are moving down a
humid soggy page in tropics

someone – the breeze – is
banging the door as if
    to interrupt my solitude.
Ups and downs we want the man
to give his best in real feeling
that way...
I am bound to respond that
way. Please go all out –
I like it he said.
"Are you lecturing on 7.1?"
How did you know?
(Read my mind?)
"Saw it at
the top of a page."

My notes – Krishna speaks to
us. He is the best speaker
and every scriggle in a muscian's
heart of creative energy comes
from Him.

Musician Madhu touching
people who hear.
That's good. I am on
the corner too, blowing
an inspired hymn
of paper and pen in
soggy tropics.
You go up and down so
sad an idle moment blasted.

He's expressing himself.
So, I said, yeah I am lecturing
on 7.1, probably straight it will be.
you know that reading
the books is required,
get them to feel it as if
as if I read a lot
you liar.

You broad
          liar.
I do read to prepare
a sit up straight lecture,
get a few jokes off...
You want to hear more about
Madhu and Irish traditional
music? Ask him.

I am the
quiet one, worrying on
pages, melodeon, soggy
tropics, pineapple not so
great but the water,
the frogs, the audience.
You think it will be trouble
in Guyana? Well, I've been going
there maybe twenty times
and so far...But if
it does...We don't
want to pray for safe passage
but for safety in devotional
          service.

7.1 is good for *japa*
reform too. Tell 'em
you guys and folks black
and Hindu listen. Hear in
the early morning still dark
is best. You chant and bring
mind back.

  Pray God I love this.
Please give me an inch or
an eighth of an inch or whatever.
Some little toehold
of hearing.

You'll say that?
I'll say Krishna says hear from
Me and that includes you
say His name. It will be
interesting the points I'll make.
Here I can't tell you my
secret love. Because I
have none.

Just the experiment, the
scratching, the knowing there is
better than this, the
expression of self as honest
as can be,
is this Love?
It's my offering...
So, stand by for 7.1 fun
from the assured sit-up
guru he's gonna get one
more shot at it and
it will be that Vedic
conclusion before Radha-
Gopinatha.
Oh, I give this to you
on altar with rice in bag
bowing down
only a lecture
    *tac chrnu.*
Me too
    tootin'
my Lord's message
numinous hear.

*pp. 11–15*

Always unafraid the great
*bhagavatas*, that's not me.
Heaven is spiritual world
and he knows it, knows he's eternal,

yeah, well I'm in this body
and do my duty, fearful
but here.

*p. 30*

*Memories of you*
I can recall while I'm here
but you can see,
 that black girl was so
young, just a child, hair
drawn back tight, rings on
fingers and sniffled as if she had
a little cold, yet she was
the Government of Guyana
 to let me in their country.

I've been here before
slats on the windows, my
fears, Vedic teachings of
Prabhupada from me the GBC
initiating guru.

Can't capture it, the big
river. The return to NYC
as if that's my home and
I'm a hero returning.
Memories of Krishna conscious
ethics and *lila*?

No, I pretty
much forget it all
someone like Guru-prasada dasi
meeting us at JFK
with a bag of lunch and off to
some temple reception.
Jaya Gurupada.
Prabhupada what about all
the memories in a river
like muddy, what do they

call it (can't recall the
name)
    forest jungle muddy
tide here in Guyana?
What was it?
Can he hear it with me
my friend and I pointed
out, *hear* this nice
part?

But he says, Oh but the
headache behind the eye
since 1970s and the
time they zonked you
    Who? I never got
zonked, just sweated
waited, and a little red ant bit me.

*pp. 33–34*

*Krishna protects His devotees*
I'm from NYC.
What's all
this race? Aren't we all
souls and music is free
and God too the people of Guyana
are religious
    Islam
    little ants
    "God reigneth"

The people don't leave me
alone, only an ant on a page.
    But love is where you
find, I didn't say "hello" at Immigration but
say it here.

The clown,
the shepherd clown,
the poor goats and birds,
"Meat bird for sale"
and me not doing much to
save anyone but myself
give me water
and give me death
on the installment plan.

Yes it was me in your photo
gone now,
and I heard the news of
armed robbery in the
temple and avoided it.
I heard they sell slit
throats and said I will
be saved by my God
    but in reserve I
here pray the present moment will
never be as bad as you
think by virtue of it
being now
    and technology nowadays is
so wonderful and Krishna
protects His devotees.
So, I am telling ya
this man let me in
the room I preached
ex-temporaneous
and he said thanks
(forgot later)
another had only a few
of Srila Prabhupada's books
like missing teeth
in front and
I wrote in my *Japa Reform Notebook*
"This is as good
as surrey with fringe on top."

Black and white
duty free
we're up for it.

And this year it's Madhu
with the earphones hearing
Irish
even as we rode
around potholes and
I couldn't even drink
without spilling.

But we didn't get
robbed. Thank you Lord
and thank you for water
air, reception
and I remembered You
stealing Rukmini,
lessons You
gave the *brahmana*.

*pp. 35–37*

✣ ✣ ✣

*I can't see Him everywhere blues*
We don't want anyone to know
the black men of Guyana
advertised in record store.

Don't know. No one knows
the old strains
The conversation I had
with a friend.
Then were kicking back.
I said I can't, can't
work more than this.
"Go into old Krishna conscious memories
then." Tell us.
Krishna ate the melon.

Krishna did in *Krishna* book.
Paint a picture in guru's
ashram.

Krishna was king of Dvaraka
anyone doing anything is a
part of Him – this
philosophy I don't
grasp. Does it mean
if a gruff and lovable
trombone is playing
some human blues
of the levee.
    I'd be Krishna conscious?
Yes, he said. Smiled.
Tell me more. I don't
want a tack on Krishna
but really coming.

But doesn't it require
a godly person and
where does He
come from?
He's the one you knew
long ago.
Oh? No girls? Not if
monks religious play it
in sandals that'd
be fun too. You can
smile but they know
celibate blues,
death of God and me
blues.

Then celebrate cute
real stuff you knew
in your liturgy
I know the whaling was Krishna conscious
    from *sastra*.

This: we say *caksus*
*sastra* means put on blinkers
like black shades
and say I dig the world
in Absolute Truth colors now
    four miseries and
Krishna at top in Goloka.

All right.
But *Bhagavad-gita* 6.29–30
says whatever he sees
    he sees Krishna,
and God likes him;
he is never lost.

Young Krishna carries the
cow calf, and
I love Him;
    effulgence
    is His.

*pp. 50–52*

❦ ❦ ❦

*Message to dear ones*
Don't forbid me, don't watch me
I am in Guyana and the breeze
moves the sheer curtains –
The men outside dig holes.
I am in here with a weak
inner head.

    But I am not sorry.
This is the day before another
lecture. I made my outline on soggy paper...
I want to say it's nice, something
Krishna conscious. Yeah I read of
our Prabhupada and his relation

with Bhaktisiddhanta Sarasvati – it was long
ago 1920 and '30 and I
picked it up from *SPL*.
Tell these people who
hear me simply – blankly?

Take it easy. Be easy
on yourself.
The master guided us,
and I tell them he was
guided by his master –
imply they should hear
from me
but what can I do for them –
I am not sure, duty life
in their little houses in
Guyana, so countrified,
backward,
Hindus and blacks and *tama* –
But we can rise above it.

We've got the mission of Bhaktisiddhanta Sarasvati,
but now they're not so keen
to push with local ISKCON
temples and politics as they see it.
Or maybe it's just that
they are struggling to run a family –
Saw one bathing his naked four-year-
old son, simple in backyard, one bucket and smaller
bucket pouring over his little brown body, gave him a
cloth to dry and some
instructions...
as I watched from above.

I don't tell these people to
make a charge of the Light Brigade
on World Enlightenment Day.
Don't tell them to dwell apart.

Just say what the books say
They do as they like
as they are able.

Crawling along. The ants
on flesh. Ah, the flesh-mottled
weak head whitey –
Don't follow *me*
    But they can say
We read in your books
you say just do a little
but do it real and
so we too keep distance
from others
and may
    preach Lord Caitanya's message
wherever we find a chance...

Can I deny that's what
I say by words and
actions. Dear ones,
dear word, expression
Find something strong and live by it.
Silent
    struggle
    as I do.

*pp. 55–58*

⁂

*Very early morning jog*
Now this light forsooth
is art on stage
please pray for me.
danced, mimed
for folks
audience – Please
Listen this man
prays feeling.

I use you this is the
way. There's a special
wail. Little boy
presents.

Lime juice for sale
two cents each on stand
in front of father's
house.
Then we met our Guru.
Remember? Same things.
Look at slats in ceiling
and die then, in some
room.

Has cloud of grief passed?
Yes, he said, it's much
better. They decided their
son wasn't meant to live
here long. Astrologer said
*he* didn't mind dying, but
it was pain for *you*.

A pineapple
smashed into jam and put
into three-sided triangular
baked
    *samosa*.

Dance lessons and music so
when she grows up and
may leave ISKCON she
won't say she wasn't ripped
off by parents' religion.

Don't ask me. I am giving
all I can. Got a ticket, got
room in my passport
for a few more stamps.

Then will you go to India?
Run out of ideas?
No, never. We gave
no veto on imagination.

The train ride
    that ride
"I can, I can"
So, Krishna muscled in
on me. In time and
pain and bugs.
Everything is Krishna taught
it forerunner.

He said it's over
and then
    we went back
to bed, me alone
    only to sleep
and dream
    forever.

*pp. 64-67*

⁂

*Night coming on in Guyana*
This way pleez / night action
not NYC
guy-Anna
this mud-baked canal bank
this sweated body
melodeon player next door
Next door Kazoo
me head
    Careens 2
His lotus feet
Now this way the same
aisle down by Guru Maharaja
laugh

laugh
he's on the high seat this
brownie do-goody
    writer of many
homespun books.

Don't we determine your
reputation?
    No, I said I go
on my own.
Forgetting his self he meeks
the meeks shall inherit
the bang bang of a stick
on a tree.

This way the night
the ink imprint on previous page
The man said even if I
was not a Negro I'd
make this music
I tried hard to hate
the white men but one
good one would come along
and ruin it.

Be peace
be at peace
accept your President
Janet Jagan
and Cheddi Jagan
international airport.

*pp. 82–83*

⁂

*Blessed are the creative musicians,*
  *blessed are the peacemakers*
This way another act
soft we can make it

bananas cut up
give one to each person
then I'll you
what.

God to be with Krishna your
protector like a teddy bear
He's the one
I don't mean in each
one men's rooms toilet
they say that way
Got your ticket you expect
a good ride
sweat in departure lounge
remember old days
Krishna is the king almighty
Madan Deity in
temple behind sheer
curtain
Brass Radha-Krishna
You are waiting in a bed
for me to return.

I will return, let me
worship You again
let me say the Gopala
Kesava and heard the
page to give them.

That's good, it's good
they surely are
and I want to hear good
sounds as in a church
or temple
    God be praised
    Krishna be praised
The same moves but new too
we limited worshipers like
me giving an initiation lecture.

I say here folks is a *sloka*
say it sometimes,
see in my wrist the bones
see no tricks
upsleave
see bolibar blues
see *yesam tv anta gatam*
four rules, sixteen rounds
    no other way
ten offenses to avoid
He said that's all right
he's a little behind
he's a little off
he's a little weird, eerie
his grooving too we like it
that way
off but on.

He's going to go – but
suddenly we hear bad
men menacing or
imagine it
    blessed are the
peacemakers,
but they have to brave it
sometimes.

My Lord, my sweet Lord
Pert pretty for Krishna
in spare time we are
happy creative urge
is given by Santa by
God
Teasin' you
He's the Lord
    Reigneth.
Raineth down at
night that shower
my doors are locked

I pray for Him.

Remembrance at death
*brahmana* boy cursed.
Maharaja Pariksit was true at end
It will end me too
tag on Swami
your false but real student.

*pp. 84–87*

*Body and soul*
Body and soul this man
I like.
He wants me to be happy
from his suffering comes
a light that fears no
darkness.

The saintly person must
suffer just between him
and God.
    His way isn't yours
But you've got to go
find yours.

This work we do
for God / we pray
to Him.
Warm weather and cold
nice people and not nice
the indifferent money-
makers
    Engines, inane TV
The art soul
    and body
He's trying...
And I've got burden of

God consciousness
    Topmost.

Smile with me brothers
and sisters, daughters and
sons as I make light
aside
    in Krishna consciousness
    books
    looks.
I'm no angel
this man
though he's just telling it
as it comes the lovely
rhythms we are born with
    if only we can
    be loving –
    it costs.
Now the dawn is not
far away and will turn
to tropic heat, trucks
and angry persons
    the goats and ducks
the baked river bank
the Plethora
beyond your grasp / you
    eat and rest...

Sing your hymn to God
beyond and hear
Krishna in all things
Krishna in the heat.

Build a fire for *yajna*
give spiritual names
your soul's in heart
They say
and body you know
is here, your sweet

and burdensome
    flesh and body
and blood
given by God
'cause you wanted it
Now my Lord I bow to
You. You are my
body and soul.

You are my preferred rank
sweet slow chariot
May You see me at death
see You in holy names.
Holy names, holy names
is all I can do
at best.

*pp. 91–94*

⁂

*Staying Calm*
There's a calm, but you don't
know if your nervous talk
is reality.
I mean if this man can
keep the worst elements
calm
he's a peacemaker but
others are not.

So, I sit it out and hear him
and think of profound and soft
mood of God conscious
poet.

Will he run out of patience
Hear the siren now down
this road. It's an ambulance...
Could be a man lost a limb

but we keep on praying
There's a way...

We can't live in peace
in this world. Peace
*Param-santim* is with
the soul and God and His
beloveds.
Please Lord
Let us remember You
So, we move along each
day. Destruction of life in
this body doesn't mean
soul dies.
    Believe in *Gita*
it can't die
the Lord will protect
    He reigneth.
And I am just a tiny
part.

Surely, He can give peace
and strength or disruption
seems to reign.
Hare Krishna Hare Krishna.
Hare Krishna.
    Soft tones of the
strong one do well
each moment
of breath
    until end.

*pp. 101–3*

*Body and soul (take two)*
We are with Krishna and got
music to accompany us
Not drum and bugle for war

’cept war on our fear
we’re a body that has
to die;
    sweet love attachment
to day and night and
    heat best
    *let go.*

Soul is real person
learn it your *Gita* lessons
from the masters
    they are your guru and
Krishna in the sacred.

And they practice as
    here in Guyana the
room where we meet
the seat of Vyasa
the submission inbred
Indian spirituality
    Bharatavarsa
No sentimental slush
you improvise
The sweetest thing
I want to be with
You, dear Lord Krishna.

He’s a good man.
They just want their sense
grat., cock crows,
I leave it finally
hope not abrupt on floor
like RFK or JFK
but you don’t know
    never know.

Let go even this
charming melody body
and soul got to part

until spiritual body
in Vrindavan Goloka.

New new newer
be safe with Krishna.
Group your *abhaya*
mottos
    like *japa*
Be with
us Lord
Sharp intake
adrenaline fear
flee and fight.
Anger and hate
    all bunched
I can't know
the pure peace.

But pray for it
May I see it in your
face and feet and name
and recall Gurudeva
Prabhupada
coming to me in light.

Your unworthy son
"Do something practical". Yes
I'll speak on *Gita*
I'll tell them
Fear is brought by...
Love Krishna, love devotees
they have heard it, and yet
say it my best again
twice today.
Lord of all
you reign.
    Body and soul, Ah, Krishna
be my *mamata*.

*pp. 111–14*

*Stick it out*
This is a slow man walking
where it's fast.
    There is no way I said okay This is the stuck in Guy
blues – the police barricades – heavily armed – Janet
Jagan is a Hindu – they won – blacks in town angry.
Don't foment on me, guy-Anna.

Let me out, me and M. and our
hand luggage and our plan for up north in
the prosperous good karma
    want to see that ten week
old baby Rasa, and the snow and
    lay back
    the the the what?

Freedom illusion, new books
records you can't enjoy
    can't eat a big meal
Mix lines, M. is pumping away
on melodeon good cheer, near
Christmas. Don't blow up or
burn down the Election Hall of Freedom House
    guard them
    "vicious bunch."

Fly out. He is a semi-invalid.
Got blues in toes, but he's a
rip-roaring
    the sweet and lonely
The all alone but facing reality
with non-devotees in a lumber
business.
    I told him – Not
said you decide.
They said okay guru,
and I opted out
sit it out
day after day

A horse / a horse pill
a herbalist comes to see you.

*pp. 122–24*

*Byeya*
(Oh, I like to say Bye for real
to Guyana – hello to where?
Krishna.)
Merry men squeak
we want home, We
want our pres!
Recount!
Not now, I'm from New
Yawk
    Yeah bye Ya
to this place
    Not yet

I can say bye
because I'm a sold out
servant to my master
    This sound leaking?

Police barricade
and pellets shoot
his eye lost
save it
    his sight.

Mr. Philadelphia Q
and Bob Rains and
Reebey Good is
all in Georgetown hospital but not me
    I'm for Khyber Pass
rifle not
    my goods.

His riffs fit him, and I
could make peace with
rioters in my heart
in a distant place.
Telling you he's in a
theater / clear your throat
Monk will play
the monster is dead
    is dead
We happy in our
routine
    until *our*
end.

Ends meet / Got enough
chowder enough butter
and cheese and no meat
O let cows and goats live
all creatures got
    a right.
Byeya well I am
happy mate
when our
bee wee climbs
the soft clouds and tropic
blue sky above green forest
lumber cut down not
the muddy river below
and funky passengers I
don't mind.

Headin' for T. and T.
is good enough.
    Only if Krishna chant
is your wisdom notebook
of joy on lap and
nervous lines "here's
a portrait of last
passenger 1995."

Here's a pic of the pianist
playing Stardust
    trinkle
the rioters helmets it
is distant
    I'm a privileged karma
case riding high
you can be brought low
Krishna suffers not, His
devotees do suffer
to purify them of
all last tense
I'm singing to say
Free
we love Lord
whatever He gives
    I wish I could say
Fearless.
I no Citra
But his *cela*
bye to blues of
the low.

*pp. 131–34*

⁂

Don't look out the window
so much, look down
look down, that lonesome
road before you travel
on.

When you look down it –
the supposed future, what
do you see?
Can only imagine
it.

Active imagination

over active, hyper tense –
the milestones of death and
rebirth, the Krishna conscious tests.
Look down that road
and hope to meet Krishna...
all we people of the world
crazy, wild, police can't
contain them with pellets,
resort to heavy arms,
even that can't stop
the angry slogans
    they're allowed...

*pp. 138–39*

*Camptown races*
Good morning, we are shaking
our little crew
we are in Camptown
    going to the races
somebody bet on the
bay.

I bet Sats will make it
awright to Bee Wee
counter. But I can't
say it will be pain-free
ass-per-in.

Then he will eat pine
jam crushed
    then will Krishna
be in my life – it's up
to me.
This is the way
we are given down a
narrow pass

you enter prit-it
your way
    your swinging band
Hallelujah
America the great.

*pp. 144–45*

*Camptown races (take 2)*
& We tried it again. The
same time? Well we did
it differ.
    We held up a banner
took a urine bottle in
back
    Swami said take two
we took all

    Krishna consciousness
waitin' waitin'
remembering – pains
joys, perks, the tunes and lucky
I got a travel mate
who loves music and therefore
*he's* happy.

We wait. Today and
careful slices of
papaya and mangoes and
a lush banana and
    then the Sounds
of goats and cars just one
more time.
    So *you* say
but Krishna may have you
delay
come back
    so best is to

abide in His name
    if I could
    sixteen at least
    bee bum
    bee bum.

*pp. 145–46*

⁂

*Prayer for safe passage*
A country's got to be free
and a black and white and
man's gotta stand up and
all of that.

But I am just a one
a one soul with my friend
and small circle of friends.
Srila Prabhupada put us in this circle
said don't go with
nondevotees.

But also said go out
and preach
So what to do? The timetable
    the...the day ranting on us until we sweat down our sides. She is telling me come back to visit and we'll install fax and e-mail, whatever you want. And I am thinking there is no way you will drag me back here...

    But why not. What have you
    got to do better where you're going? What do you do up north in Pa., you sit around and eat and sleep...
So the gremlin tells me
    continue I pray for
vitamins.
    for release of endorphins
into the blood.
I pray for the safe passage

to airport and pothole over
    over ocean Carib,
    Atlantic
    Styx
    fluto
    religion.

Pray take me to Godhead
But I don't deserve...

There is the one man's song
I leave a trail
for other ones
to take
    us back.

II

We will go / we will go
this smart ride
the passport good
right look of face
got pills to back me
up and money and phonecard
yeah, we got friends
    Lift us up.

But if Death calls
the jingle jangle of bones
skeleton dance can't
save you for this life
    ticket's up
    Cheddi went
    Forbes went
    Janet too

Abe Lincoln, everyone
has to die,
    as Hemingway said.

But we are devotees, know
    Paradise
    of self in Lord
    We war against madness
    and want peace to
    righteous
    Please give us safe passage
    and if it's rough hold us
    up
to go as a soldier monk
poet without disgrace
to the bottom Davy Jones locker
    praying Hare Krishna mantras
bubbles out
mouth
Hare Krishna hand up
    scissors
    Swamiji.

*pp. 150–53*

*Now's the time*
Now is the time sweatin'
for fathers
we hope you enjoy
thanks.

We heard in '66 and they
say he's a genius
the bird of many notes.
He's playing that way
riffs they learn in crips –
for me it's just Krishna
repeated "Jesus Prayer"
and I don't want no interference.
Madhu sees me looking down through
bifocals.
  Hearing Burr chippin'

Now's the time –
    it's time he brings
dob juice early
I heard it before
well, not like this –
In Guyana? Why not, sweat
is sweat, and Janet said
the government will be inclusive.
Same and new
Krishna consciousness
is revolving.

We want to be with our
master now and later
sweatin' no jive but
all eternal service.
Arid. Desert. Heart of
this reader of Jada
Bharata who was great
and Bali Maharaja was great
and Lord Vishnu who is all great.

Yeah, they were the best.
In those days when
*devas* visited here
But now (used to be one flag
empire Yudhisthira)
now Krishna consciousness is floundering
yet flourishing.
I don't condemn or judge
but as master said,
    "Encourage them more and more."

If I play then Madhu picks
up his own horn and the
cow bellows most unhappy –
everybody's awake for the
while a few days before
Christmas.

Play man, trucks roar you
can't hear much. But I say
Krishna, Krishna in a trance of dull
routine sweating sticky bare
feet on wooden floor.
He was doing that back
in 1944.

Don't be woogy, the Now's
the time. Fade out.
But not me, I am up for
a full day travel
remember you
as old timers who did
give art joy
    and God is source.

*pp. 156–59*

# CHAPTER TWO - GETTING THROUGH

December 23, 1997 – January 13, 1998

I'm in America right
now always end
in *dandavats*
my natural crawl.

*Part Two, p. 55*

The Christmas holiday has arrived as Satsvarupa dasa Goswami returns to the United States after his demanding and difficult journey to both Trinidad and a very turbulent Guyana, in light of a recent presidential election. Winter begins when Satsvarupa Maharaja begins a stay at Gita-Nagari Farm in Port Royal, Pennsylvania – the first of two settings within this, the twenty-first volume of his on-going literary project, *Every Day, Just Write*. After extensive deliberation, Satsvarupa Maharaja has chosen the title, *Getting Through* for this volume after considering a number of possibilities including, *God Reigneth in America* (which would carry forward the title of the previous volume) as well as, *Volume Twenty-One on the Run*. Undoubtedly, *Getting Through* suggests movement, but it seems to this reader that a distinctive mood is conveyed with this title, that of challenge, stress, and even fatigue. This phrase possesses all of these connotations, and the title is sufficiently broad to include every possibility. In addition to particular moods, this title also suggests shades of meaning. For example, through what is the reader moving? Both the prose and poetry of this volume suggest not simply "getting through" a trip successfully from the Caribbean to the United States, but a journey through life in its deepest sense as well. If a *sannyasi* is traditionally one who travels from place to place as an itinerant preacher, so too is the *sannyasi* one who bears a particular witness to life before the horizon of the spiritual world. So, it is for Satsvarupa Maharaja, whose "getting through" embodies both aspects of this phrase for he is a traveller in every sense of the word.

The poetry contained within this volume represents the work of an artist whose writing displays one and at the same time aesthetic discipline and genre-crossing patterns. Consider "Flute Song" the conclusion of which is cited at the opening of this preface. The theme of movement is wonderfully expressed in terms of devotional practice. Here, Satsvarupa Maharaja describes how his own movement will "always end in *dandavats*", the prostration of the body in humility before the spiritual master or the Lord Himself. But here, the author describes his personal *dandavats* not as a singular moment in time but as the manner of his movement itself, "my natural crawl."

"Let's Go Alone" is an embracing reflection upon tears, both those that flow authentically in moments of repentance and feelings of separation from the Lord, and those "squeezed out" in a self-indulgent display of false piety. In this poem, the referent of "getting through" is that of the spiritual journey within human life in pursuit of love of God. With references to Bhaktisiddhanta Sarasvati Thakura, the Christian Desert Fathers, and St. Teresa of Avila, Satsvarupa Maharaja offers to his readers a spiritual primer on tears. The movement of this meditation leads the reader to the author's personal recollection of his own tears as he prepares for his upcoming deployment within the United States Navy. The poem approaches its conclusion with a lovely reference to movement once more:

> let's march on this
> *bhakti-marg* and
> pick flowers for Radha
> and Krishna.

The poem then ends in the same manner as did the previous volume of *EJW*, with a slowing of the pace of this movement, effectively created by the actual shape of the stanza on the page:

> Don't despair. It will
>     come but not before
>     you...
>     cry
>     for it.
>
> *Part One, pp. 100-01*

With a slower cadence, movement and tears intersect, thus informing the reader that tears born of repentance and love will come... but in their own time.

*Well Down by The Riverside*

Well down by the side river
we're going down by Riverside
oh joy
    oh bo

me and Mo
oh boy
 the joy
 of Manhattan Bullshit

this man a little siphon
pours our ink and blood and headache

Bullshit
damn

oh man
oh man
Bee flight 42 and black folks pretty in Trinidad
and Guy-ana all be-hind me

Now we're going into
a new year this is the way I died
in Frankfurt

He said
Adolph

He's a reneg artist
He's a peed out 60-year-old
fudgesicle in
sick bed

Riverside no sick sic
no sex celi bate
sell a bite

I am smart
enuf
got my Guru
deva
(to you)

Oh, sob
Down by the
Riverside we're
goin' I wish
you could
understand
He's so good I just wanna say
He's that way He's our man
He's got the blues...

*pp. 1–3*

*Jackson Heights*

Where are you going?
I am going to the Bar
on December 23?

There's this
Dec. 23
my heart and sweater
 skinny
M.'s out there
I love his approach
buy a short
winter jacket in Macy's
 and go out busking with melodeon –
Paddy in New York.

Bless dear friends
preserve their skulls

and lungs
But he...
that
car accident.

Did ja hear?
You're going for it?
I said you better

He said your book is
too slow
white boy
I said wait
I'm a universal
soul neither black
or white.

Okay.
That's what you say.

II

Then what about guru?
One
he's Prabhupada.

Is the way I know
to write faithful odes
coming from myself I
said wait and listen this
has to be better.

Unbroken unit in
cave, that sound controlled.

Hard priest
soft corn
my ear is hurtin'
I want the best sound.

Krishna sonic
Krishna cowherd
in your life I
said.

It's like this
God is *sastra*
and I speak it to you
tell you there is nothing
 but free spirit
Krishna is God and that's all.

Repeat it as you like
but come home on
time, be careful
subway
graf
rapes
you take care
and tomorrow we'll go in car safe to Pa.
highway I'll be listening
to the
muse and
Krishna will come out of me
the only way I know it.

There's this *Gita* blues Sreemad
quick
code
my friend
in Australia
ISKCON folks
 madness neuters
you chant better
please.

*pp. 4–7*

*An Answer to Thomas Kobes*

You are your own man
but you better
get with it
in Krishna
Cons.

You better swing low
beyond down those trees
and dreams
and old Christmases with
your Dad and Mom
and sis.

Yeah, I went down the
road Samson Ave.
and disappeared
in Art
and foam.

I lost myself
 crying
in self-pity to recall it
 But
the salvation
 theme is real.

II

So, you tell them now
Folks, disciples, devote-tees
you just follow
the path
But what path
Thomas Kobes
ask me

I tried to see it but
    now I'm unclear and
    too ill to see it.

I say well it'll clear up Or I say (take 2)
your folks
your Bible (*sastra* Vedas) I
uh say
Something comes
out maybe genuine
of my own searching
that's it
we're searching

for the light in heart
and head
Friend, we need each
other.

The scripture and I went to sleep
on Christmas Eve it was I
wrapped my sock
around my wooden recorder
 because I couldn't play it
no privacy
 no women
  no men

just me and the rules
and my master distant
 and we'll come home
  but the path has just
   got to reveal itself
like an interstate
 coming up fast.

*pp. 12–15*

*Did You*

Are you happy?
Yes.
Can you live forever in
overall?
No.

Will you go back to Godhead?
Yes eventually.
Will Mr. Nair
Charlie

Will you hide the fact
 Will you play kazoo
Will the chickadee
eat seed
freeze?
Will you?
get a headache?
Fart
tell that truth

Will you embarrass
  enormous
   superb
      wild
Krishna consciousness

Did you
are you the guy
were you true

in the gut did
that true
did you ride from
Pa. and blather

and you / did you
 find a means
  will you say a
   prayer for me?
Will Krishna
and Prabhupada criss-
cross at death will
you mistake
      press wrong button

Eighth chapter *Gita*
trills
   remember
I read a guide book
to Vrindavan / author says
I thank my guru
- for what

did you tap your toe,
is it allowed
Did you break through
grape juice?

Does it come from God?
Does it come quick

So they ended it
that way
      Vrindavan things
I'm getting back to basics
with my Radha-Govinda
in temporal
Ireland ah let
me live and die there
thinking of Vrindavan Krishna
and going nowhere.

*pp. 17–19*

⁂

*Somewhere*

There's a place where
 I'm going with
  my nose into the ground

There's a place
in my heart
no dart

There's a place
 where fairies die
  and angels wither

yes a Brahman
where Arjuna and Krishna went
and beyond that
there's the place
they go over and over

yeah
there's a place for
devotees
in hell
where they
remember.

We chant the Hare Krishna mantra.
There's a heart and a mind in
rapt decision.

there's Vrindavan of course
and there's a girl and
guy hand and hand
it's Krishna and Radha
 and the *gopis*

and *sadhus* who earn
it Syama

and Syamini
and there's a
*sadhu*
under a tree
thinking of Them

my Deities
Radha and Govinda
waiting for me
in Inisfree

there's a play
for us.

*pp. 19–21*

*Tonight*

Tonight, there'll be fun
no doubt
Tonight, he'll fall
in love

but me let it rain
creak house
walk in goulashes
in my mind
tonight a rubber band
a curling worm
in my intestine
and yours

Her-nia
tonight
Padget and I
play
ball

Krishna in Vrindavan I said
   for me is here in
where Port Royal
no, it’s
Pearl
     Street
Mott Street
Staten Island
our car went
through
last night

Christmas night is over
the presents are
wrapped

tonight is love for God
His son best is
born
in a manger

we want permission to
go back to Godhead
but joke
let go
Radha-kunda
turtles on Christmas
 Eve
      green scum on
surface

me afraid
“Give me comfort!”

So, this is the night of
the Iguana
the night Christ was born
pouring rain and

me in a trailer
in Port Royal writing this
letter to you.

Please Christ
(in vain)

Please let me
call God Father's name
Abba!
with a drop of
*your* sincerity.

*pp. 24–26*

(I want to write)
You can all alone there's no way except your own
no, you can be a man in
a *prince nez*
pinstripe
suit

bold over bold over bowler hat Baladeva
comic

there's no way known of course. There's no way.
A whale friendly
there's a certain

Christmas is here good cheer
ring the bell and offer
Ekadasi food
There's no way I
say.
So, he said Be of good
cheer punch bowl
foot falls eventually
he'll interrupt me

but
small wonder Krishna Krishna
occurs so rarely in
your pantheon
sob and squeak

yep he interrupted you but backed out when
he saw me writing.

Spring the slob
the seal
on Christmas is
cold again

the Note
squeaks
the Krishna is all in
all
Krishna
cracks
the ice.

"Tell me when you
are free."
I'll tell you
when I'm in love and
don't mind Krishna
demands more

when I stop blathering.

*pp. 30–32*

⁂

There's the hollow sound
There's a man alone How
would it sound?

To the crowd
I mean the group
of disciples
They'd flip
out
they giggle.

Alone alone there's
the man on the street
lower
depths
 suffering
  Bombay
   movie stars.

Please accept obeisances
squeak
mouse hunt.

Please leave me alone Please watch the movie
go to bed Xmas
nite
the dog is put out
don't hug and pet him.

The cat is gone
Don't refrain. Don't interrupt,
they're talking and
displaying a fierce
determine.

They leave me alone to
roam

in a school room with chalk
boards to myself
practice
on Danish
radio
a truck driver says
"What the hell is that?"

Hare Krishna is not popular
a mouse screams
Hare Krishna is one of
many even in Mumbai *Back*
*to Godhead* magazine

Anyway, we get
our
quota
small
200,000
visit Krishna
Mandira on Day.

And this is Christ's
scream
    descend
    it's over.

*pp. 33–35*

⁂

*Playing Alone*
So, he is playing alone out there in the night, and I don't know who I am in a sweater, but I'm indoors and got friends.

Here's the truth – a man in the
subway playing alone a long way away no support. But
this

man
me is
soul
from Krishna

Feel for that devotee who is working so hard and mourning that, "I'm working real, real hard, real, real long hard..." What to say? He "ruined" the easy conviviality of our lunch together.

Say Why not get out of it if it's so hard on yourself and say but I've got it easy staying away from women and family and begging off others so my day is to collect money and spend it on scholarly pursuits.

He's out there playing the
 improvised tune
cold subway station
give him a break
or appreciate in a packed
theater for his squeaks
he practiced thirty years to get it that way.

Now I'm taking a break
to drink and eat
it was tough the dead layers of
a soul who neither
wakes to his despair
or can pay attention
to *nama*
and remember she
(old devotee said) "I fell down
even when fully engaged
in service and *inattentive* chanting."

Then the longest note.
And he performs the art
of blues
  squeaking.

*pp. 37–38*

*Cowherd Boys*

It can be rendered in a different
way jaunty and crazy
monk style – I mean
 Benedictine monk
Skippy peanut butter
 march of elephants
going away with it
there is fun and frivolity
in cowherd sports
and demons coming,
but Krishna our very dear
friend can take care of them.

He's the sergeant
captain drill
kill the Agha
kill the Baka
Arista
and the *gopis* may claim
His heart attention,
but we boys know
 only our *rasa*.
Pee pee pee pee
the flowers are bloomin'
never winter,
no cops, parents just
cows, cows and calves and
unending wandering into
the grass-field woods.

Forest fires
serpents, giant ducks
and a python statue
as big as the sky

He's the
Lord and master of

us pee wee shoots and
"I can out wrestle my
dear friend Krishna," says Stoka and Balarama.

The march of the
donkeys into hell
or actually liberation
throw up into the trees.

*pp. 38–40*

*Sad To Recall*

He's sad such a good
creative man died
suddenly
We say noble
and love.

We it's strange and I say
I'll be okay
my headache or no
 remorse.

There's no way around it
tears coming down
he was a good man.

Now we've got his music...

II
What about your spiritual master
and other great souls...
he was so great an institution
 formed around him,
we have to forgive them

bodies strewn. He taught
the soul eternal
and Krishna conscious Krish
Supreme Personality of Godhead.
Now that's worth
the price
of your life
lives
many times
so, stop griping.

Rather I'm just sad to say
I couldn't come up to it
and an awful of
shit has come down
in the name of
institutionalized...

Wow we miss you
Swami
we miss the early days
our sentimental
watery heart
you could say.

But it's more than that,
it's strong men and
women
and children
and souls going back to
Godhead.

Our unique expression
and contribution to the world –
your Krishna consciousness
as you taught
Gaudiya
Lord Caitanya.

Oh, I'm sad but
happy and secure in
knowledge and work –
besides
you are giving
me an almost
free ride –
I'm grateful
grapes of wrath
chant chant chant.

*pp. 42–45*

I'm preparing a grave and
 a lecture
Get me a kazoo and I'll
 compose,
get me a free pass and
I'll enter Vaikuntha rabbit (*sasi*) in the
moon
get me Buddha drops Krishna droplets
force
pretend, pose.
Get me pencils and crayons.

*p. 46*

*I Just Met*
(Now wait a minute, old man, don't start romancing.
Transform.)

I just met a girl
named...he said
Romeo and Charlie and

we are not marching
soldiers – yes, we
are.
We met and then danced

by the light of the moon
and suddenly –
he met his guru – another
romance.

I just met a girl was
Radha bringing him
*prasadam*

I just entered a woods
(Dante) lost

a woods where
Krishna dwells.

This is the non-biparte
he just met and improvised

chords and themes
and struck it had nothing
much to do with the
original Broadway school
"He just met a
girl named Marie"

But they were happy in
their own way
and suddenly I find

Suddenly an inch –
or much less
opened up for me
and I saw daylight

My Love
my attention
fix it on divine
holy names
and I love
you and faced the wall
Zen Zazen
I face
the wall

glad my love...
Hare Krishna.

*pp. 46–48*

⁂

*Flute Song*
(A child made up a simple tune with a flute and played it to her father...)

Well I took that song and
made it complicated into my
 own life.
You mean with a smooth
band or what? Yes, something
like that.
There was always room
for an angry man
who spoke in his own way. Horn a human voice

riot and burns down
but we don't want to
rip up smear over
we want to be a
fellow.

Ha let them laugh I
went out in cold
slippers

bird feeder
Madhu in his shed.
Yeah what I heard
guns of day after
Christmas "One more
week of massacre" deer
season.

Get it right
Krishna season
the night will be your
time to

Scar scary folks
scar yourself how much
you can surrender
I'm not sure
nervous
shots
the cattle.

Call them over and speak
straight
100 disciples in a room
no big surprises
keep the lid on.

I got no secrets
a bear rips through
a cabin tears the place
completely apart
looking for honey.
The drummer keeps working
oh my
the Swami is alone
he (the other) went to
France and Morocco and
join SWAT team

to attack extension
guru in Siberia
if he goes there.

Bears
fears
headlines
dreams

He's a friendly sort with his
friend sharing the inner
secrets on why we don't
go into *gopi-bhava*.

Look whatever he
teaches of Krishna in Vrindavan
that's it
don't think you know
more.

You don't you don't
rip and throw out garbage
be true to one only
I don't know more
than what he teaches
I only *heard* of it

Don't louse up her
game

That's my way too.

Vivid picture of Bhaktivinoda Thakura
I just happen to be staring
at it
jump out and reality
move it.
Look at that picture of
my mentor when

I die "Just wanted
to reeve up."
Get away from the
repressors.

So, the girl's flute song
pleased her dad who
put it into a composition
and I said
    we'll savor
the *Krishna Book*
when I go back
to my sod.
I'll be simpler
I'm in America right
now always end
in *dandavats*
my natural crawl.

*pp. 51–55*

*Mangala-arati Take*
(Well sir you want to rise early and jump and shout
your God consciousness! *Kirtana mandala* is the
perfect bliss)

Listen people gather
come on have faith
it's rollin' the good
time religion.

Believe in sweet pains on
emporium of temple
Jagannatha
and Radha-Damodara
it's so good to
see
no flies on You.

Brush Them off with
*camara*. No peacock
feather this cold
morn.

Now one leader sings the
top broadcast of Hari
*nama,* and we follow in
a little cubical
  of flesh and bone.

Mad I can't get this
pen to work as I'd like
we're going so fast
how can this be religion?

Well there is more than
one way, you get to
see your soul as
the fire
bright to defeat
death and ice.

Shout blues *haribol*
Hare!
Come on save me man
I want to chant
hey! Krishna
I'm in hell.
That one shout
O Lord God he's
mocking in vain
well he's at least
calling out.

Hare! Krishna!
deliver us! This

pre-dawn in dark temple
with Deities dancing
*tribanga*, He's a
smashing young boy.

By riverside Yamuna
background peacocks
peahens calling, better
change to a pen
that writes in
dress and stress and peels out under.

Hide all that blues
it may be worldly.
But
this old time
*kirtana* is best.

II

Swami allowed even the sax and the guy
with frankincense in strainer
smoking up Lower East Side sky
under the tree –
and drummers –
Flutes!
He come and hear the
Swami in the park
drum.

Gets you higher than LSD
      unbustable
shout *sahajiyas* pre-mature...maybe but
he's saying just chant
and it'll clear up.
Whatever happened...
We are on the last stretch
but there will be many more

he's offering the conch and water
curtain, candles
The last
is blow that conch!

I know
you'll save me in this
black church a Syama
good news
oh yeah cleans
and cries tears if you're
lucky. The standard
Gaudiya dance done in Turkey
and Detroit
oh yeah...

Now the end is sad and formal
because we've gotta move on.

*pp. 58–62*

*How I Feel (But God and Scripture Comes First)*

There's no way a guy can
be a burnout in this Movement
and not go back to Godhead.

I say stay in one place
and listen to me
I'm the one who has to stay under
control
this is
my day to
tell you the music
people don't understand.

God in scripture comes first
and then how *we* feel
about it. I'm sorry I
got stuck onto so many
things.

You should understand
better
this is the way I want
and a good fellow.

This in the tune he made
my hand writ
lost all steam
lost all Krishna consciousness
Little Rock
lose all sense they are
pounding my head.

I just want to give a
sane lecture a sweet talk
straight *sastra* /
that's the best thing isn't
it?
And keep this other
to myself to myself.

Gee it's a danger zone
that when you go
you are an artist
of your own.

We got out of Guyana
in a
travel year
this is the way
we want to tell you
man.

The dam busted loose
just a little
feed birds
I'm the one
who doesn't know.

Take a shower and
be calm.

You'll be known by
your act.

All right...
peace...

*pp. 65–68*

⁂

*Dumbo Becomes A Hare Krishna*

There is no way I can get out of a tight syndrome
guilt they project to me.

Listen to the love of art
art musicians
they cry without
tearing
        you down.

Hey I like this sound
you say and toes start
tapping.

But when you get down
you are sad  herring
he's happy clown
wail out all that's
coming down.

You cry you're so sad
so happy don't know
whether this baby
drooling is *maya*
or the center of their
    home
     angel
      fat cheeks.

I wished I had
a wife like that
a fat wound
an art vocation
a reassuring angel
a taste
for the old Familiar
Hare Krishna mantras I cry out.

He sounds like Dumbo
on a bender
Dumbo out to fracas
lunch lurch
Dumbo of my starry
boyhood in Queens
Dad and Mom and me
and Dumbo and his mouse.

Do you see what I see?
Raunch
I am that way too
cry together
tcch tcch tcch.

Dumbo goes Wet West
Dumbo becomes a Hare Krishna
wears a *kaupin*
*dhoti*
and switches to a *sari*
a braid a –

he don't blaspheme
Dumbo
mad elephant.

Hatta matta hasti
here comes down the
aisle
I am the ant
I am the flying elephant
    you never know.

So it turned out the sad songs
the snow melted after all
I got together with fine players

and we hurted no
body
but played.

Until we couldn't remember
how it came about.
He was a merry prank.

Wait serious ex-GBC
raconteur *emeritus*
ah that's the word
now enter your office
with Tempora paint.

Srila Gurupada you left us
holding the bag of *Sadhu-*
*bhusanams.*

You on your youthful seat
thirty-eight shit years I can't
remember all the silks
with abuses and privileges
you took.

Did you fall from the
spiritual world? (with
Dumbo)
She writes me and says "That is
a demoniac version" *tal fruit
logic.*

So, we're working out okay for
awhile
knit hat
band aid
baby pamper
hole in the foot.

Man writes she got arthritis
and Joe writes he's got a spinal
chronic and we're closed in
I spread good cheer –
she says no to it
doesn't work what if you
go blind?

You prance so slow and graceful
like World War I marching band
now
they come grinding to the
scratch finish line
full of good cheer.

Oh beep me a mantra
I'm game
to revive my hopes with
old friends if only
they be
indulgent.

*pp. 69–73*

⁂

*The Promise*

(I don't want to be outside of Krishna consciousness.
Got to bring it in.)

So, listen friends I'm here on
the ranch and say help
we are not the same
    sittin' in a row.

We are dispersed
Diaspora of ISKCON
many have gone to
heaven or even hell and back.

My back tow please
he wanted another guru
a better break
we defended ISKCON
GBC
as best we could,

Then, then the master
plan of the Supreme did
it reveal itself well yes
sort of
bodies strewn

Vietnam vet.

The wall of names
who died in the
cause
shot leaders
say said bad
new kids initiated by
the hundreds
splintered...

He's writing his blues
sing the anthem
unofficial I said he
could be like a bright
black man
who forgives doesn't
blame *all* whites
for all his ills.

But he said I got
misused
we are waiting for the
return of the master
the self-effulgent
one
the best.

Then he comes in just
a little jaunty and nothing
great?
No, we decided to
wake up and love.

Love and freedom he
said his followers
said...who you
talking about,
Prabhupada or
someone great
you think
came after him?

The promise
was we'd all live in
ISKCON and all come back

all be saved
happy, prosperous

(without much work?)
never grow old.

He didn't renege
he said I'll
take no personal offense
and went out and
distributed a book
got a dirty look.

He said I dismissed.
I went around asking others
what's your experience?

What an array of opinions I gathered! Then I decided to chant my prayers in private before Gaura-Nitai, but nothing happened, so I said as in the desert tradition I'll wait on God. He'll reveal if He likes, and if not, I'll just stay and wait.

I'll broadcast His glories on His song, as Lord Caitanya
and I'll be kind to others. Not
dissimulate and I'll be a
peacemaker
keep the promise
the faith
science
smile in
my master's
feet
I am
a toenail watcher
forgive me my
excess and offer
*pinda* to my soul
        errant.

*pp. 78–81*

❖ ❖ ❖

*Burnt Orange*

& This happy day infectious
happy birthday
he was a lovin' man
  in best sense. This man
is lonely thinks he's
not good at art poetry
or his religion.

But give him an intro
to other leaders and he'll
come back alone ASAP.

Soon as he can
Now is we are saying
Krishna I chanted a little
there in the garage drive
pebbles, sun cold
and a farmer in shocking orange
(don't shoot me)
moves in his tractor
I thought he'd
see me and think who is
this man or woman in Hare
Krishna pale orange

Burnt orange
darn peach
saff-Ron
He's a member monk mark him.

Return to You Lord in
all things I couldn't find
You
why does my ankle ache
why cars on the road
could I hack if if I

had to go to work every day
in that little car.

It might be nice here in
summer. Violet
crawlers on that wood
piece against the old
trailer...wife and child
waiting while he goes
to work.

The dredge the drudge we
each feel
The worthless self-
estimation and then suddenly
    a lift.
Suddenly and then
back into your working
groove.

You are the priest for
a flock, expect you – "Please accept me,
please detect in me
and give me the juice carrot
batteries wisdom of
Prabhupada.

Quirk man
we wish to God
we could end in
best consciousness like a
musician in his last
album
now it's just plain
good for everyone
Take it folks
my sinceres.

*pp. 87–89*

*A Letter*

Now there's no way I can be without you dear friend. I'm writing from Czech. I want to go back to Ireland early, get away from controversy and into that quiet routine again.
Poems
A brother writes after India pilgrimage – but I'm different – why go to India if you have to come back? And why lecture if you don't know yourself?

You squeak heart secret way to evince
a Western mind
car horn
just leave me alone
he said
I'll give you a good story
full of cheer in Krishna consciousness
so saying he entered the ball pen.

"Dear Guruji, please initiate me. You are the most sincere of the lot. No one else but you for me."

Gee wiz, he kicked sawdust with his toe
and said
Just leave me with
Radha-Govinda again.

*pp. 91–92*

*Fooling Around*

Now they say there will be a big
snowstorm. That may be
clouds on parade
this is serious enough.

Now this is done by many
times going over a tune until you know
it so well you can play with it.
Dixie
let's get serious.

This is riotous fun. This is
the end of the fun. Now the seal,
the clown, is playing.

It's because they're so well practiced
in Krishna consciousness they can do it –
like the back of the veined hand of the old
*sadhu* who knows all *lila*
places.

I know snow drops will come
and I'll be out there catching them
    cider
Nero
book on Saint Paul
in Krishna.

This the way the fellow spends an afternoon mooling
around, then call with whistle for study of
*Bhagavatam*. Gather students and get them down in
rows.
(Same rows we eat in.)

Got our tickets for going back
early to Ireland as I asked. "Your
word is my command." The
music is to be true
the danger is to one day pass
through despair careening
and come out like a car
washed like a kid through
a scare house.

Hey I saw it the monsters
peeked out jumped out
and we made it –
scare house
by mouth of clown you
enter.

School days
the pizza club
devotees know better
than fool around
may die in Vrindavan
favorite place when it's
your time
the serious lectures.

Snow flies
front-wheeled drive – let's
get over there before the
storm and then...we can burrow
in and not worry, enough 'tatters and
color crayons
alas.

You don't keep straight on Maharaja
Pariksit and Sukadeva and Suta.
Well I tried but you see I had the marbles
when
I was a kid
and saw a young woman dancing
    got loose as a goose
from tea
He said, "I read your book
it shook me up you were
like an LSD head and a Mrgari
and now you're a disciple of Srila Prabhupada so I
figure you'd be a suitable
guru for me."

Guppies. I just think animals
should roam free. But he
explained that bulls are
unmanageable and must be made
into oxen. I don't argue.

This coda comes around
we promise I will rise with
hope to chant but Lord's not
letting me, once tears or something
I'll not give up
I'll not
give up
chant Hare Krishna.

*pp. 93–96*

⁂

*Let's Go Alone*

Lord.

(Hang on I want Krishna consciousness)
We will go to Ireland in a little room with Radha-
Govinda. No ghosts. We will. Help us,

This is the moanin' part of life. When you go guttural
and pray and cry to Krishna please help.
Well I'm too much of a polite fellow to get into that.

I thought he was going to shout and make a fuss. This
the truth. He wants to see Krishna
– and no one seems to inspire him so he goes alone
and cries out to Krishna about that.

O Lord! Saint Francis's tears,
Bhaktisiddhanta Sarasvati Thakura recommends tears

Desert Fathers speak of its purification – tears. "Not a dry eye in the house."

Saint Teresa of Avila mocked persons who squeezed a few tears our of their prayer session. So, it's not to be imitated.

No sir.
The Navy rack
I cried at Doris's house after my first few days in the barracks. And cried all night on LSD in my Suffolk Street apartment, after the Navy, partly because I saw my paradise was empty.

Now end this song
was good news to
all fellow Christian-Krishnian
soldiers
let's march on this
*bhakti-marg* and
pick flowers for Radha
and Krishna.

Don't despair. It will
come but not before
you...
cry
for it.

*pp. 100–1*

⁂

Oh yes oh yes
the ghosts are gone
the dancers here are souls
they want me to
prepare a feast
but who's gonna offer it to God?

Well you can do that you-know-how, you're a
*brahmana*, you're a Vais-nava.

You think so? I don't think
I am,
but there's no one else
so here goes!

*pp. 118–19*

⁂

*Pannonica*

Oh, a blue day I mean a gray white day, he
painted his side out.

He horned his way in
you can't get in that
way. You can only be a
true devotee if He lets
you

compose
a lecture to arouse the sentiments
But we've heard it so many
times
*krsnas tu bhagavan*
can you do better than our
guru – of course not.
Love goes that way...

Hiding out in a Pa. farm
in snow-bound
There's no way
I can find the buried
treasure in palm of
my hand.

Snow blows wind flakes
of snow
yeah my man,
the wind picks up blowing
that deep
dark color of
Tuscarora
sign "Yamuna River" covered
in snow.

I'm sorry I'm going astray. But your
*brahmacari sankirtana* drama and
dance didn't move me
I preferred my secret
thing going on
They said...

Pannonica was a duchess
patronized the arts
This is the way I said
That our father in heaven
(I) drink water more
and said this little
life I jam with
hours and colors – he
gave us jam for
bread but we preferred
to listen.

The time of snow
coming down on us. This
was before the epic
*Ramayana*
or *Mahabharata* was
conceived
What?

Yes, long ago when Krishna
spoke to sun god

when I had attention
which I intend to revive
I intend to be a good boy
again
at my desk.

You'll see snow
You'll see clouds
the plane soars over
the president of the Un
ited States
in trouble but worse
are Iraqis
"It's not over yet."

The morning power comes
from God – see Him
there and nowhere else
in Yamuna
Govardhana.

That's right. That's right.

So we stopped to listen to
the brook
our ears alert
so alive even though we
is a dead fifty-eight years critter
can't revive.

Even though all is gone
out of Gita-nagari past
I am in an instant and
Madhu plays Pannonica
on his melodeon.

I am reading
(in a make-believe)

*Gita* verses as intent
as he is playing his music
I read
and say Krishna thanked you for coming to
us favoring our lives and finally taking away
last illusions.

Leaving us so small and
naked and finally I
surrender
yes, we look forward
to that
only if He wills.

*pp. 120–24*

⁂

*Bhaktin Donna Lee*
O Krishna there's no way
he said but to be in love with the
Krishna conscious preacher.
There's no way but to go
with that preacher
downtown and follow
him in giving out books
or what he does.

There's another thing – a cookie
he gave
he said work hard
your art influences me
said Donna Lee.

She said I can't go fast
so don't expect me to be
in with love with a Krishna conscious preacher
in a right way
attach for a *sadhu*.

Then we ran around the
bend. Snow fell so
heavily I didn't know
what was going to
happen.

Donna Lee, will you like
to be a devotee?
But what will my parents
say?
Hide the Deities
rent a flat
move into temple.

Donna Lee Anabell
went to France I'm not
saying you should be
a devotee that way
but at least chant.

But do *you, sadhu*?
Yes, I do yes I do.

I said I don't refrain
from that sort of thing
not madness
too fast
spiritual life ought to
be slower,
and I don't jump
into it too
cold freezing creek.

Anna Donna, may
we call you Dinabandu
may we arrange your
marriage
and carriage and *sari*.

Dina do, will you
like if we plan
the whole thing for
you.

II
We imitate Prabhupada
sound like
wear cane
dress
tough
sound English
and can't make it.

Be a puppet he said
let's all be puppets of
our Guru Maharaja.

Donna Lee agreed and was
the new generation of
disciple. She twirled her baton
a last time
and became *prem*
transcendental.

Then I said
I will be the initiating guru
of everyone in NYC no
more
too many peoples'
    karma
            it's not 1960–80.

*pp. 128–31*

⁂

*Clown*

O pretty miss the snow is
quiet and I'm quiet the medicine
works
you keep your trap shut
please be kind and easy on me
all these loving etiquette devotees
open up *my* heart?

I'm not insincere stalwart
tell your sister and your momma
the clown is louting
and I love him too
he's in Krishna consciousness.

I heard you discoursed
on *dhira* tell us more.
Well it was like this –
I was clown indeed but *dhira*
Christ was tolerant even
on the Cross but not
making light playful jokes
and ribalded
Lord Nityananda was
cross out the word
you made a mistake.

"When is it okay to be
disturbed?"
Okay? I have a right to
feel bad, I have cancer.
Yes
sir
that's my baby.

He said the empty spaces
indicate where they will
build houses in the future.

So I said *dhira* is okay
we cannot advance as *adhira*
But Goswamis were
loved by all even dogs.

It is disappearance day of Jiva
so good you spoke on it
Get it done the
program the schedule
of work performances
the poetry reading –

Can they see in the shadow
when I pee in the toilet
there's only a light curtain –
never mind we are leaving here
soon enough.

Can they see into my
room paintings of jest
and I read a guru's newsletter
and say, "All-high persona."
Am I better
prolonged fast
This tat-tat-tat reprimand.

*Dhira* is the way
self-control
drive your car steady
Don't get distracted
corny examples
Me I'm a regular man
saying Be *dhira*
by flowing
with the Now in Krishna consciousness
    be pleasing
*parampara*

*pp. 140–43*

*Dusk New Year's Eve*

Now it's dusk blue I mean now the columns are sinking
before my eyes
Don't forget it's God.

Roll
The sun is gone
the peahen is white
she wouldn't like this sound.

Say oh is he wounded is he
crying? Peahen as white
as snow goes to roof
snow crust.

Krishna, I heard *nama*
while walking outdoors
it was better than
indoors.

"I listen to him very
closely." And?
Something universal but
cacophonous to me.

Let loose
they want to put a fellow
like that in a cell
not Benedicting.

Now calm down and realize this
in time when this is
normal, but you can
also expect
a reaction.
Krishna sets the patterns and
makes fun when you
can't get out of it.

Krishna Krishna I'm going to call
on You, and the effort
will be dusk the
water in creek could
freeze.

Stalk white patters
like to go out and walk
yet indoors read *Srimad*
yet I can't just a little
Be calm and cool
and just take it in
the tendency to.

- Look! Wind moves that
ten foot tall evergreen
thin
branches shivered
snow fell off.

Look it moves me not
I look through sheaf
of colored drawings just
to enjoy the messages and
explain to a friend how
I did them.
Krishna Krishna Narada the words
laid on or pasted on later.
Krishna
Boy wants devotion.
Be a sport.
Control senses.
Worship Lord.
Be a haven run mad.

Don't break this thing...
Whew all them words
don't hardly make sense as much
as you might like.

Squirrel acrobatics
my master said you can
do it for Him.

The words in Goloka right now, in Vrindavan in India. Some *sadhus* have very little clothes old ripped burlap for bed cloth, some are not *sadhus* but Vrajavasis and the animals no clothes at all and no mercy either as they attack.

You could hear *their* sounds
and say, "Sounds similar to your praying to God" call of pain pigs' fear, monkeys' war and fear and rituals like that.

The art of *vaidhi*
the sweet *bhava* the
rocks holy
the dirt eternal (they say).

Well you can say all that but I figure best for me to go where I can find a routine peace and when day is stolen from me I'll make the best and go in and accept the mere pain and say Krishna in this way sweet you are taking me along, please be in my life in the way You like and give me to perceive it.

*pp. 144–48*

❖ ❖ ❖

*Your Signature*
He's got his own signature
we each have a way that's
ours – it's his
intro theme.

Why is it quirky mine?
Now is the time
the people

like it.
Krishna, I'm walking on icy
 crust You will help us
each step even if
we fall and break a
wrist
You are never lazy or
neglectful in our
care.
Now is the
time to spend in His
service
my motto use time
well
means.

Let's not mess with
women don't let
them lean on you
or you on them
or smell their fragrance
even in a dream –
no dirty looks.
Keep on guard don't fall
and if you start to slip
call Krishna!

No compromises. Take a
pill only if you have
to go
may you die in
Ireland in Vraja consciousness.
May your pen not skip
or heart
except for Krishna
may the earth rise to
meet you
    with a smile.

New year go away
your way.

*pp. 157–59*

*Ugly Beauty*

Real beauty is in Krishna, and we should know that
        The tender is for Him
our sweet Lord
        a *gopa* in Vrindavan.

He taught us in his books.
I go exclusively
down a death walk
no melody, but I can
use it in his service.

Oh stand sway grace
gently on your old legs
for the Lord and His
two *sakhis* on either side
of Him and Radha.

Thank you he said and I'm sure grateful you praise me as an exalted Vaisnava although I am not. My time runs out but we are all here in a new year dear. Praise your dynasties laugh and thank God.

They already pledged to their guru who brought them here – they didn't know for a month that they were Hare Krishnas – he tricked them with love and black grace.
*Smile.*

So they don't need your ugly beauty
you are an accessory
*alankara*

even if the *alankara* is
wrong, stubbed if it's
*jayanti* – praising the Lord
it will be accepted.

Ugly beauty is the world.
If you forget him
Keats
I got the pocket mantra
glove and at all times on my beads
he's not left us, everyone's Founder- *Acarya*
Krishna

I'm just piddling away I
got no sense it's now too
do right or believe us
Lord we are
going to walk in snow to
the temple
I'm only doing
  what counts.

I'll be a good man
this morning talk what it
takes
do the thing for Him.

So, you all, if you want to
help me print and sell these books
okay but I have to do it
for Krishna

or I'll feel wanting like
Vyasadeva
do you think you'll be
satisfied thinking that the body and mind
is the self
or not *dhira*
or not kind to the *adhiras*?

No, it's not possible if you
don't go direct to Krishna
you'll suffer
dis-satisfaction
be a satisfied
Satsvarupa
trooper
in real beauty of service
to find Krishna
master who rules
take this easy path seeking
sun to task, easy or
as you will.

Now close this poem and
be a homing pigeon to
Gita-nagari
temple room
conch
  open door
    Radha-Damodara.

*pp. 159–62*

*After the Clubhouse*
This meeting was okay, until they said you are swell
and my pride swelled. If they put me down that would
have been worse.

So here we are in Pittsburgh ink shining on the trail runaway from familiar but stay safe – you know it's like when you're a mother and your son still wets and craps in this diaper
  but you hold him up for
the world to see
proud football player.
You know my secret fun
in the clubhouse I said

"Little Lulu and Tubby" and love it
she said your memories help us
to throw away our memories I
thought Oh, well maybe we
want to keep them as delight
in letting go
the Lulu balloon
goes up and up
over 5th Avenue
Ratha-yatra.
Lohitaksa gone to
next life such a handsome
and talented guy a credit
to ISKCON he and his wife, Rasajna
break stereotype of
cultist dull.
O whale bone O save
the black and white
make believe whales.

He's his and hers
what else happened
in your clubhouse when
you gathered in your crowd?
Oh, they said
the fruit of this can be
  made into juice and jam
    anyone not present today
can join later.

Your great intellect weighing
in lightweight. He's a
self-effacer beep beep
get aside – kid
hit me from behind with
his smart cart he was
a Jew or a Black
at least he wasn't

a Hare Krishna – ouch!
Didn't even say, "Sorry."
Blues the mood piping along
no is loverly best
the champ gets defeated
you better read *Srimad-Bhagavatam* and
talk *on those* subjects
bubble gum,
playing marbles
won't get you
heaven,
  spirit soul.
The sweet time so
haven and laden with
love the tune that
gets you set up to
say
Monk in cell prays
*gopal* mantra and *kama-gayatri*
and Lord Caitanya
ah
um
Krishna Krishna we love the
Lord

*pp. 162–65*

*First Day of The Year Blues*

I have nothing very special to say. This band is okay to take us back to Godhead.
I'm a sad fellow a sad case wrote a disciple from a big town. My reply is cursory.

I can't seem to take time
you say oh Ireland will be
the place I'll think of Vrindavan there
    but won't it be
the same...?

Maybe the thing is I'm talking to you

I'm not the strongest man in the
world
like *he* sounds.

My oh my we sit on a seat
and speak the ideal and make
a splice a knot (boy scout)
to present cases.

Here is how you do it.
Talk to me
alone with the scriptures
and everyday talks.

Krishna Krishna you can't do
much how silly people sound
and that includes me –
so I like when a voice
cries but not for himself
but
yes, just one but
for all.
  Louder make it louder
just for a little while
today first day of year
blip blip music
from the
place.

He wanted to go back to school
to work to play at

night alone in a room
get a best girlfriend –
what? Daydream "All that life of past it
garbage to throw out" said
a reader of *Memories*
But is that the point?

We wobble
cry
fierce
but don't hurt,
Feel the melodies great
composers have given –
you can ripe it up –

Radha-Gopivallabha
Radha-Damodara
"I found Lord Nityananda's mercy this
year in Mayapur" – I find it
hard to believe my brothers
find what I see no trace of.
Sounds like they are talking of
something
nowhere.
Where is your heart
new gloves, shoes, too much
pampering "A pair of boots
for Gita-nagari and a pair for
your travel" pie dessert,
ladies cook for you.

Everything is sad, but
music makes us merry
I'm telling this for
the benefit
return
*my* Krishna.

*pp. 168–71*

(Part two page numbering starts here)

*Resisting*

I was resisting it but
this allows me to write my
last day in Gita-nagari
you can separate the pain
from feeling it he said
But
I know only a few things and then
you will be with me
fly with me on a breeze.

Just sleep and relax and
draw a free pic of a man
facing another man extending
hands to each other.

I haven't even looked
out at the sky or trees or
anything, why don't you
take a walk.

The man in your soul
in you as taught by *Bhagavad-*
*gita*
then this will lead
you all the days running you'll
be dying down the same road
as young Lohitaksa
    your time
`   will be.
Then the piano won't play unless
you recorded it but your
unknown self goes on to another
life I can't keep time exactly
straight.

Pretty sky ugly road
and layward wayward forbidden
areas for celibate monk
in his birthday
the holidays are over for
*karmis* and flu is going around
    get a BMW: "Stop
dreaming, start driving" on great
lease terms
don't cover it up.

Don't remember all the
things you didn't want
now let's
remember to be ourselves
commit a good act of contrition
the Krishna conscious way
your master.

The truth spoken the
way he likes.

*pp. 9–10*

*Tonight*

Tonight, there will be just a
warmed bed, and I hope I can
sleep all right.

There's nothing to cry for
Krishna is far away
and very near
that you know
how little you know.

This night a star a bunch
of them clear in the night,

and you under the roof filled
with peacocks.
Snowy, wet, melty world
you're inner dreams not
ecstatic, worried fellow
I think you're lucky
lucky.

You are loved, cared for,
and your group lives
under shelter of Supreme.

Knowledge we accept and
embrace
follow the Krishna teachings – e-mail from
Osaka, Japan, "We distributed
one thousand *maha*-big books at
the Red Light district in Christmas time."

And I say me too
sweat it out each day
clipped back you can't
do better, keep time.

Oh, it's like this in a bar...
no I'm a clean head
empty, take off that
sweatshirt
bed down
tonight I admit
I'm simple.

*pp. 16–18*

⁂

*On Leaving Gita-nagari*

Music hath charms. I go my way
tapping a toe as long as you are sound in

head
oh, my poor head
    you can't know.

He sounds like a disciple of a
master he's following.
Well what do you expect me to
say something original is he making the
usual changes
and what's the sense of that.

Please don't intrude on me now
not just now
I have to create
leave me to do it
heat cracks into the room
I'm the person who has to cry
out in way he never did before.

Music man of Gita-nagari we will
just stay here and leave early no more
temple participation, the community is fine
    but I'm too hurt
too lone
too blue
too new
too few to be
part of it again in this lifetime.
Just a little off from it is my campfire. The sound we
make is a little cacophonous and sweet you can't raise
that in the group.
Got to be apart
yet a part.

In – we are
all *Prabhupadanugas* hard
strident interpretation of the
master

we come down the street,
    down center aisle of Grand
Cathedral led by *Bharatanatyam* 16-
year-old girl, two hundred Indian and
American Hare Krishnas lead the
way, and the old people turned
half-turned in their seats to see
what was coming – same as
the caterwauling in the street?

Laugh at it / cry out
we know how to do it,
everyone has his way to find the
heart of Krishna consciousness
now present, we
are Krishna conscious troops until we die
    see you in Vrindavan, man.
See you when are you
going by plane and train to India?
Don't even ask if he's going
to GBC meeting / chant in the van
betide be woe oh oh, Krishna.

*pp. 21–24*

*Sunday in a Closed Room*

Now I want to be a Krishna conscious person *but* free. But you'll get it all right. Don't worry. You can see Krishna all right.

*I don't.*

I don't understand how a fella like you can get away with this.
It's easy. Krishna lets you, and you recip-ro-cate givin' it back.

I see. I see you'll be
all right. He's the higher note.
This is the home boy sock
in two pair of socks
still he's on edge of twinge in
eye high price tag for
life.

Pain isn't hurt
Pain is a picture I remove
it's a Sunday matinee we're
at a feast see, crowded room
I wish well for all
devotees ethnics varied
men and women.

No no there is good and
bad there is familiar and
I spoke at cabin on
leaving said God works
to deliver His devotee
from out of place by removal of thorn.

If on *parikrama* you get a
thorn, sit down
at once and remove it with pin,
or it'll drive in deeper
with each step...

That Parasurama dasa doesn't
like me, and I make a
demand on him – some
people just don't work –
go as best you can
serving your master.

I'm going back to Ireland
and even before that I

can begin *Bhagavad-gita* reading
the groovy Lord said
the Arjuna wise heard
and I partook.

If the GBC comes down
me, I'll them
what Arjuna and Uddhava
and Narada and I got
a headache leave me
alone
that's all right.

On a Sunday in a closed room
a quiet man gets to
wail in his own way
That's melody for two
we're also working
for Krishna
to free self
be self
throw off tedium.

And die in the arms of Lord
that's the truth isn't
it give me a
round extra to give
to my Lord.

And walk in senior citizens
park concentrate on
what you really
are
really – a servant!

*pp. 28–31*

⁂ ⁂ ⁂

*Special Permit*

I am here and would fall asleep if I tried to read
*sastra* so I'm telling you.
Stay awake in some form of
Krishna consciousness
memory music yearning plan.

You recall the squeak which uttered a way to tell
people we wanted peace at any price.
This was what I said.

Come on, be a devotee, go to Goloka. In your time,
you've got it made, answer a letter, take a shower and
in there get a good idea.

Krishna said I started it all,
I finish it as Shiva, I take
My devotees to Me, devotees
are My heart.

He gave the strict orders
through guru to avoid non-devotees
and sense gratifiers.

I've got a special permit
    special mission
special price I have to pay –
I wanted to share the sounds
left themselves
he's recalling his master and
I recall mine even as I go my
own way
gathering in what I can for Krishna.
And did not go to the weekend conference at New
Vrindavan, and don't want to hear about it, dodge,
Brooklyn Dodger, in between them so before they ask
for you you've gone.

Who? My name is disconsolate,
no, I'm truly satisfied
but don't know, Lord,
if You'll be satisfied with
me
that's the thing
You are in our life
at every moment.
  Stop fooling yourself take
American Epi Airlines
Allegheny USA don't
crash but pray just
in case
and slip on ice disc got
medical plan.
Beggars take money to
help themselves on plea of
being a devotee of Krishna.

Now I believe you've got
to make yourself into
a silk sow purse
of money gathered in
checks of SDG road
travel houses stay
kettle warm in bed.
  He's gonna read
his way to heaven
    you just see
won't disappoint his Swami
we'll sing the tune to
please
the secrets put out
in his own way
ladybird shed time
surrendered soul demanded
freedom
given.

*pp. 40–43*

*Short Portrait*

There's no way a guy like me can be young again, and
the truth is head fogs even on a sunny day.

Wow is the splayed out nature of mind and taste
(inclination) which you might expect would be better
after thirty years.

I'm just happy to be able to write some ditty daily lines,
hang'em out to dry like in a backyard.
    blues sweet every housewife
or daily worker can find
if he's a little intro-
spective to God in his
life.

No, it's *maya*
but for myself I'm never
away from the Krishna conscious strain.

Wish it could come more
vivid / short lives/
"We are here for such a short time"
 that's *too* short.

*pp. 45–46*

*Embrace What I Can of His Teachings*

Hello he's got a hot front man
they're crashing through I can't say
it's my time
But when they swerve enough
traffic

it's far too fast for me I
sit back and feel my
pulse.

Hey man I pardon you
and believe you
swagger not, slow down
for this man makin' his
way through a day with no
pills.

He wrote an open letter to
the Maestro which is the
way we should do it provided
he can lead us to freedom
from death / simply believe.

At this point embrace what
you can of his teachings lean
walk/talk/write
cry would be nice
but it's all got to come
natural.

Follow rules
look at old memorabilia
of Swami in '66
moving to loft, Mr. Paul
irritated, take caution
working on typewriter...

The past I excavate a
note Steve gave one hundred
and then three hundred, moving fast
again

Going to India? No to
Ireland don't follow me
into a sylvan cave

and I content to face self
“My way is introspective
and personal not like your academic – “

Honor them all
saints
stop the *aparadhas* to
leading preachers.

Then.
I just limp sorry about
all this crass and cross
down shuffle
I'm really merry just need
    a break.

*pp. 46–48*

*Make Krishna Known My Own Way*

Back from a walk a singer
me toes his arch
for Krishna is God.

Complain: No one knows
my God as God
well you got to make
it known.

He better first please the
guru group his own
if they put him down...

Phone: Whatcha doin'
man? I'm disappearing
I'm telling you that.

So we never heard you
or saw you as we wanted
than this –
you better play
as best you can.

Sorry he couldn't do
more he trampolined
in *sastric* garland
umbilical
chord.
You
better get on the
line
e-mail preferred.

No – only to God
and guru and all
honestly people
there's the
answer
you bet
betta.

*pp. 56–57*

*Wail and Control*

You can be alone with a man
sound threatening? But an artist
a devotee...now that sounds
better let's say he just wants to
convey Krishna consciousness in good way

He's got a groove. He's got
a sound. The sky is gray and so
warm you just hope there'll be no
bad time hate flashes and what to

speak of.
Please don't bug me about my
entrance of a Krishna conscious theme. Here's
the boy thinnish from the
painting by Madame Heng of
China she didn't know
Krishna except what they told
her and showed some prints –
well organized.

I am on crowded on all sides by
repercussions and censors and what
seems right. Cages.
Boundary walls – are
also to keep out dacoits.

So, you don't know what's the
best thing. You wrassel around
with God who could
kill you in a moment.

This themeless seamless
seamy desire to play?
He's the sound in ether
"Is ether something or nothing?"
It's something, subtle
occupies time and space.

So, although sitting silently I can't
say much at all what's
from cubby hole to cubby-
hole sorting paper clips from
rubber bands, taking off a sweater
opening a window, then
closing it. The wail will
finally come.

I was attached to one brother
to talk honest our doubts
confidential, faced even
blasphemy – faced and said
I want love of guru and Krishna
But how can one like me...

Face displeasure with the
institution. The letter back
and forth but I don't want e-
mail. He's peaceful but what
man is without the honest
wail of confusion and has
to let it out, control it –
I appreciate hearing it
calm down.
   Like a demon in him.
He moves you to your own
honest investigation – why am
I so quiet? What's under
the cover of man
who washes mud off his
shoes, keeps identical pairs
of shoes and tries to go as
far as he can
without disturbing
himself?

Vibrato. Deep dark secrets
some scandals I won't let
out even at death, it'll
help no one – Indians who
respect me don't want to
hear what all I went
through...
            And so, the Grecian urn told
its tale. Krishna conscious prose
format.

*pp. 60–63*

*Thinking of The Longest Retreat*

The Krishna consciousness that brandishes the
memory. She wants it to come out
that way. I do too. I want
to tell something
not for novelty
but what comes
faded rose
know hurricane he said here
only it happened in England
only Ireland is cool.

You are welcome to come here
safe land
touch and Ani will greet you with two hard apples and
old banana don't expect scones.

Small car and ride in back
happy tired jet-lagged but heading
for the longest retreat ever
don't need koan to
explode satori
just go with invisible
Acintya
Lord Krishna
   is inconceivable
Lord to pure souls
and me in practices
I got it made
the longest retreat
a few months
withholds Lord
until I show more stuff.

*pp. 66–68*

*My Master's Class in a Classic Groove*

I got to keep aloof
keep in *Srimad-Bhagavatam* my nose
keep count of
the money.

Count assets / here's a system
I'm out of ink
dream and dangers and wake in
safest places imaginable.
Don't write so hard it goes through
the page / these are simple times

Krishna consciousness is like that
good beat kept us steady
makin' the changes
as they say – sun and
sunshine, *Bhagavad-gita*, go out and
preach, whole world's in
ignorance, Krishna calls them
*mudhas.*
The same tradition as Rupa is
good enough for me
Vrindavan dirt unchanging all these
years, monkeys...
But the world is crying out
*karma-yoga*
bring them into
hear from you as the
beet reet
yes, my master's
in a classic groove and I
don't tire of his "Body and Soul"
*aham brahmasmi*
Krishna says
chant Hare Krishna
go and preach.

*pp. 68–70*

*Open Letter to Boss*

I'm not feelin' so good
Boss
well still you gotta
 work.

I'm not feelin' so blue
not so Krishna conscious
that's the main
not feeling so much because
I play it safe
I'm getting old
not feeling for people
'cause I'm selfish

my sound is my own
I know the idiom and
have to innovate

Boss I'm not feelin'

the love but you told
Srutakirti the main
thing is service itself

I'm in the tradition
your servant but
gee after thirty-one
years in the business I want
to shake out my own
thing and reach *but*

make a suitable contribution
to your Movement
so, it moves
moves just a society
of rules and big shots
mow 'em down,

the opposition in the world
is so
powerful seeming
and apathetic

work as one going out
the music of sound
principle?

Boss, Lord, your *cela*
wagging, tagging
his mind
sons of his
own daughters,
granddaughters –
can I tell them
who I really
am?

And why, boss, do I
lag so in central
Krishna consciousness
why
no love and you know the answer is
I didn't work
enough!

He wants more!
said Saint Francis and
naïve Brother Leo said
why, haven't you
done enough? No, not enough. He wants me
to go to my cell, and
He'll tell me next
what more.

I haven't done enough and
you want to push

me through just when I'm begging you
please give me a break
peace, my space, my own room and
no demands...
Boss I'm a sad case, but
happy too
departing from
strictness
not too far, I
hope,
taking a chance
with these
improvisations.

Your memory your picture I'm
telling the followers of the
fine times you suffered to
    bring us Krishna
      helpless it seemed you
        endured
          love.

*pp. 75–78*

*Back and Forth Jiva-Cela*

Alone sitting reaching out
 wanting my master
but then you have to go to him.

You can't go somewhere else
and so oh I'd like to be
a pure devotee. With crows.

Straight up and up is
reading *sastra* regularly
same old format reveals
Krishna in the casting.

What's in you, "Is there
a sound, like 'T-O-N-G!?'"
the guy asked and Srila
Prabhupada said Yes, it's
Hare Krishna the piano tong!
AUM – Radha
Krishna
*Jiva*

me struggling wail tomorrow I'll hold high note, blue
note no will know I'm not perfectly straight – tong!

My TONG! is to simply
repeat and tell of Swami's
early days including when
he initiated Satya-svarupa
and Steve gave hundreds
he was a washed
out skinny dude
(locks on window grates)

Swami had a phone gave
it up, "Always disturbed"
disciples phoning him at midnight
Swamiji how are you?
Is this the time to ask?
Oh, I'm sorry

I'm sorry, regret I didn't
send you the *murtis* and
hundreds of thousands
to buy a temple in Manhattan .
A laughing stock hopeless.

“I am not
satisfied.”

Paul Mr. Paul Steve
Don’t play the horn or
bass anymore unless you
can join in *kirtana* and
don’t disturb.

*Kirtana* is main thing
chanting the holy names some crazy guy at the door
don’t
let him in
no! Elliot! He feints a
punch but doesn’t deliver, only leaves –
I’m glad of that.

What was I saying?
You are straying from master yet
saying oh I want him and
Krishna.

That’s what you were saying
and drawn to storefront
days, nights, as if –
   No, it *was* and is true I’m
made of that my memoir
is not of music but of
stopping all and doing only
transcendental loving service with
him from New York to
Boston just went enter it
and all else left behind.

That’s the spirit for you
out on Second Avenue that
evolution of Krishna consciousness
from Hayagriva to ISKCON Communications
and back it’s evolving and

the one master takes
us BTG.

*pp. 82–85*

*Irreversible Commitment*

Oooh listen to this my friend before it gets too dark to
see the roof and chimney.
I'm a little boy lost he said
The baby was playing with *karatalas*
in the other room and I
was...

in here resting lazy couldn't
move said just relax for your
big days tomorrow.

Krishna consciousness is like that
where you got at it in the
best fashion. You and your
friends. You get together and
admit stuff that may be
scary and vulnerable.

Like how come I don't
love to hear my guru
like I do used to how
come the temples are
so empty or filled with
a sound I can't bear?

Where's the...nature of man and
pudding? Krishna is in all things
dogma, we are in a background
that secret confidential
avant squirrels and screes

"Violinistically" he said I'm
nowhere going along a track
on something when he suddenly walks
in on me.

It was irreversible once I took to
Krishna consciousness I made that kind of promise
not to be allowed other
dog barks no Ravi Shankar
anymore

No mistakes.
I said I'm about to
go at it. He's talking to ya
the nerves I don't mind.

You'll be left alone. Krishna is the God we
    recognize the
tired riff wakes us and they
all sound a lot wilder than
it ever was

rile us awake us we want
to say the hell in us is
disappointment I can't write that
story yet (just now) of
entering the feeling of being
lost along the way

lost my ticket ticket nerve
the Movement got screwed
up by crazies and no one ever
said what actually happened
Can't get the history straight
never will
They're all going about
it wrong got to
explain it for myself
my own history anyway.

This groovy improv
is helping me to understand
there's no truth in the
driveway. He parks the
car nice. Over warm
winter morn walking in
mist dark pre-dawn where newspaper was thrown on
senior servant property.

This stuff *is* Krishna conscious
too because the whole world
is. My one-hour talk is just
a certain direct way but
ink flies all over in
coherency vocab
shrinks

Krishna Krishna baby plays *karatalas*
*sundara-arati*
Radha-Govinda
mine waiting for me
to come home
Ireland
land of irreversible
ire direct Krishna conscious
I'm better and worse
than it is.

*pp. 88–92*

*Praying with A Friend*

Alone alone he said in his lecture reading, and I'm
reading *Srimad-Bhagavatam*.

Now he actually is. With a friend. He (friend) said I'm trying to express the sound holy I hear in my head and dream of sometimes. He finally got it out?

And what about me? The flashing images on the slide show of *EJW* covers got a little too tedious.
Now we going our way too – it's a Krishna conscious trip for sure.

The ladies approve. Men too. But it's in the exact *milieu* they recognize – I'm pushing it freely, whoever saw abstract paintings in Krishna consciousness before?

The playful...That man, that creature those swirls the joy, you can't express in words, and yet he *says* things we all know. "I am alone, I'm sacrificing for *Bhagavatam*, I saw the
deer..."
He's hard he's soft he's contrary blues faking it.

Take a deep breath, junior.
"Will you gather us in one place when the earth changes take place?" No, I don't know about it, have no info.
I say pray to Krishna
learn to turn to Him
I can do it myself in
Guyana when I was afraid
in a car accident a friend did.

He said the earth changes
needn't
The siren
the rough, bluff.

Got their names mixed up
Caitanya dasa, Caitanya-roop and
Syama-goopa-rupa –

"You're under pressure"
  holy climb to Everest
   Meru, Brahmaloka
   go up
guide book
fighting me, I say, "I'm weak, let me go for now." To
fight alone
room with a pile of letters you
can answer, sweating, glad I
did it, day one
day one
pray the Lord is great
Krishna in our lives
That serene tough
of a church man who bows
down and praises Uttama-sloka
    peace in God reigneth
    Krishna dances
and Gauranga protects His
nice devotees O devotees
in India, excuse me as I
seek Krishna on back trail of
Wicklow and secret place
and send you these pictures
in the album
of hearts
mantras
Krishna clean us
Swami I'm praying in my
    way with my friend as he
prays
and we're under the
crescent full moon lotus
feet of Syama
Radhe-Syama.

*pp. 99–101*

*Wise One, Dear to Krishna*

End of day the wise one is
my spiritual master and like
him Narada and *bhakti*
masters following Lord
Caitanya...

Their qualities are so
transcendental and *audarya.*
Teach from where we are at.

Wise one, teach me, accept
my child-like offering. You can
do it, you gave me *prasadam*,
it's the memory I'll always
treasure.

Serene you are,
white clouds
clear pond, you are like
that and give us blessings –
to work for Krishna.

Lyric,
music
universe, little life...
God comes through you.

I'm hoping to go to a cave
comfortable one where I
can worship you
by my arts plentiful
scratching.

You bring peace to this *jiva*
he wants to love and feel
it, the spiritual dimension –
read what he wrote.

Let it get cold, let
breathe in deeply
on a winter walk I'll
be protected in boots you
provide and if it gets
rough in this *jagat* –
I'll be your *cela*.

Wise one, dear to Krishna
you are, lover of God
please include me in
your embrace of all
creatures.

Take me to you and not
too hard but the Lord
as Caitanya prays even
if You make me broken
hearted I'll be Yours,
the way is paved
strewn with flowers...

I know it's cruel and hard in
the *jagat* but we are ready
to take on what You send
in the mood of Bali Maharaja.

I'm writing by lamp in a little
clear space you give me.
Tell them – don't follow
me. Leave me be.
From my cave I'll give out
to share.
Lord Krishna I love You when
You let me serve You as best I
can.

Wise one, dear to Krishna
please let us work unto
dying day in some way
Your *seva* is vast enough
and we can do it if You
let me.

Wandering now, ready to
take rest in your shelter
once again
even at death and
after
serene, wise one let
me be with you
as serving.

*pp. 111–13*

*Same Old Hope*
My own way, remember the old days when you...not
yet delivered. You've got to be more hip?
No now you've got to be more – serious about next life,
not to return as best drummer.
Not to come back at all. To be instead a *parisad*, and I
don't mean prematurely thinking of *gopis*,
"A good idea."
But you have to wait
    for it.

While waiting,
you are not gonna blood
shed and hope
don't lament over the
lamentable sure-thing blues
may it go well you pray
God in our life.

He read poems but did
they listen to the message –
God in our lives
I'm not sure. Did I?

Once a boy was growing up and
he entered ISKCON was fine did
all duties for master then lost
something along the way? He lost or
the Movement lost? His guru lost
him? No, he's lost and
found by your grace
*etti ket*
don't blaspheme
me or your brother.

This is a story of what he
lost, grip on pen, ability to God
into street and stop someone with
a *BTG,* ability in man.
Can he find,
go back to where you lost
the car keys look on
ground with flashlight.
Look with therapist into
your past flash
life or is there a way
I found my lost love
an eternal soul
guts to serve Krishna as He wants.

I found diminishing power
and cynic is improved
I found I want to be
alone I get hurt
by any criticism of my
writings.
It ain't Kerouacian so
you're wrong there

by Cracky
those guys too...

We're inspiring in us love
improvising and sad into
happy by art
and now that can be
done for Krishna I sure hope so
or we're lost.

(Lost again) well He may
accept but say it's not the
best – karma to *prema*
hear the sparrows flit to
the feeder and fly away when
I loom too near the
window
old Manu dasa, here I come you still got only
that one dented gray car?
Is it the same old
with hope?

Here we come back
our same old we
don't have a new epic outlook
or speaking more in *bhava*
as natural supreme love
from *japa*
put our finger on wrong
 same old yearn
for writing free
even.

*pp. 128–31*

How long how long how long
don't ask. Just write your

best and follow that lady
who said she wants rhymes
and romance like Yeats
a cracker I never ate.

No more Beat what's
your Totten-tots
have no place in a lady's
heart. Old yes old
man staggers down aisle
in jet bus to toilet
*toilette* piss and wash
your face isn't pretty
to a young Irish pug
nor is he to me
but I'm glad to be
alive mummy
a little longer for
my master
roundelay.

*pp. 138–39*

# CHAPTER THREE - RETURN TO QUIET HEROICS

January 14 – February 1, 1998

"So, how come you call this book heroic?
I say quiet heroics. I'm saying that to deal with my
spiritual poverty is to "return," that is, to come back to
the spiritual standard. This is my fight. It's my
battlefield right now, not another. I'm fighting to use
my time properly."

*Part Two, p. 46*

The term heroism is typically used to suggest an action of bravery and self-sacrifice. One thinks of enormous, almost superhuman displays of strength and compassion, actions undertaken without any self-regard. Given this common understanding of heroism, the understated title of Satsvarupa dasa Goswami's twenty-second volume in his literary series, *Every Day, Just Write,* may leave the reader with an intriguing question. What might "a return to quiet heroics" be? In this volume, Satsvarupa Maharaja will share critical wisdom for the spiritual life. The spiritual journey is not characterized by dramatic acts of bravery. Rather, the humble devotion typically hidden from the eyes of the world will be defined by the author as "quiet heroics." The spiritual life is characterized by a daily effort to maintain a spiritual discipline, or *sadhana,* of faithfulness and commitment. The reality is that to embrace and maintain such a discipline is heroic indeed, given the persistent demands of the ego and the allure of the world.

In this volume, the reader is introduced to the term, *vaidhi-bhakti,* the significance of which is immeasurable. *Vaidhi-bhakti* refers to the practice of devotional life with a commitment to observe and maintain the regulative principles of spiritual practice ordained by the great Vaisnava *acaryas,* and in particular, A.C. Bhaktivedanta Swami Prabhupada. Within Christian devotional life, *vaidhi-bhakti* is expressed by phrases such as "the ordered life," a life in which specific parameters of discipline provide boundaries for the pilgrim on his or her journey. Lest one think that such boundaries or regulative principles stifle the life of the spirit, one should consider a fascinating study conducted by child psychologists.

A group of children were given access to two playgrounds. The first playground was enclosed by a perimeter fence, while the second playground possessed no such boundary. Significantly, the children on the enclosed playground were observed to play freely, using the entire area for play. Then, on another occasion, the children were given access to the playground without a boundary. In this instance, the children played in a very limited space within the playground, that being its center area. The conclusion: boundaries actually and perhaps counter-intuitively, provide the safety and security which foster conditions for freedom. Conversely, the lack of boundaries actually stifles freedom, resulting in minimal playground space being used for play. As with children on a playground, so it is in the spiritual life. The carefully constructed framework that is created by the observance of *vaidhi-bhakti* principles provides room for advancement in the knowledge and love of God, and in the context of this world, faithfulness to its precepts is nothing short of heroic.

Within this volume, through both his poetry and prose, Satsvarupa Maharaja details the characteristics of his quiet heroics: reading, chanting, and the worship of his beloved Radha-Govinda. This life is pursued in the pastoral setting of Geaglum, Northern Ireland, to which the author has returned from his most recent travels as chronicled in prior volumes. As the Irish countryside invites a soothing solitude, in the same way it's natural beauty shapes the remarkably tender passages in which the author describes his relationships with his deities. For this reader, these meditations form the centerpiece of this extraordinary reflection on devotional service in the spirit of Srila Prabhupada's teachings. The following passage captures the mood of this volume in all of its elegant simplicity:

> The puddles, the walk, looking down at pebbles, looking up at Syama-colored clouds.
>
> You've still got a piece of the morning left. What will you do with it? Try for another *Srimad-Bhagavatam* verse and purport.

*Part One, p. 51*

As with this volume's prose, the poetry ranges across a variety of topics from self-discovery in this return to Ireland, reminiscing and reflections upon both the author's past before meeting Srila Prabhupada, as well as his time as a disciple as well as initiating spiritual master. In addition, the writing life itself is considered poetically:

"Krishna! The *Vidagdha-madhava* was written in India
 under the tree.
Lord Caitanya asked what are you
 writing Rupa?
 He wrote that way because He

gave him special mercy."

*Part One, p. 92*

We might consider as well this gentle stanza detailing worship of Radha-Govinda:

> The cry call of
> Krishna's flute I
> place it in His hand and
> don't shake Him my
> dear *murti*
> delicate boy
> *manjari* dress Her
> good night.

*Part Two, p. 125*

A "return to quiet heroics" is a return to the foundations of Krishna conscious practice as delivered by Srila Prabhupada. In this volume, Satsvarupa Maharaja quietly and gently imparts to the reader a sense of *vaidhi-bhakti* not as a moralistic matrix of rules and regulations. Rather, the principles of *vaidhi-bhakti* provide the coordinates for a style of living that is infused with the potency of the *acaryas* and the boundless mercy of Radha-Syamasundara whose side-long glance not only colors the Irish sky to which Satsvarupa Maharaja lifts his gaze, but brightens the heart of every devotee.

*What You Need*

Well you needn't go in a
rowboat to Inis Rath but he wants to
you needn't be t.p. and climb in hierarchy
but maybe you need to.

Maybe you I need to be alone now,
listen music you need?
Need the trees? Your knees?
What do you need besides
sliding into watery death...
you need only chanting and
reading
but you say I need
more for awhile
even a saint...
  to preach...

Sprinkle them stars through the heavens. Listen awhile
He's rowing across the
chilly strait blue ripples like...

Green shiny sunshine on
grass water rain I
was out and rainbow
came.

No sex for us monks
it is best this way
they have their fun
and grimes
and work for it
rich men's sons don't
work
play in the garden
park.

You needn't preach so much
but take it first yourself,
    work on that.

I don't mean alone
I don't know
but just got this feeling... He's economical see?

Learned best is less
learned in his bones
moans...

My way seeking in this lake
region "Lord don't let them
rip me *and* us out of Your
*sankirtana* van unless You want
to make drama glorifying
Your devotees... Of
course, You are the Master.

The will of God
is the way he tried the
bow is bow down truth
I'm a fellow of trans-
cendental camp
    pitch our tent on
borrowed land.

I want to be a going-down-road-
alone knowing someone will cook
my lunch and I can wear
a sweater
you needn't tell us all
    this
but you want to it's your
version of front-line.

Thin barbed wire on fence
no cows in sight

alone in clear
    circumference.

Conference of one you and
God talk to yourself
can help folks best
this way
I'm waiting for you
to re-enter *Srimad*
you need that
and the other is not so

important to keep talking not
enforced by some
agent of *maya*
or hesitation
    staid
your people there
are your people
the devotees
receive
pleeze.

*pp. 7–10*

*Opening Intimations, in the Shed*

Take your time. Do it to represent the guru and Krishna and not your own self. But we want it with the self of Prabhupada, not just the message. Thus I can say I'm okay too.

That's all right but...I've got the previous knowledge of what the Swami taught me. I'm not going to ditch that in favor of exploring with people (artists, explorers, mew-zissions) who go clean-slate entirely with all their talents.

We gather and try to hear what Narada did and said. He's unique so great, but we can also chant Hare Krishna. Can you pay attention a little better than you did before? The window is fogged over. The painted pictures in the Gongbi are very nice.

I'm tired and alive
I hope not too old to have hope
to create a new best Krishna consciousness of my life,
shouldn't it be you get better and better?

Go inside the house and write a story about what got lost. At that time there's no violin playing. It'll be fun, me and Finn.

Wow just imagine how it used to be.
Now Krishna is here. I'm just a little snot. A shining
star pennex I mean
apex part
servant
I've got to find myself
and thus find the world
I'll tell you, this is going to
come in these weeks
if He pleases
and I get in touch.

*pp. 12–14*

* * *

*There Is Hope*
I don't feel like writing, for a start. That's the thing
when it gets dark in this shed. You can tell your mama.
I heard she's dead, and you died all in a flash over the
ocean.

I hear once you start your serious Krishna consciousness it's just a matter of time before you'll be back in your eternal home. Krishna wants to see how much I move at least a few feeble steps to Him.

There was a time I came back from the travels and said leave me to this crowded little room but you can't find all you want so early. This was the period interval between two points

like
heaven and earth
"It's January" said the boy, and we laughed.

It's January '98, 98 Olds '98 I'm
hearing you I'm hearing

I'm not sure where to go but that's all right it's just an over-flooded meadow with no pictures by me no horn blown

by me
my mouth
he looks pretty good for
60 years.

Open the wound
stuff it
the words can be rough,
but I prefer to soothe both
you and I.

With superior knowledge that
God is with us a Friend I am
your friend only in this sense –
I can't prevent suffering I
can point to Krishna in your life

I recall now in my big coat
what it's like here in
a moment of reflection flowing
with it.

❦ ❦ ❦

All fogging window of tiny drops becomes
    a...I return to pet the dog I figure out he forgot me or never really knew me and yet he made a little effort to walk over and get the special petting I do over his long face, over the slightly scabby eyes and collie snout.
"You remember me?" "I thought maybe you were dead."

Live a little longer
bouncing haunches as he
goes away down the meadow,
ducks under the lower rung
of fence

Go and do better just a milli-
inch in *japa* or is it
so engrained that you rush
through them mechanical
all the way?
    That milli-inch.

Lament and sad and peaceful
too we are all God's
and under His rule seeking
Him we do in *Srimad*
*Bhag* and I just myself
am just
in line to read the
sacred book
sweating
and unworthy, but

not so hopeless as to drop the entire enterprise, "Oh no!" and head for the pub. No my brother reminds me there's hope in a day like today.

*pp. 14–16*

What's your point?
Felt point, gold point, Greenpoint, Greenville
Mansions.
What's yer reason?
K.C.
Oh, K.C., I hear that all the time. You Hare Krishnas
are not theatrical enough. And I am not
self-pitying Narcissus.
Yes, you Are.
Y-R-Toys-R-Us.
You are teasing us,
I think
therefore, I am made after God.
Gawd they don't know say bad
"Stupid to believe in Him." Never mind,
eat yr lunch
offered to your Prabhupada
Radha and Govinda, slightly
tilted crowns, honestly, little of
that too, worship, ask for
mercy, hear Godbrother talk
*Srimad-Bhagavatam* as I eat quickly.

*p. 31*

*When You Go Alone*
(In the shed dark sky)

Now when you go alone you have
no memory but whatever you read
this morning
someone slammed a door
    bright eyes ideas

We're back in rainy Ire
Back in the shed
singing and dancing in the head
know most wonderful thing.

Maybe what happened is –
you're offensive to devotees
or to holy names and no one
will tell you you won't
let them and it's as simple
as that
shut out.

Maybe it's not so bad
but you're shutting yourself out
preparing a wall around
your house and get ready
for a solitary's desk
and stove.

And ramparts and reasons
to do it. Merton went
back and forth in
his now 5th volume
 never sure
dancing in the waters of life.

*pp. 32–33*

⁂

*Improvisers Mean*

Improvise means truly you start
out with each other listening with
esoteric ears public says ah
baloney!
you say it's art it's
epiphany and noise filters it
as we intended
something free but

if it's not connected to Krishna
(isn't everything?)
you'll not be happy it's
Maya, all those early books
of Vyasa not directly
praising Krishna
and where can I claim
I'm at
      by comparison?

The lake flooded looks
gentle water spilled onto
green weeds half-submerged
and trees but the people are
     okay.

*pp. 33–34*

Happy tune in juke of Spanish
eating place at counter stools
they're all talkin' that language
    around me
I think the city is a
     happy place.

But you're not alone you're
the brother who said Feelings is
what counts he came out with
*élan* when he was young

As for me it all comes from
contact with Swami but what we
were before – we hurt each
other with words "You jerk
you write like imitating Kerouac
who I never liked. I liked – "

And you hurt back it gets
darker by the minute in the
shell of the 1958 I was too
dumb to know that
was going on
in free jazz.

Now they're all dumb
to KC despite or
because of some devotees
pushing it in airports
and despite my light
emanating out the mid-
night window.

And I'm dumb to Krishnaloka
and to "I'm not this body"
give us rain and a new
day.

Master is saying it in
the writing he left – death
comes to all and if he the
wisest of all also
succumbed or demonstrated it
then why do you think

you won't suffer it in
a rough worse rash?
  Oh take me a swan
carrier bed, and don't
light incense but let
me break out of the mold
of all I was in this life
even though I'm filling up
with it even now.
You expect a dramatic
rescue like that?
Naw you'll just go the
same more last poems
and they can interpret

A *maya utsaha*
devotee like Bhakta X can
say, "He died thinking of Krishna
set perfect example."
he says *therefore*
you must cling to lotus
feet of a bona fide spiritual master.

Somethin' else
you were right then and
merely have to hold on.

Now that's what I call
origin is
not so
Krishna is in all things
and you can call to Him
He'll send you to the
place of your actual outlook
your master allows
in the veil
    of suffer
            all.

*pp. 35–38*

*Will I Be*

He's in there and I'm out here
This is the way I wrote in Pembroke
There was no fun for me anymore
in games
I was a devotee

In next I wanna know
will I be a covered devotee
and unhappy like a kid nobody
hangs around with while I wait for
reincarnated Prabhupada to come
and be my teacher again?
Will there be another Kali
yuga holocaust and I be gassed or
the recalcitrant Nazi
writing poems

Will I be the hog will I
do my homework

Will I rot teeth on Clark
bars in Care packages find
Mary Oliver will M. be
there with his lute
will Radha
cast her sidelong glance of
mercy

Everything could start right back at the
beginning right? Lower species
no joke
you discover *Bhagavad-gita* in a
barber shop in Great Kills
*déjà vu*, "I heard that somewhere... was it a previous
life...
Swami comes down the
street to Hayagriva and me"

I just think I'll be a misfit in
this world thanks to what I
took in of transcendental wisdom
I just want to go
back to Godhead

I want to kill no quail
in the shed write
I want to be a good boy
make noise
I want to be
with Swami telling
me to go back to Godhead as soon as possible
as his Guru Maharaja told
Go

Go
be serious chanting can
do it in this lifetime
yes you and Mr. Nair and
Siddha-svarupa Stevie
you and all the guys
and femmes
and the unpet pets
   go.

*pp. 48–50*

*Song for the Unwounded*

I came out here to do something, look
at water in quiet heroics or "boast
our weakness" (Saint Paul).
    Then...
I decided in favor of water and
sky, land too or Inis Rath.

You decided in favor of painless,
but not always. But since you opted
for it today, what is your gift to
Krishna? (And His devotees)
Don't you know He wants only
    your devotion.
How do you give that? You have
sigh, exhale, endorphins work or
not, depending on chemicals or
not, You Krishna
I'm Your servant
even though I can't mean it
now, I read it in
his book.

In rainy season roads are overgrown
high weeds even trees and travelers
can't see...just like a *Brahma*
forgets he's eternal servant of
the Supreme Lord Krishna

Read these truths you'll find
nowhere else.

A lion roaring, woundedness "I
speak and preach so often I tell my
fellow preachers unless we can
heal (by words) we're not truthful
to the mission of Krishna."

Rough and salty
to wounds / sweet men
strong and open enough to sing their
shout gut bucket

Krishna, your best followers
influence us
I'm completely under influence of
my master, his puppet but

lately this puppet weighs down
by age and health and cynic
warfare, let's see him
"Let me see God or else
I can't follow so well... Don't expect."

He's sad he couldn't be true
to her, but I'm remaining chaste
in outer forms at least
repressing the vice
the vise too by pill today
and come to tell you
if I am well
I say Krishna is the best
form of God
the one not wounded
always playful
rescue us.

*pp. 56–58*

*Paid for This*

Now it's getting cold out here.
It's free to move, the spirit. Do as you like Krishna said to Arjuna. That's the difference between a living entity and a stone. He comes voluntarily to God.
Wow you guys.

You make a noise like thunder, you shock us with your combined freshness toward new songs, scuttle and scutter.
This is the way
you keep saying that

The rainy season brings a metaphor
of temporary – Rainbow without

string, like Rama and Krishna appear with
no attachment to the world.

I think I understand said the bemused
audience. He was not anchored
enough to a recently read *sastra*
Funny furrowed smile,
what do they expect one
said you look at me so
penetrating and harsh as if
you were disgusted with
me. Not true!

Now there's no one and I'm waiting
for calm strength to face
my suffering
it'll be a story of some
kind spiritual road
pat on back
sufferer for Christ.

Squalling animals' rights Negroes'
white saucers women's gays
and cultists too, Rwanda
an Obsession Bosnia
get me outta here said
K when he'd come all the
way to Kumbha-mela and
Swamiji wasn't there just
wise guy gangster *sannyasis*.
I too would have
said that.

The story of who they escaped
went back to their farm.

No wonder you think you

lost something hair raising history
and you defended say the envious
demons just didn't under-
stand.

Nor did the antis.
Like just come down to
basics of chanting holy names
as you walk
quiet heroics.

Lake calm or ice mirrored pond.
No human in sight just now
a little walk you bought this
time pain-free to write as
much as possible.
Paid and you'll have to answer
for it later.

A big white cloud looms up
a familiar melody
over the island shapes of
green brown trees, the Irish
devotees at Govardhana little
kids hot spiced *kicchari*
head cold at least one
of them must have and
think of me under the
same moon
see you later.

So I tell you
the peace we bought says
Hare Krishna mantra
Lord Caitanya Caitanya *mantra*
peace on earth
in one heart
until it expires

did his best
the quiet.

*pp. 60–63*

❧ ❧ ❧

*Happy Tribesman*

So, we can expect you to go your own
way. What's in a thing? It's the message.
I want to be a devotee and take in all I
can learn of the world and give it out
in more pleasing Krishna conscious ways.

There was a man in moon
danced. He pranced? No, he was serious
in a classroom with chalk toast dust
I mean. Tenure tears, he had to
mark students' prayers in red ink
many hours and went and ate in restaurant
with women he tried to sex-conquer
and he wound up in Manhattan.

That's not my story. Mine is
different. I went to college at 26
Second Avenue. I went that way.
It was easy going. We crashed we
fought the cops? No got
along as peacefully as possible, but
not deterred in our giving out
*Nama* and books and *prasadam*.

Then you've got to provide for people
who come join your temple. It's
like that, rules and love and *sastra*

this life is very nice
this life is very nice
even when tough you read "I'll
take it as happiness for serving the Lord."

And you? Don't smoke that cigar
in my face. I belong to the superior
race. We are Krishnaites. In this world
for awhile before going on to eternity
Don't forget it.

Taught a seminar. Taught a Krishna conscious
theme happily little man of the
tribe, smoke a peace pipe if
we did (our version),
eat a milksweet *prasada*
give cheer to the others.

And Then a heavy note and we say
oh yeah okay we'll take that too
I'm describing the Krishna conscious life for
you, it happens that way you
forget he's Sats
he's coming on fresh
in his homework
if I have to come back next life
but for now let me
do this life enjoyable of writing a poem on home
themes relaxin'

Krishna is the best Godhead
better than Unknown
Love
He's a cowherd
loved by *parisads*
Radha and all
the grass, land, water
*everyone*
that's Vrindavan

Krishna
Krishna
finale before he simply
starts another sport
beyond all religion
the God of *prema*.

*pp. 69–71*

⁂

*Clowning Around Looking for the Lost Treasure*

Young they were and so that's
what you examine, *élan*
I may have heard this before
I don't know for sure.

This much I said I didn't know for
sure. He is such a funny man.
We all like a lurching friend,

usually fat in belly who
can make us laugh
The Clown.

But I tell you it's like that.
The sad story put into music. The
funny part of it is, a man is simple
in one sense
Don't let him get angry
paranoiac turns the whole thing into
something ugly out of hand completely.
No don't worry it's only
music a movie
an illusion
  a Buddha
a Buddha trick
it'll be void.

There's no hell eternal
well you'll have to endure
a hot iron bar. You brought it
on yourself. You brought it on.
You can back out now.
    This is the story:
He thought he lost something sure
enough, diving for it. He went
under water, that's a laugh.

Prabhupada
gone to Krishnaloka
and the resident place is
infiltrated by students and
Vraja-babas and you are
exiled.

I have laugh at the seal
in the zoo, diving
into the wreck.

I have to sing alone you look
for it

And so, he goes outside and hums a tune,
Hare Krishna tune and
sings Oh oh if I
could be great but I'm not so

I'll go to bed by P.M. and hope
to sleep, expect some little
minnow of a dream
and give it to y'all in the
morning.

Then in the shed
he sings, "Time will run out on
me and I'll tell you I'm a devotee

of Hare Krishna
here's a *Gita*
tells one soul in each
body." Joke on that
you'll die soon enough for all
your wit, you gut-bucket.

Yeah Frank-Hank now has the
upper hand preaching aggressively
to end the bout in his favor
but let's all be friends
I do appreciate your effort
come back next
week or sooner I'll have
a session free with you
look for the lost treasure,
eh?

*pp. 81–85*

*Clear Science*
This is your time to praise the Supreme Lord Krishna. Perfect knowledge.

They are sad men because these are the times. I remember how they go far out it comes to no other way they can play.
That's good.

The *Vidagdha-madhava* was written in India under the tree.
Lord Caitanya asked what are you
writing Rupa?
He wrote that way because He
gave him special mercy.

It is a sad ruthless world.
But the spiritual world is
beyond this one where there is
no anxiety
we want to fix heal
no so now we are not wrongly
angry
but
there's another world too the
    world He points to
Srila Prabhupada says
Jesus, Buddha, Krishna never said
this is the place you can stay
and be happy.

pure water, the truth is
emanating out a pipe
a smoke
a cloudy sky – I'm going
over there by a rowboat
blessed forms
only a few know great secret
inner sanctum
        *Caitanya-caritamrta* tells us
Lord Caitanya tells us
Swami tells us, we sit
and hear and think how to apply
    Bless me Lord I'm not
perfect but I know
perfect knowledge
telling us how the Supreme Lord came as Lord
    Caitanya

and gave us this knowledge
    He gave the import
put
bureau words
spiritualized dic
the

Man said I go
to worship God
science clear
    Krishna.
That's it / that's it
then you come back to your
house and salvage day
  in holy way
you are let free awhile
Bro
it's all yours
and you pay.

*pp. 91–94*

*Swing for Krishna*

A rainy day and soggy page don't smear
it you are just a man in coat with
no great circulation
"You look great."

says happy birthday in sardonic
way like a skeleton dancing really
loves a departed leader and doesn't
want to sentimentalize.

Now I say we've got to swing even
a marching band down Gifford's Lane
does that
Cubs, Boy Scouts, Brownies
Girl Scouts, Barber's Association, Vets
of Wars...
swinging band loud and brass
and drums.

Heard they won't let Hare Krishnas
in the St. Paddy's Day parade because
they don't dance in regular rows
don't dress right
I's right
show good rows even
happy birthday
death.

Remember Krishna is the ankle bracelet,
He's the way we have to be
each day
Dress Him and Radha,
your eye blinks.
Auspicious omen blinks
dress Him in a way
He'll make a set of clothes
please
for "my" Deity.

May I speak on Lord Caitanya may I be applauded
allowed a mistake of 20
seconds floundering trying to give
examples of humility
sleep on stone pillow
be here now no
sweets, Don't eat on
Fridays.

Be here a sandwich a *laddus*
not too many.

Serious I say we will
swing the way the
dancers do
God in head, body, gut, heart
copied

God Krishna is the best dancer
even Siva outdoes
*pralaya*
the Lord is the
socks
Kaliya / who bleeds –
I found a long quill feather picked
it up but it was stained with
blood put it down where you
found it earth rainy Northern Ireland
helicopters

Sing love Krishna was the
people got a right this why
we Krishna's not allowed
Don't dress in ironed clothes
*tilaka* smeared
women heavenly unwrinkled
but sloppy with prams too old
some just too
individual and not magic
  theater

Well I'm at home writing in
this way / pass the test
swing from Krishna to please Him
not the official Board
you say happy birthday
Supreme Lord. Every day is to give to
Him while He gives breath.

*pp. 102–5*

✣ ✣ ✣

*From Ireland, With Krishna's Love*

All alone this way the famous
song done "lustily" the reviewer said.
You can do a different

past.
Just stay with it. This jive hive on a Sunday rainy
day. It's not always a sad thing
you can run through a *kirtana*
happy as a clown.

Old bee in shed salute last life
Now Mr. Blue I ask you

When the heater conked out you
had ten minutes to write something
to Ireland-America mother
and ask if you are dead I
can get *maybe* the papers
and if you are alive I wish you
eternal verity in Christ
and Mary.
Hey mother chant Hare Krishna
Hare Krishna you don't like to hear but it's
a *sraddha pinda*
blessing like a novena

Midnight Mass
'round midnight
the monk plays in Hare Krishna
ghetto we *dhotis*
wouldn't recognize me
no teeth and you?

Ma, I got to go and you
too from Ireland with
Krishna's love

Big stars
loves God.

*pp. 106–7*

⁂

*Crisscross*

Crisscross
just a walk with thee
this could be our theme song I'd be narrating pictures
or singing Here we go
dear giggling shy *celas*
of my master

They don't know these references
old time man in Bermuda shorts
identity crisis
where's your *danda*?
That plaid stick?
Oh boy I'll report you to
the liberals pipe and scoot
boil and shuffle

This has got to be beyond
the *parampara* limit

No, I won't do that to you
goof off is not
right for a guru of my
sort
real person but got
to be limit

We walked on border
of Radha-kunda like Swami
with B.S.S. saying "Print
books"
like these / picture
rain
my private life
is private

Before you I look good
in pressed linen don't
even recall worse I
did answer in the positive
don't mess with Mr. In-between

This is for Hindus
and American converts
Afro-Bronx-N.Y. –
crisscross, Irish-American

Slide to be with you we
expected

Each year a new show
There you go I thought
you'd like that so
crisscross and more

The solemn hour
I expired
with no smile on my
face forget
all *maya*
    turned to God

"Juty"
Scottish Churches College Swami we are with you
still...

*pp. 108–11*

*Brilliant Corner*

This doesn't have to be heard by anyone
but me.
So, this way the truth we
uttered in springtime

Krishna was a young cowherd boy
our voices sounded thin in Vrindavan
this was the
year we lived there long
enough to see white blossoms on two of the trees
exactly as described in *Vidagdha-madhava*.

We were happy dizzy sometimes
the world seemed tilting
you are in harsh Vrindavan
in your mind.

This was the reason I bought
a ticket. They're going now I think
oh, will it make them
different?

This is the brilliant corner
where you turn off to Bhakti-
    vedanta
Marg, corner of
your room, mind to
see *hari-nama* face to face.

Turn that day
Swami says you got
I'm proving the truth
will flow until the pen
says
"We have no further orders"
I'll never leave the Swami
and he'll never desert.

You can rush it or not
it turns out the same
but karma can be changed
you have free-will a little
I ask you

brother, are you content
to stay below?

*pp. 118–19*

⁂

*Little Zip Offering*

This is...me in a
pants of pink.
I dress Radha and Govinda
in lovely pattern blue tack the
*pujari* secret, secret wires.
  I'm the *pujari*
  informal
This is me, writing for Krishna the
habit of nun
and priests lecturing "Brothers and sisters"
become enlightened
in sorry-joy

Makes me want to tell
our version go faster and
better to love
but I don't feel it

I am responsible
he says
I say it's okay to sing
for the Lord
in flowing measure
any moment it can stop
heart attack, call it
Krishna Bang

Your obit – he passed away
in peace on LBJ ranch

writing “Wichita Vortex Sutra”
backyards in
Sanskrit
Script is heaven-sent
Swami
Bhaktivedanta
made me
hope he’s not ashamed
of little zip offers
In 60 years he’s come
to desert picking stones
*silas*
and got his Radha-Govinda
    dress ‘Em
smart.

*pp. 120–21*

*Making the Changes, No Ghosts*

Did you hear who died? Did
you hear we have to work overtime?
Crime. Bar your windows. At least
we have a place to work which is
city field office.
We go out and see clients
    write them a check
who is cheating whom?

Then I became a devotee of Krishna, and the boss called me in the higher office to talk it over. It is my religion, there is another Krishna like me in a Brooklyn office.
Then out to see the clients with shaved head, they can’t even notice in dark tenement
hall.

You’re doin’ it for Swami. We’re
talking about old days

sad and so sweet
makes you want to cry.
Tender. But it has to keep
changing. Some insight that comes between
two lovers
to be taken away
the gentle, tired touch

Up again rousing, prowling, it's
like that...
Then I met the Swami, can
hardly remember, he came to see me in
a dream last night after I
scratched his *murti* – both
real Srila Prabhupada and *murti* as if showing
me they are one
and I'm writing this from
Northern Ireland, which is now
    my home in exile
from Vrindavan where I can't
enter
from U.S.A. where I can't go
too much communication
exile from spiritual world
and from ISKCON
diplomatics
and truth escaped me, kicked yourself out.

It's got to be you are another fellow who makes the
changes,
they'll say something good about you
after you leave,
"He made the changes" he
wrote that one book...

This (look over your shoulder)
you've still got time. My man is
the Supreme Lord and the
truth I found

I've got my beads
somebody talks about meditation
or modern hurts, healing, etc.
– and it occurs to me I've already
got the best thing in Krishna consciousness just
have to work at it
open that window
man.

Srila Prabhupada is behind me
I take care of him, see?
No ghosts here, our tender
moments are not for sex
I say it's beyond that
and beyond mere God
Jesus is ours too but
Krishna the boy...
I don't know. Hold on, you do
know. You've got to tell people, it is
Krishna
my crisis quiet
of doubt or lack of taste
of trying to find truth in everything

My colors from any set of
crayons. I'm telling you it was
a little hell living with that pain
so, I can sing my blues
of relief in a natural way
I did not have to find it in a pill
so many hours in bed...

*pp. 132–35*

*Siddhanta*

Met the minister's son
the 31-year-old *bhakta*
(newcomer, beginner, don't know
how to put on his socks matching
or a carry a *danda*
    a conversation)
`   etiquette toward a *sannyasi* is
to bow down flat.

O master we are sick of etiquette
in superficial sense
I'm not a *sva-tantra*
just a puppy-dog
but needs my leash
off sometimes to run
away and come back
to you.
Write at night at dawn pre
before anyone up to see
my Radha and Govinda
His shiny complexion
so nice and sweet

There's the drummer makin'
a nice sound
who is that playing?

The cornball past the day
is mine a little longer
with veins stretching across
back of hand under thin skin
Fog in head can actually
be pleasant.
  Handwriting exercise.
I too dig it listening in my own way
have you forgotten Krishna

is in this energy too?
Be careful
I got to say this is
His realm and I am a
Krishna conscious monk
meditating and praying in
a faraway cove
to sounds that may not have been
addressed to Krishna
and yet they were
it takes a godlyperson
to appreciate it
that way.

We are free of the days of
the Navy – then how we
would cling to this sort of freedom
sound
wanting to be free ourselves but it was not enough.
It could not deliver us.
Please don't cast us down
please take us away from
it if You think it best
I come here to be with
Krishna conscious thoughts and bringing
them out of a kind of
rhythm of handwritten prose.

Ornithology. The birds
soon rise and fly away
Geaglum unknown
unknowing
*sastra*
it's I who add
to *siddhanta*
and you can decide.

*pp. 143–46*

❧ ❧ ❧

*Maze Enter, Find Krishna*

This is me writing in my shed gray day. You've got to remember what it was like when you let go. I don't think I do.

You knew it was refreshing to dovetail your tale. You in secret.
Launched a missile. Wanted to be the best fellow actually. Heard a priest lecture – you have to leave your town and learn something. Well, I'm sixty years old and have been around so much that my almost-ten-year passport with additional pages in it is already filled up with stamps. Give me a break to sit among the rushes.

This talking about self. Talk about the other. No, that's violence, they say. Got no choice.
Mr. Abercrombie went on a gig to sell paintings; his car fell apart. He donned saffron and became TP of the most famous preaching center in the world. Forty people a day attended his class. He joked and shouted. Get the idea?

They were an angry bunch. I don't know their names, but one at a time the came forward and said thing like
Wow
Gee
new new
all is included
hold the wound (as
Christ did).

A Krishna conscious entry said Jaya Nrsimha
I'm preaching to young
get'em in the fold

He sought the theme. It

was a worm came out in rain
what's the story? I showed
a guy, a brother what I lived,
could he understand the story
of my drawing.

Those forty people wanted
straight Krishna consciousness so how can this
stuff satisfy? I am not
sure. They signaled to each other.
This must be understood
in the right context. It's tension and when you are free
of headache –

Glory to God
and the teachers of the master Krishna will pull you by
the coat
what do you know?
Start again
maze enter. Find Krishna in
there, go through.

Give me *murtis* of your altar
give me gold
(to print books)
I'm your guru Do you
love me and me you?

Episodes beliefs doctrines
alone festers dangers
together festers society
He better not waste precious
time or won't advance.

Give him a solo peace but
we want substantial Krishna consciousness
at every step
this avant-garde we suspect

want to know about Srila Prabupada
says in his senior man about
you – too late.

*pp. 151–54*

⁂

*Who's a Saint?*

I'm telling you in quiet way
there will be a telling you this thing.

Krishna
build a bridge. There's a
telling.
The quiet scene belies the truth

of danger / but I'm okay
he said
they had to move into a
better
house / government paid
Read a little
pack your own back.

Read at desk but go out
and strip get initiated
wandering
find guru
or his rep.

Could be a racoon
annoy from him telling
this is what master
wanted of us.

Oh, I'm tired I'm not
go back merry man it's
all right you'll be
happy as you go.

Me
I met a brother long ago
once every 40 years I
see and mean to say
hi.

Maybe he's a saint
against odds
help out all others
Mother Teresa died
and he translated 14 hours a day
for Italians to make
money for his *grha*
- is that saintly
too?

Who's a saint
he grinds ax
wants himself included
for listening to hip sounds
and writing what comes.

Won't accept the judgment
of the board
got his own way.
Mister you bet get eye contact on bosses
rush.

Free of that gremlin
goat
Vietnam pigs
little legs on
open farm.

No words condemn me
He's in fields happy.

Your words condemn you
no saint
graffiti

We is telling I is hiding in pseudo-name Henry, Hines

I flat out barfed on them
I sat back shat and then wanted.

Too rancid to tell to scare them away from cave of Haridasa.

He keeps saying he's a
saint
self- advertise.

*pp. 154–57*

*For the Creator – Our Creative Joy*

This is the way we came into the picture, I mean to say empty yourself and be happy that Krishna consciousness has come to you,
they all learned it from him
as we learned Krishna from
our master.

Flowing flowing joy of creation
what is it? It's God touching you
to dance for Him
thank the Creator – He has
a plan that we should serve Him –
in this world the mission
to rescue the many downtrodden.

Serious but I don't read newspapers
my friend sleeps in and I'm glad
for quiet time
and for breakfast.

Better appreciate people
the time is when I forgot
to pass
an earring
the *rasika* readers with
thin voices, me and two friends
in a peeled wall house
no thieves at the moment
while we read and shared
hoping Prabhupada would
contain us.

On top of it a melody painter
waiting for his own head to
fog like curse or time
run out warning – you
got enough, man.

Now say good-bye
and merry chanter
you are so glad for the
freedom suite
and maybe it'll be rejected
I offer it as best
I can today.

*pp. 165–67*

*Teaching the People of the World*

So, I'm staying back in my safe old room. As soon you
say "safe" you worry that you
should be doing something daring. And yet, you can't
even walk to the shed for the fog in your head.
Live with this, man.

Yeah, I have to see it that way. Building
up the pressure by monotony to where we are
waiting to hear a big sound to bring relief
come on...
come on...give love a chance
or whatever it is you want to say.

You want to say freedom for everybody
Bring happiness to the people, tell
us the words of a song you want to
utter.

A caterwauling it may be
a horse neighing and roaring
it's a whale got to hear through...Burton Green (in
*Srila Prabhupada-lilamrta*) said
we had to break through this capitalistic
egg
Somebody else said it's ugly and harsh
I turn it up

Say, I believe in your basic sincerity.
The truth is not a simple easy
thing
and when you do return to the
love theme I know you mean it,
I hear the overall coherency
you propound

Me too in a simple way wishing
to build up in my reading of Srila Prabhupada's
books. The people of the world
have to come together
and he says the only way –
not a compact for sense grat
but teach them service to Lord Krishna get it?
some day...

*pp. 173–75*

*I'll Walk with You For That*

Take a serene theme and just go with it never
mind the imperfection. That's like the "spirit
line" in a Navajo rug...
but when your our own master speaks
you try to represent him right.

When you chant Hare Krishna mantra there's no
alteration
in those lines
you
are one old headachy man, well you
look and sound okay to me.
You are looking for a
good sky of good news from God
the Creator, the Narayana and beyond, the
inner form of Truth is Krishna is known
only to Krishna's dearmost.
We want to accept God's plan somehow
you tell me how to do it
and give my turn to tell you
The Creator has a plan.

His plan in this age is to
sing His holy names again and again
but the art is to do it
with grace and surrender if you
can you're doing fine
in the West and South and East
and North.

You are moving right in that freedom
groove of 32 syllables, I walk
with you for that, back and forth in this room.

And those on the street are doing
the right thing I may join them
again and encourage.

Oh, encourage your own hide, Junior.

I do wish you to grow up in
spiritual pants (*dhoti*) realize
you've got a long way to go
but by singing you move along
right now going round in it
yeah right now I'm a chanter
 the unripe
  growing eternal.

Roll it out yeah in your tongue
the master plan is peace and
happiness won and fought by us for
Krishna consciousness. It has to
be won. What voice can
utter the unintelligible sounds
of a God fearing
crying
on knees
sounds funny to some folks
kids start to laugh...

I don't believe it comes in
tongues like that
beyond English or Japanese or
Egyptian...
Even Sanskrit, flute,
drum. The Creator has a
master plan
called *bhakti* and we are
called to give it
His one command
surrender to Me and
do it for pleasing Krishna...

*pp. 175–77*

⁂

*Astral Travel*

You thought you were tired and should go to sleep after your fourteen rounds and that would be better. But I don't know.

Could you astral travel? Could you believe it? You should do better moving from left to right in some outer space...

We want to see how this is Krishna conscious, does that mean trotting out the...*parampara* message and print it in the Hare Krishna newspaper that such and such a devotee named did

a program of astral music and wowed
the punk mayor of Nevil
 Nebraska
and was given a *prasadam*
 medal for his synthesi-
zer music is that what
you mean?
When you say sleep that's
*tamo-guna*, isn't it?

So a better student never strays
is strict under the grip of his young
ISKCON guru
who tells him no nonsense
no astral travel don't even
notice your dreams
 laugh at you
  get a whole audience
   to laugh at you
    - neophyte.

And don't forget it well
I'm no such young guru
I don't believe astral
either but do...uh
to dance in private
and my flute under
cold moon to a beat
that's not tragic
but got an elegant bounce

to it. This is broadcast to
you from Northern Ireland on the
old radio show
free
going out there to the cold slither of moon
  Ekadasi
wolf
            Krishna.

*pp. 183–84*

*Relax and Spiritualize*

Well you can't repeat and expect
excess success. The thing is to direct
you back to Krishna memories.
What have you?
I say the truth is that you
better go to the bathroom and wash your
face and come back here and worship
Radha-Govinda while hearing the
*Vidagdha-madhava*...

The truth is beyond any mere nice
guy vibrations. Please pay direct
*kirtana* always with voice on top

Hare Krishna Hare Krishna
Krishna Krishna Hare Hare
We want that sort of
romance with Absolute

Don't think you can't have
it – pears, apples, bananas,
sugar-free
sweet yogurt –
don't think you can't have fun
in Krishna consciousness—you can
But how much do you
want to pure please Krishna
Himself?

How do you picture Him in
terms of this earthly dance?
Is there a music a sound
like Tong! or om!
"Yes," he said, "that's Hare Krishna."

But the sashay and wiggle hip
oh, we'll laugh and kick you
    out
ex communic gate

"Don't follow me into
this house this is my place
we're going in the door I
don't want you to follow me." Raise eyebrows.

I say the Krishna planet is
entirely different but exists all
music not electric piano and bass
I don't know you'll know

when you get there.
This here is spiritualized
energy if pure devotee is
in charge and delivers it
now.
Relax I take it
trust in me / I'll offer
it to Him
(give me some money)

Trust in thee he's got
a good heart and head
plays chords and if he
doesn't know Krishna Supreme
we will stamp it for him
on passport transcendental
since I am an authorized
guru for this here
international society.

Going higher / don't put me
on
I'm serious ironic
not the truth you
used to but we do mean
Krishna is God of all.

The *Bhagavad-gita* is the scripture
par excellence ABC
God is bluish
aura is gold
all over
teach you if you hear submissively next week.

*pp. 184–87*

⁂

*Paying Easy Dues*

There's me by the Chinese shed and the river is rising.
I'm painting on my scrolls and say it's okay, hunky
dory

I'm paying my dues every day
a certain kind of
mellow way.

Get bored and then in the middle
of a day by talking to a
bushy eyed boy I say Hey
I'm doing all right don't
complain, this is a good way.

Everyday blues just right
sages find the path
everybody's wisdom sick of it
find how you can follow
your master and yet...

Paying dues easy enough
sometimes it's like that in an
easy life suddenly
thunderstruck you're always worrying
that water's creepin' up to
my back door...

Krishna is raining and reigning
and reining me to go on the
path, up the hill I'm
complaining "I can't see!"
I can't taste nectar.

Rain streaks down window.
Aren't you glad you're you
Ain't you glad to be in

a shed...where you want to
just be here with the
expert blues conducted
by reading *Light of the Bhagavata* about
cranes on mud banks,
floods over fields

and pictures of the rolling water
in BBT colors it's all
real nature
and the purport of a transcendental place where
Krishna and His
cowherd friends live eternally.

Chestnuts on the sill
pens in a jar
paints I haven't touched
since I've returned "no energy"
But my Lord,
You'll be so good
You are *so good*
*to me.*

*pp. 194–96*

*The Promise*

It's getting cold in here / so warm it up
the promise, you can get it.
You gonna get it.

Your mamma told you
you better it
this way I told a

man I'm a devotee of Krishna
he's all alone wants to be told
he's right.

Wants the Lord to say you're
a good tootin'
devotee one of the best.

But (knots in wood on
desk look back at me) it's
not so easy. This life
you went through trials
to get where you are.

What's next? Tell the world
this is the best way I have
you can get it from me.

Krishna is the summit
get past the ego in a wall
a man I know wants...

Strive to go up chanting holy
names was I okay in
Trinidad was I laughable
in Guyana was I cool
restrictive, bloomin'
in Gita-nagari and Baltimore?
Where am I? I know
coming on, coming on
Did you tell the truth
the promise Krishna makes is
good
you have to do it
yourself
you have to hold up end

You have to hold your end
you have to give your end
this is the way

Krishna is summit is truth I'm
running out
go deeper
deeper I haven't got the
truth deeper than I know

Krishna help us to be good
shout!
I am warm the promise
he kept you are each
doing raising up to him directly
God. Now I want to
say I chanted in a warm
place

He's a man of regular proportions
come back to Krishna and Radha
*murtis* on a shelf

And break and *dal*
everything I wanted to come out
okay but it came out its own
way.

You gonna make a mistake
sure but you keep going it's okay
this way

Krishna in ethics
I sweat it out
am going nowhere.
This is a service royale edition of Krishna.

Words non-superficial
render devotional service
to your master.

Way overboard
rap on knuckles if
it comes to that
Details from the
semantics
Krishna love Krishna's love.

*pp. 196–99*

(Part two page numbering starts here)

*I'm Just Glad I'm Free*

People like it in Japan
weird red light
dist.
Rama-raya distributing *maha*-books
there.

And now he's in Vrind
with Radha-Syama and
his best *pujari* favorite

Here I am a
lonely boy happy days

Got my sec to go over notes
Hey what's this return
my stapler
do we have to live forever
in a land of horizontal
rain? I mean where's
the sun?

Everything is temp
you got your K.C.
so, why complain?

He's left alone and they can't
drag him out no way
always can say here's my
medical but in wartime
Army Doc can decide
"You're *in*" (1A)

They can. Hold in. Bring
police to prevent riot
guns over the hill
in Rathdangan it's
only 60 men I
better make sense.

You mean you're reading a little better yes I read
of Ajamila and he didn't
get carried off because
he chanted
without offense.

*Nama's* power
be true
be true blue
to *hari-nama*
(I gave that name
to a brilliant boy *Harer-nama)*
whose ears stuck out like
mine and then *Hari-nama*
of Santa Fe and

Then he came to Boston
influenced me with his
hip skinny voice –
"You don't chant right,
too proud

three chickpeas for each man
for breakfast."

On Ekadasi the man jives
serious radar said I
couldn't understand in
Navy ship dipping
danger to ocean up by Canada
I'm most glad
I'm free.

Sit and look out and
appreciate your freedom

Tension on he builds the
space everybody tantalizing
but keeps it
serious as possible
they can hardly appreciate
with the rhythm

Ajamila was good to
chant Lucky and I
the same in fourteen
in a burst no sleep
no love, same walk
the beat is kept
the beat of heart
in Krishna chant
fourteen rounds
two to go.

Them I'll do out on.
marsh walking
the beat is the thing
be peaceful playful
prayer in
rhythm

the trees wrapped
in clover of winter.

It's okay *you* say but
what does God say?
Swami lecturing on
the high *NOD* in
yard of Damodara in
'72 recall KC is happy, powerful
the world better get it.

If they don't, the world
can get bombed,
like a drummer's sticks,
no, that's his love.

Let 'em say bad things
but we won't be stopped
Hare Krishna is always special

Trouble ahead in next life
but you resume KC
where you left it
- said the unwise
philosopher with legs crossed
 thank you.

*pp. 5–9*

*Summoning in Postmodern Blues*

We are after high speed stimulating in postmodernism, deconstructionism blues.

Now, now, no history. They say. But I don't know, some of my good friends...may be called postmodern... "Profound distrust of metanarratives."

I must have Krishna consciousness as the main course, and our ethos is we can see the Lord everywhere. But for the special original form and *lila* we have to go to Krishna conscious persons in the Gaudiya tradition of Lord Caitanya.

Well said. Summon the people
(and animals) to come to *kirtana* in the
open hall of a Hindu temple in
Trinidad
your drummer struts in Diwali
parade grounds past blazing Afro spirits
playing on pan drums that
80 rum Guiness stout
  We prefer straight *kirtana*
with ching-ching-ching *karatalas*
and Bengali drum.

We prefer the ordinary lecture, which
can set someone dozing in boredom
or put off someone as Hindu
"karma," "reincarnation," Krishna as
God, *Bhagavad-gita*...
well...
some few will wake up in
their wooden folding chairs
and say Hey.

They may come to chant with
us Hare Krishna Hare Krishna Krishna Krishna Hare
Hare summoning the tribes,
waking the eternal soul –
"Oh, that's what *you* say."
This is not the best milieu
in which to tell you of Krishna
I suppose but it's what we've got.

*pp. 16–18*

*The Winding Way*

Now we are under a desk lamp writing for
dear life finding the truths we need.
Each person has his own voice
and all that.

How to be a sweet devotee of the Lord
how to be a fighter for Him
stay close to Prabhupada,
speak to your own people
and yet beyond that
- but who will listen?

Stay with Krishna conscious Vraja
conch, *gunja* berries, peacock
*kadamba parijata*

Marshmallow I'm made
of hard rocks, semen,
blood, those arteries that
squeeze and then go wide
to cause pain because your
brain thinks you are
this body.

Now this is the quiet way he said.

My Lord, please visit me,
please in my chest and bones
when I die
before then millions
of words
notes, tunes, running
out this way has to be the way
I'm seeking.

Way – Way – Tao
*marga* – path is it
dark it is winding –
the path is narrow but
when Lord Caitanya walked. He
didn't go from point A to B
He walked in ecstasy
going nowhere except
zig-zag
to find the truth

In my own case we left
and right not out of ecstasy
but confusion and there's
no other way
no way but the Krishna conscious
winding path.

O, thank You Lord
for bringing us to Your lotus
feet I see sweetness
  in
this tune "*Naima*"
written by a man for
his wife
but it's more than
  that.

He wanted to be a most
dedicated servant of the most Supreme Lord
and couldn't always find
his path the
  way
at once lotus feet
Krishna
  at once
Srila Prabhupada says
you start.

*pp. 28–30*

So, I'm just my own sort of man and you go to realize that. Roll along with sunlight that comes in the window on your right. Krishna actually carries us but we have to do something on our own with what He gives.

You've got to work. Caught you pausing as if you'd quit for good. Well, that won't do.
You've got.

Krishna, I'm reading *Light of the Bhagavata*, pictures of Krishna will run out then back to bulls, and cows, and trees, and leafy leaves, and water the Chinese artist depicts.

My own pictures of Krishna. I'm so poor. What if someone is coming to interrupt? That would be a shame, I suppose. We are doing okay, and I'd to have to quit.

You strike out straight ahead, he said but can't for eternity and anyway you can't for more than, say, seventy or eighty and it's pathetic after that.

You can't keep up zesty *sutras*, new novels, spring forms, another
winter, but then you just
give up and I don't mean to surrender to
Krishna with love –
if that, you'll be lucky
If it hurts, I thank Him
I figure I got it coming to me
bif bam
the *gopas* give Krishna a
sweet and the more He accepts
and gives them what He had in
His bag

I'm trying, man
to come up to a standard you'll
accept. Shout it. Please
keep going
carton
please. Put a board on wall,
and I'll draw a snake-headed
man. I just get tired and
beg Krishna to accept me

He says keep on coming My son
Krishna is guiding you and guru is
your father. I accept your home-
made offering
as far as you gave.

*pp. 37–39*

*Romance at the Time of Death*

Some fellow is a romance in a castle in Spain I can't spell to remember you when you never did sit with devotees in Spain and you forget or go easy on the unpleasant ones like the time they asked you...

The sweet house by the Arroyo,
the night under the cypress tree
the woman with flashing
Catalan eyes, the romance
of the guru illustrating his point
by shoving coins across a table
in pre-dawn when they sat
at his feet to see him off on
his travels – to Italy but
fifteen minutes after he left they
crunched a rabbit on
left side

Yamaraja catches you in daze
of past loves you forgot
your God and all is lost

Good-bye, good you want
to have memories of the Krishna
conscious activities – if you can
string them together
it 'twould save you at
end.

My Swami walked into the room
and didn't disown me
we stayed awake in his lecture
or if we dozed we came
back,
we went out in our vans
for him,
door to door.

That history...pause and
look out at the drink today
in 1998, a year to go. Ah
yes, we used to chant loudly
and lecture to the friends and
blast 'em and smash 'em
and laugh at all the fools of
the world, never think we
had such a long way to go.

My romance is like a castle in
Spain; it cannot last but
the lyrics bring Krishna to mind,
we hurt and were hurt got no
choice but to write a letter
to a friend...

Dear master,
no *sutras* I know, but
who was the red incarnation
*ante narayana smrti*
let me never forget –
but did I ever remember,
if so
'twas your mercy.

*pp. 40–42*

❖ ❖ ❖

*Three O'clock in the Morning*

I am here lonely thinking of you dear puppet
My love goes out I want to sit back...

The thread worried / the sinful person said I don't
know how I'll return to hell and back.

Sure, you can...just let it roll.
Well, the Krishna conscious persons come in the door I
never knew I'd be disobedient
to my master.

Then declare it as holy. You
can be with Krishna in all things.
You are complaining lost

I never wanted to tell my
mama I'm sorry for all that...
   drop out and just give us
*Srimad-Bhagavatam* gloss.
   We heard you...We heard
you. Oh boy, this is gonna...

He was so dedicated, and you can be
too. The gentleman that he was...

so, man
This is
a drop out, I'm alone
like it's midnight. This is for my book
don't feel strain

Ajamila chanted Narayana
I'm stressed
I want to be holy and maybe
should give up all attachments
except the direct Krishna conscious ones

Or, you'll bring on another headache
and send yourself to hell Kali-yuga
shove it down your throat
can you help other people
make them merely smile

Okay boss, I think I know what
you mean – you'd like to be a saint
but not if it means too much
*tapasya*
and not doing what you like
pay the price
make your bed and lie in
it – with a headache.

*pp. 49–51*

*The Temporary World is a Picture of the Eternal*

This is for you to write if you will.
This man is an artist and I'm just following
in my own way
Sun glancing in the right
hand window.

Now, this temporary world shows
the spiritual world. How's that?
A searching man wants to be
heard. He says I haven't found,
I'm a bit pressing and annoying
I want you to listen
to the beauty of creation

But Srila Prabhupada says those who want
to matter or art are
not getting the top full
*ananda*
they get the bitter they
get it taken away.

For that *ananda* we need
Krishna in His many forms.

I say, Krishna please be with me as
I carouse, peruse and be
with heart beat
shake my pen so hard it
may splash the page with dots...

What? What's the Krishna conscious
recreation, the thing is to serve
Krishna with whatever you have
Don't pay attention *so* much
how to make it relevant to
the tricky, sophisticated mind.

You'll get there,
you'll adjust

Ah gee, I sigh, there's no way
I tell you.

What did he say and how to apply
he says clean dishes

sell books, *Do* – life
is not don't, it's do
Do fight
Do serve Me
all recreation.

Oh, you better believe it I'm
just
rambling here, the terrace is
smooth
the temp is spirit pic two.

The yogurt is treated and
becomes a medicine
the thing is a bad bargain and you
use it "a Hindu master said
everyone dies but not me, this is
the most amazing thing."

Little do they understand our master
the hard-hitting thing he's got,
save yourself at death
you can't have it without God.
You're a person and so He is
you've got to act.
I am praying to know Him best...
Give yourself to the rhythmic best
they are giving and you can live up to it.

I'm sorry (oh no, he's gonna
apologize) I'm sorry I'm not better
didn't point to you
Krishna in all His glory
But He's supreme cause of
the comic eggs and
the oldest tradition
and can expand to the new
you are yearning for.

As for ISKCON, I'm sorry
about that, but we are maintaining
    he's in the center
his books
lots of good people
and they do speak on these best
nectarean scientific books...

May the new millennium
in a hundred years it'll all be new people.
See the new pen from Staedtler "liquid point"
also runs out but you
see it go down inch by inch

Don't you cry
little baby
you're in Krishna consciousness
the "summertime" of
love.

*pp. 60–63*

*And the Blues Will Pass*

So, the man didn't hear too well when he grew old. But these days people get to live longer until they get cancer or dementia, Alzheimer's, many, many, you don't know which one you'll get.

So, we're singing a kind of slow blues
in the feeling that life is a dry sort
of hurt but we can all move along and make
something of it.
For me, I sometimes feel –
can't put it into words – that I am
going nowhere. You know what
I mean?

You go attend a lecture by some
learned preacher of your cult, and you'll
feel better
or do some own work,
work hard up a sweat,
take a little risk
or just calm down and accept
your lot...

And the blues will pass.
Some make a music out of it
but if you want to entertain
other blues people you've got
to make it
not too overbearing
give it simple structure
something familiar to us all
they'll say, "Okay!"
and buy it.

Me, I've got a built-in captive audience
of one or two, some people just
read because they think they're
supposed to "I don't buy that
hype," said the man on a
boat cruise with 3,000 people
on board honoring him

So, you are all alone sirs, and
you ought to turn to God the
ancient, eternal scriptures and
buy the whole thing in faith
the absolute – Don't buy
some deconstruction teaching
that nothing matters.

We walk down a road
playing around I feel pretty

good each early evening, I come
out of the shed – when I'm
writing I have no idea –
I get thirsty, slug a sip
of Volvic water
swans as ever
water
the man is a short-
lived dance.

So, better make it as positive as
you can. You can't figure out
love and wisdom all by yourself
better to follow this swell
tradition from India
it's good groovy with
*bhakti* and words like that.

It could very well be the far
best of all world's religions and
saints – I mean Krishna and Vrajas –
why not? Consider it
all the other or just accept
it, a lucky take –

Don't mean the others are false
but this *om purnam...*
scraping a cello,

a chair in Vrindavan guest house,
I'm up at twelve and one, still going
strong on beads.

I've been there, so need
right now to take a trolley
back there to see if it still
exists
the travel stay at home
blues they say I ain't purrfect

I can't hear
the same thing blues
where is Krishna,
the beloved?

*pp. 64–67*

⁂

*Constant Kirtana with Drone*

O Lord, this day under the
puddle of desk lamp light,
there's a little circle where
I can write the bird marks in
black ink and I seek Krishna's
beauty form. And I
want to Krishnaize whatever I
do. Let the doves fly up.
Let us chant over and over
 with Swamiji, you can join.
It will reach, sustain.
Look to him to guide how
just how far we may
express our own.

I don't remember those days
except to say it was good
and I'm still seeking that
youthful and excessive and
off...
But must have life of
self happy or how can
you plod on without.

*Om shanti* Hare Krishna
all glories to the assembled
devotees. L.A.-based

Swami Bhaktivedanta what do
they know. Please be with us
in separation. When you return
we'll straighten out the *kirtana*.

At least know we are doing
it each day and we don't
forget you / we work
for you, tolerant master
to uphold the Krishna consciousness
play that harmonium.
End.

*pp. 75–76*

*Dusk Dialogue*

I can't be so sensitive with an ink mark on the back of
my hand.
Mud solid
I wanted with Madhu and told of some
very minor disappointments I'm feeling.
"Therapy" – is art and music for
us, you get absorbed in it and uh
just forget your troubles.
What are your troubles? I guess
it's the death question and all...

The talk of the years you spending in
this way away from the fray and yet you want approval
and breakthrough to
Krishna's love. Can't have your cake and eat it.

Could live alone on an island
and yet miss the point – those who
give all to Krishna.

I do hereby redeem myself. He
said, Krishna I love You. I chant Your
holy names but the kind of monk
I am I want to work in *this*
world and make these art objects
this flow and yes to be
myself I can't be a *gopi-manjari* just
now or a prow setter
or ISKCON dike buster.

Oh, he's singing alone fine but we
each want our own space and a guy
who can make a contribution as we
see it.

As we see it.

2

This is the way he handled it
he was angry I'm telling you what happened
as I see it, it was miscommunicated.

Okay, sure but listen I think you
missed the point. (These two persons
are talking it over)
*Naima* didn't come to
 an end. It just went on and on
  the source-force.

I said you better take it
these scat voices making so
little connection
they tell me
you are okay
I just gotta take it easy
as dusk Lough
Erne, you know? Yeah yeah
I like it very much
Krishna is the center.

*pp. 82–84*

*Any Earnest Moment*

I am not spending my time in
the wisest way
he says
Let's just leave it at that...

Let's get down to Krishna
conscious brass tacks. Why?
He said even spreading paint
is Krishna conscious
or Irish music
ooking certainly –

Thinking of Krishna, what's that?
It's – He and Radha and *gopis*
joking in *Vidagdha-madhava,* so you
just repeat that...ah, but who is
left qualified?

So many earnest moments
work, fun, human blues
being
(splashing the ink)

Well, I mean...
I don't want to depart from the
norm unnecessarily and never shall
Prabhupada become a stranger to me
 he's mentor.

Don't ask me
I'm just paying the dues
I did already
am waiting for the latest headache
guilt
fear
gauche
shame

to overcome me.

I want to be a devotee pure and simple but *yukta-vairagya*
is a real embrace and let go
We have a right to the past
and let go all sins
chant Hare Krishna on beads
don't die just yet.
O *sannyasi*, you better be
there on time at curtain
in temple and sing the
right tune *samsara-dava*
but in your own
private
mind
soul is within that.

More later.

*pp. 91–9*

⁂

*Spirits Rejoice*

Well, you don't sit back and listen
man, I'm too juiced out to write
a neat monk's *EJW* just now
I'm glad only to stay awake
you fall asleep talking to
yourself.

This way doesn't exclude us from
your club. I was there back then.

Prabhupada said to me in effect give
up all you are doing and concentrate only on *Srimad-Bhagavatam*, *Bhagavad-gita*, etc., and ISKCON work if you want to escape birth and death – work to preach.

So I did for twenty-five, thirty years, and I'm still doing
it... But?
Button it's a little different
now writing in the yellow pad
for dear life
worshiping Radha-Krishna in the
normal way living in separation
from Krishna in Vrindavan
Sounds okay to me.

Yes, it's that way. A subway
sounds through. Stand back. Don't
die yet. But be on time
with your little sonnets.

He races through the airport carrying a
box of books.
You mean this is the inner record
of even a straight face repeating *parampara* –
repeat *sankirtana* lines
"Hey, stop and take a look
check it out
you believe in God?
Check it –"
Behind that mask and wig and
hat is a staccato, crying...

He was so free he had to come
back in the other way. Wounded beasts,

the pig in Vrindavan tied by four legs same
in Puerto Rico – screams we go
by on a *rickshaw* say, "Oh what a
shame in Vrindavan." Muslims.
Untouchables...never think *this* is
our *kirtana* too.

I think I see your point. You are
saying spirits rejoice in all things that
are going on and yet you maintain
the protocol and right-look behavior
too but within churns,
the crying, sighing.

The rebel lives / the rebel needs
to be redeemed / the dreamers can't
stop dreaming and sighing and drools on
pillow and doesn't even dream like regular
chapters of *Gita* overview.

Write the timid rebel lives / in each
one of us there is the wild center of
confusion which has alternately a
nice fugue and neat and can make
 sense even to a child or
  priest.

So, spirits rejoice we will serve Krishna
 explaining how to do it better
    he just lets go and plays what he
  feels
we are waiting.

He's the man in an ordinary way wants to tell you
Krishna consciousness is here folks, *prasadam* served
at the table of hors d'oeuvres, please understand the
Lord is the person behind all that happens there's an
intelligence it doesn't just happen automatically.
Take it apart see God lives
and if you inquire further
our guru
These things are ever hard for most,
but I say
  come on chant
   with us.

*pp. 93–96*

How long can I run on in Krishna consciousness
this way? Recalling. Krishna was my
master long before I knew it
in this life and another.

I knew it in the hedges and
before that throwing a ball against
the wall house stoop.

I knew it in my face can't even
remember Srila Prabhupada
or my mom,
wearing knickers
trying to figure it out – how
to hide from big dogs
(on 76th Street).

I was with Krishna in my
hugging and crying and lusting
I didn't even know but
I believe it now.

Now I hear the Lord
comes before Goloka
a big book presented
only in my 26½ year.

Got anything new now?
Well man, it's like this
you've got to believe.
I was with Krishna
in previous lives
Sadaputa says proves
planets maps UFOs
Joe-blow proves
inspires
gets spiritual name.

This was the time when

I recall in *my* room above
parents in the house on
 Katan Ave. all that was
before I met the master.

It's like a story you believe
swinging a lead
bat then you take the
lighter one, lime
on hands (all archaic)
then get up and strike out
before little league was
invented.

Boy Scouts little
Mickey Kelly vampires
now, now Strawberry
festival at church is only
a memory and
don't do a rose-covered
spectacle's job on your life.

Leave behind not remorse
  you
old times were like that
you played back and forth.

So, I'm saying I went through
the changes quick *ashramas* and
life is more gone over
you got nothing to do.

But practice, practice the Krishna
conscious way is extant there's no
truth but
  KC
banners waving in
my face

I'm waving them from
rooftops

Please God take
my service I
don't want any other
but service to You
See people join ISKCON And it healthy if only
in a dream –
next life?

*pp. 101–4*

⁂

*If You Believe in Me*

Yes, I remember being alone in
the room and they used to speak
sing to me and with smoke
filled John Young and Tommy
one happy and trapped, Navy
still ahead
and now I'm free in the
old last years
the same.

Krishna is trumpeting
I'm steering, I'm being steered
He saves even from old habits.

Old Swami stern master
tasks give
and now I allow
a little at a time
rebellion? Difference
I am who I am.

Letting it out
let it out.

I'm so happy to write
this and want however my
Lord to be pleased
or what's the use?

Sonny was a friend
so warm they knew
what they were doing
it is authentic.

It was only a paper moon
the changes nobody knew
for sure what was happening
freedom
with fences around it.
The high wall Swami
put up around his disciples
keep out Godbrothers
and Mayavadis.

Stillson Judah thanks
for no royalties
But we are righteous disciples
think we are best on
beach at Juhu, Venice
saying
we know, we know

But you knew, Srila Prabhupada
tin soldiers fearful
laybacks
soon to quit you.

Still I'm righteous
still here!

It's only a paper disciple
    paper tiger
    vibrato.
Please please please
you
are the best.

Please accept this
nicest I can do
please annoy excuse
the crap.
    You Krishna is nice
        really nice.

*pp. 112–15*

⁂

Swami low level fellow
you are grateful you have no pain today
and start to think
I could do much more.

Swami, do you remember Guyana and how
you were nervous in that country
thinking there might be riots
and you'd be detained in your exit?
Do you remember your headaches there and
sweating and playing the guru and

talking to Madhu how to get through it
all honorably – what was most on your mind?

I wanted to write what was
happening, and I wanted to do the whole tour
and come back to Ireland.
So now here I am looking

out the window, and the day is
mine to use as I like.
But swami, can you get your
airship off the ground?

*p. 120*

⁂

Swami, do you still love? Swami, can you rescue me?
Swami, leave me alone to my own devices.

O master-Swami, Prabhupada this
little swami you made in 1972 is still
yours, if you'll accept me please put
me as you like
yours in service,
  the outcast.

*pp. 143–44*

*Wherever You Are*

Did a painting of Radha and Krishna
and now
we want to tell you don't
listen to anyone, it's carefree the
man said.
You infect me, and I'll give
you a little Krishna conscious wisdom
  I picked up not from
Typhoid Mary.

Where did I get my Krishna consciousness
  good looks? From the
same place you got your strength,
father.

Father, where did you go?
Why is the page yellow?
truck – in the snow?
    Hello

Come over on the radio, I
love you too. Work for
our cause.

Itching nose. Stop a
moment and listen...

You've got to give your love to
the one who's giving his best.
The critics listen differently,
but I'm an artist lover devotee
   thing is put your heart with
the Absolute.

This is the way. Right here
we will tell the people note the
time and space in the upper left...
   they say Let us enjoy it
for ourselves.

Eerie ear
the world could shake earth
 and fall apart just when
you were enjoying yourself.
Practice Krishna consciousness, practice chanting
"O, my God!"
Practice "O, my God"
I love to try to chant Your
holy names.
Then wherever we
are in different parts of the
eco-system we'll die
off and come back.

Hayagriva and Srila Prabhupada meeting on
the street, Second Avenue again?
I don't say that I say –
No, don't claim he's shaven his
face, got a young *gopa* body
well, it's possible.

Eerie, sweet, the rid of all taints
the impediments
give bricks
build a house you can live
in forever. You'll be happy in
that surrender, walking down that
hill. Don't try to get others
to enjoy what you love
but put it out
for Him.

So, Swami how did you
Like? Oh, the teachings of Lord Caitanya
are in expert hands
now
for my state I did Krishna's
picture relaxed in the sweet
form words are aghast
I don't want to depart from
Him anymore
then come back
Krishna is saying
come back, it's not
too late never.

Never too late in
Copenhagen, in France, USA, China
    where devotees of Krishna
kindly give out the wisdom is
all I can say.

He is me is the perfect
God I babble to an end
tired, I guess
ten percent brain functions
where is the heart of a
pure soul
remove junk.

*pp. 159–63*

⁂

*Crossing on the Sea*

Look out and cross the ocean you better go forward old man, it's not becoming to move so frenetic with creaky limbs, bent forward.

But internally you can cruise.
You know
the way is fraught with
dangers called the razor's edge.

I believe you the *kim quo*
no nonsense, Prabhu
you are all I got
you're mine true
build up that wall and
keep in the rainwater.

Leaving the house I see Jayananda
sitting on cement front yard alone.
No playmates, no coat. Hello
*Haribol.* He's got sand castles
made from pails. His dad
will be back tonight from
painting sales –

Struggle and churn, high-minded
he sought to give his art the

best standard
perfectionist. Yeah, I
too finish a job in five
minutes or less.

Squiggle, they say and the rest
I am too fraught with pains but
twice a week but you can pop a
pill the beautiful book
*Srimad* and its derivations
and once a week you speak
on it to those who are devotees.

Ah, ah smell that fresh air
avoid the pits and bloody feathers
of an escaped bird. That's
the spirit, raspy.
You are not perfect and you
said, "Don't video me, even from
back and don't include the photo
of my ex-wife dancing near me
on Boylston Street in 1970" –
he's got the thing compromised –

Now, we write without thinking
I think that's good but you
can't expect it to turn out rough
– and loud and scoff of
neck doesn't guarantee
one...

They all died and their work
is on the discography but one
wonders what good it does them,
whereas

an unrecorded unsung hero of *bhakti*
say in India doing daily duties
at the Yamuna, not even speaking
English or in ISKCON, could suppose
    they could
go back to Godhead.

Yes, I suppose
a moneyed agent of
money belt doesn't belong so
well in that simple environ of
Hindustan, so that he has to do
the best in the pelty West – and nowadays
the West is everywhere, Coke and Pepsi
in South-est India – you will do
well if you follow Prabhupada
    encourages.

Therefore, let's raise the flag
for our internal "Marseillaise"
our revolution of be kind and be
Krishna conscious, take your boat
on the non-stormy water and cross
fifty years old and after you
can move smooth and
even fast on the internal sea, Please
pray to the Lord who protects
His mariner servants of His devotee
of devotee of devotee
scream and peace
to all, Hare Krishna Hare Krishna,
Krishna Krishna Hare Hare.

*pp. 169–72*

*I'll Say Juty*

So, I am in the light and you are where you are, we are Krishna conscious entities. I don't want to write, I want to read.

Come on, you have to be with us just write whatever comes. Forget your
Krishna conscious poems
  your McPoem
your *Srimad-Bhagavatam* ham-bone
    your influences
      and be who you are.

Or, should I say the opposite –
   forget who you are and
just give us Krishna consciousness
   be  a short-order cook
here's a *sutra*, a *sloka,* lecture.

Like this morning, I'll tell
inside and out what Lord Caitanya did on
His southern tour when He first met
Ramananda Raya.

In boots, I walk
down to the quay, into boat,
sit on pad Arjuna
puts there for me. A
mistake is allowed.
That's all right, just recover and
keep going, you are mostly right.

Now, each man is very limited and
doesn't know where to go. Here is the
cinch – Krishna is in Vrndavan, maybe
Radha-Govinda will give me mercy
and change me around
open the daylight, he goes

on and on and doesn't know
any other routine. Walking in the
wet woods
deer strip the bark
barge sunk with too much wood
on the right side.

Simple offering, they play whom?

You skunk, I thought you were a
bona fide devotee.

I am, I'm in the GBC meeting
hall, I'm in the seat of
the conference for improving
social order seated at computer
on the street in Oslo in ratty
kitchen
on cold altar
in warm-as-hell Guyana not
worried because Krishna will take
care of you.

Krishna is the sailor boy, the judge –
you mean, He's in their hearts
cruel passages
lower species, He sends the *asuras*.

I want to be on top of
the scene but when you die you'll
stop writing before that, your
*études* free exercise
J.S. will come by your bedside,
say that's enough jive

now try to think of Krishna "Juty,"
I'll say, "Juty." "Huh? Judy?"
"No, Juty. Don't you did?"

They say, "Oh, I think I know what
he's talking about," but Ganges and
Yamuna in my mouth, they want
    to get back
to their meals and work.

Swing Radha-Krishna and send me
where you want, I'm old enough to know
drooling in my porridge
O, Justice Department of Dublin
let me stay in your country
where I'll roam by
Supersoul sent
to a quiet place of love.

*pp. 180–82*

*I've Heard*

How deep is the ocean of love
felt by those pure devotees?
They quiver with delight
and willing to be sad and suffer
because Krishna is sometimes
    not in sight.

I don't know what to say about that,
watching the rowboat go to the island for the Sunday
feast in this
quiet place.
    Krishna, Krishna, Your flute has enchanted
the *gopis*. Your hurried and soft and
deep and calling notes...they say even
when the air blows through the holes
it sounds like Your flute and
once Jatila heard it and came
running to chastise You.

I heard the flute of a
man, and Srila Prabhupada said where
does it come from except Krishna. It comes
from the Lord. You have mastery of
some little thing you hold onto –
loading or serving it – but then
you lose your grip…
whereas Krishna is master of all.
*Idam hi pumsas*, use matter
to praise Him and if He's
pleased you can enter His
internal energy.

Sri Krishna, I've heard,
I've heard the flute, the
treat, the sad heart, the
rough speech. And in
the night when it's quiet…
I've also heard the truths
that can save me
  when I die.

Please help me
remember what I've heard
and give it to you earnestly.

*pp. 186–87*

*I'm a Converter*

You're running, the sun is going
down slow enough, how many degrees per second, the
man's
rough handling but means well,
wants to show his stuff.

He wants to be with God I say,
I say it because I'm a converter.

I take what passes and put
it in His service, fix it
That's all.

Don't be lost to Him. Does
the mother love the baby's
shoes? No, she loves the child,
and we love everything that
is Krishna.

You have screeched from
rooftops and that seems
befitting the age
passed and now we
are showing them we know their
    anger
not cold, heartless or
    staid.
Can't find sins
enough / repeat what I
read in *Soul Making* to
devotees as if it's my
wisdom from guru and Vyasa.

Tired but brave, but
tired. Prunes past expired.
"Best date" 1996 – eat
'em anyway.
  Victory Ball for fall of
Kamsa, novelty allowed
in service of the jolly Lord
*gopas* crazy under
moon, Bala and
Nitya
happy, loose *gopas*
without adults
yeah, and I scratch
hens home-free.

*pp. 187–89*

# CHAPTER FOUR – THE BEST GOSTHYANANDI

February 2–22, 1998

*gosthyanandi* – a devotee who desires to preach the glories of the holy name.
*bhajananandi* – a devotee who is satisfied to cultivate devotional service for himself.

"The best *gosthyanandi* is a *bhajananandi* who preaches."
*- attributed to Srila Bhaktisiddhanta Sarasvati Thakura*

As life in Geaglum, Northern Ireland continues during the winter season, Satsvarupa dasa Goswami will reflect upon the above maxim which inspires the religious institution, the International Society for Krishna Consciousness, of which he has been a leader. The first part of the couplet serves as the title of this, the twenty-third volume of Satsvarupa Maharaja's ongoing literary project, *Every Day, Just Write*. The signifycance of this maxim cannot be overstated for in it, two vital and complementary dimensions of the spiritual life are held in balance. Without the reciprocal relationship between the *gosthyanandi* and *bhajananandi* moods and practices, the integrity of the spiritual life is compromised. Within the Gaudiya Vaisnava tradition, its religious affirmations and practices are intended to be both embodied and shared in the spirit of Lord Caitanya Mahaprabhu's preaching movement. However, without the spiritual depth that arises from the practice of a *bhajana*-informed *sadhana*, the preaching efforts may indeed run the risk of yielding words without depth, a message without realization. However, the *bhajananandi* life without an active engagement with the world through the preaching movement, may indeed devolve into a self-indulgent salvationism. These are the valuable insights that Satsvarupa Maharaja shares in this volume through both his prose and poetry.

For this reader, navigating the spiritual demands of the above maxim, and the working out of its implications draws the reader into the very heart of Satsvarupa Maharaja's artistic project. The following passage not only distills the theme of this volume but is further an articulation of the author's work as a whole:

So, somehow even in this semi-invalid condition with hermit tendencies, I have to spread Krishna consciousness. Give people hope and faith in this process. My example is an alternative to the straight institutional life but also in Krishna consciousness. I "teach" (struggle with) how to face your conditional emotions, past life, how to remain a real person while following the demands of the Krishna conscious teachings. How to avoid the many pitfalls in religious life.

*Part One, p. 34*

*The Best Gosthyanandi* introduces a new writing series, entitled "Field Work," which debuts within this volume. These timed writing sessions recall Satsvarupa Maharaja's earlier appreciation of Henry David Thoreau's description of himself as "an inspector of snowstorms" while our author writes that he is an inspector of the heart. The title "Field Work" has several connotations. For example, one thinks of the farmer tilling the soil as well as the researcher seeking to understand nature's secrets through work beyond the confines of the laboratory. Both of these images of field work may assist to orient the reader to this feature of *The Best Gosthyanandi*. Such is the mood with which Satsvarupa Maharaja opens this series with both prose and poetry. The following poetic excerpts are characteristic of this bold venture which the author inaugurates within this volume:

far away/very near
He's with all
He's the best friend of all

I'm opening this series
serious and bizarre
we'll not quiet
                Krishna give me a sign
the truth is light of the *Bhagavata*.

*Part One,*
*pp. 29-30*

A further feature of this volume is the inclusion of intimate and tender passages in which Satsvarupa Maharaja writes of the worship of his deities, Radha-Govinda, as well as the *murti* of his beloved Srila Prabhupada. I would suggest that this ongoing and ever-deepening loving attentiveness to these exquisite forms imparts to the reader the foundational importance of a relationship shaped by love and service to the Lord. This commitment and experience tap a wellspring from which the preaching life emerges. In fact, this reader would claim that the worship and care of the *arca-vigraha* presence of the Lord is a sublime expression of preaching. In this way, Satsvarupa Maharaja brings together his own unique commitment to and fulfillment of that profound and challenging maxim, "the best *gosthyanandi* is the *bhajananandi* who preaches."

*The Pain and the Joy*

Wheel on the isle side of
Geaglum looking down at Inish Rath. And we
want to go to our room and thank
Prabhupada for allowing us to
be a good fellow and worship him

bring it out, the good in you
ask God to speak love, and
to spread love and peace
  and do what you can do in that
way, good sounds and credit
others for trying in their ways

a simple offering made from the
heart of each citizen of this
            here *sampradaya*
and as he said – When
pain comes on the ordained days (when
you've decided you won't take a
pill)
then you say, alright I accept
you, pain, I want the philosophical
attitude. I'm no Thérèse of Lisieux
but calm your restlessness at
            night in bed
even if you can't chant clear
be aware this is due to you as
a kind of karma

remember the old woman who
told her docs stop the morphine,
I've caused other's suffering
so, let me suffer now.
  To the end.
Though it's true I love
the freedom of the song, return and
can work pain free

yet, you can't always have it that way
true, there is wounded-ness,
yin and yang, both ways
the crucified, the risen,
the joyful and heartache
going to Krishna we are.

So short-tempered am I
I wish I could do better.

*pp. 15–16*

⁂

*In the Field Before Going Home*

Remember I want to go
home
    any house will do

you have 6 minutes, sir, in which to write your Will.
Who would you like to be with?

My master should tell me what
to do then. For now, I'm in the field
still. Listen, this is good. We
will be there sure enough.

I said I want to go home.
I mean clear free
  but Krishna beads I can finger
give me more mornings please,
he pleaded

and the Lord gave another, he
rode with it and got alright
  I said
Mister, can you help me
find my Lord?

Well, I sure like the company of these
people taking us where we want to go.
But Krishna Krishna Krishna
You must know I am the
best imitator-follower

look, to follow Prabhupada
is good
we don't need
a new man sound
he said all scriptures
*Gita, Upanishads*, etc. are all
saying the same thing in
different voices.

Like that I want you to do it
too. You have the resolute will
you've been given the message
now go ahead with it.

Oh, alright I'll go to a room
and take what He gives me,
grateful and be on alert when
you can do better

like the pregnant animals give birth
in autumn you'll get your Krishna consciousness
on time, like it or not
it'll come
be patient and
determined.

*pp. 24–25*

*Quick, Surrender*

Fast, so fast they go, and I'm on a
bicycle behind them. Madhu says
he's frustrated wanting to go faster
in moving into a new house,
you can move like that on
a horn or car or plane
and the mind is very, very

but still can't reach the abode
of the Lord
swifter than all running,
soul power
busts through

well, slow down no use your trying.
You simply can't do it
reach that place by any speed of
this world

little animals in the cold – how
quickly they run to catch a prey
or run away an example
of quick –
my quick of cuticle quick it hurts,
run after the pill bottle

make a joke to get them
to laugh every ten seconds

one second goes by so slow
on a drug
time change
warp
"I'm getting angry," she said
when things don't go right.
Yeah, I know you can't handle it

so quick, slow down
patience
take what comes in
Krishna consciousness I
accept my standard
and ask Krishna's mercy on
all us slow students

who, unlike liberated souls,
can't climb to You
until rid of
slow torture of
this world.

*pp. 36–37*

⁂

*In Times to Come*

He is here Stefan singing a song
on a flute made by Krishna
inspired ingredient
and the breadth

"Give Him your breath" – selling
flutes and wooden pipes,
Visnujana even before he
joined Swami's movement.

Time on my hands means
you don't know what to do.
But I have my projects

Lord of the *devas* who
teaches the herons to
fly but not like owls
or parakeets.
Breathy reed, stop up

holes and excited...Krishna's
flute is like none you've
heard on earth.

Call the *gopis* who
hear it best.

Please, Lord in the
times ahead when we feel
too much pain please let
us remember You
and find the inner peace...

may we rise to the occasion
when we no longer have this
sweet solitude and can't polish
our poems or
be treated nice
bedstead quiet and
regular.
    If and when
I ask You never to leave me,
and may I increase my
gratitude and awareness –
what I want and can't seem
to find.

I want this ease for a
somewhat broken man
so soft and weak à la
Kali- *yuga*,
but You know best how
to make me strong even as
a supple bow
in the hands of
the great *ksatriya*-like
*brahmana* preacher.

*pp. 44–46*

*Who Can Make a Poem to God?*

Sweet all things you are
like sunset, sunrise and
the Irish gray sky moving – you
Lord are all pervasive
I said it was like a movie, my life
But we can't trivialize my words
are not enough

this way we waltzed, this street
we walked, how different it is now
no more Holocaust book
I don't want to read

she herself said it would get
monotonous to read
the thing has to be done by a great
poet
waiting for God to allow you
to be another Rilke, Homer

I say that a little poet A
potboiler man who lives
in the best shelter
must have something to say

he says I cleaned a pot with
plenty of suds and sponge and
grill – uh, what's it called
like Brillo, steel ball – and
elbow grease – *and*
I offered it to Krishna
you call that a song
Yes, and you say God,
Krishna and serve You
so, practice, practice and
dedicate your brief time
poignant peace,

don't eat too much or too
little
your words of Krishna can be quoted –
Prahlada said *sura-varya*
go to Vrindavan
out of the
hole,
be true to God.

*pp. 61–63*

⁂

*What's Your Rush?*

Shed. You are the master man
Push-and-shove subway life
I only wanted to be with a
fellow who could
help me go to God

in that sense hurry
otherwise what's the rush?

Window fogging over, piano
rain. The fellow and
his wife and children returned
from India. What does it
feel like
there? Here?
What do you mean?

What do *you* feel like
in your skin and bone your
life tooting along?

Is it true you are a magical
combination? Did you
enlist in those

rare *sastras* but how
did you come out
in the end?

You are what?

I'm in a rush to pen
down sonnets 34,000 to
last the millennium
and beyond

to do me good, Krishna
beyond Devi-dhama
to Hari-dhama top
Krishnaloka in
lotus and flare coming
out is all His energy

we're heading there faster
than light/don't look
out, just be glad you have arrived

soaked in a skin phone
rings next door
man upstairs practicing
me want to be alone pray

"Save the rascals!"
Go out for that
in your hut you're the
man to do it

each day, rain or shine
He's back from India and
I didn't go, I stayed
chanting pennies
worries rounds
sleep so good, stopped
short or full of dessert

and it's *déja vu*
it's no more you can take

a lit-up cigar a
throw-away
not wanted anymore
this fool plays
havoc when he wastes / a sec / Krishna
Krishna Krishna/ sonnet for...

*pp. 66–68*

*Here Goes*

Narada said and don't forget
there's a king
there's a hole there's a
prostitute a husband
of her
a razor-like machine
cutting us down...
tell Narada you
are not improvising and
yet you speak free
    I don't know how...

No No No
the way is the way
to Krishna up a hill, up a
hill like Venkateswara
Trivikrama Balaji.
Up walk pilgrims
Nock and Lough Erne
to believe austerities prove
they love God and give
up flesh

people hate that nowadays
but stick with Brijabasis
and what *they* like
no sweets today
no lush pers
just chant Hare Krishna and
go out and preach
tell people the truth
of *Bhagavad-gita*
but what if they ask you: Can
we play music, can we hear
it, can we enjoy the sound
of rain, read Issa's
haiku, love animals and birds,
what will you say?

I'll say Hypocrite.

I'll say you can do some
stuff in Krishna's service
but I make mistakes too
and still have some enjoyments –
I'll say (smiling) why
don't you start by chanting
Hare Krishna mantras a prescribed
time in your own day.

Clever fellow. Madhava is in
the springtime

home come spring and winter
we too clever to want
dumb
fools all
Hare give us shelter.

*pp. 78–82*

⁂

*That Crazy Beat Drives Me from Gestapo to Iso to Lord Nityananda*

Can you bear up with all this
pressure and noise? You poor boy,
ol' man.
Yes, I think you can because
you are a Boy Scout
hey, come on I think you were
a tired out flag
a Walter Alston of
spirit in knickers I'm talking of
Brooklyn Dodgers

here, rest take a juicy apple and
take off your bulky coat
the Gestapo (in my mind)
laugh at me about to force me
as I believe them
and relax
thinking I've got a minute
at ease

ah, that's better. I notice you have
"McGregor" stamped on your chest
and no gold Star of David, is that
your name?

No, it's the brand of sweat
shirt. What, are you from Mars
or time warp past?
That never was. The beat drives
me crazy a little. I itch and the sun
comes in through window on my right.
Everything was anticipated and
they thought they were improvising
but were wind-up toys of material modes
  now, I said fast and slow suits me

You see Krishna (hears from *Isopanishad*)
knowledge / walks fast and doesn't
is far away and near –
how's that for a surprise?
Oh, it's *dévà vu* to me, man
I knew all this before

when we learned *Iso* in
Boston '69 and they recited
every damn day in Tarksa's
reign in Trinidad that black
emperor of the crime crew
No, he was good in his own way
it scared me so unreasonable
he could be big
gang leader of
Blacks and unwilling Hindus
and sincere ones remain.

Remain eating a big feast for
Radha-Gopinatha and staying up late
on Sunday night bathing in sweat
*kirtana* back and forth dancing

make some sense, snowball.
Okay, this is concluded,
the Supreme Father
has inconceivable potencies
    and I'm also His
ironic part and tiny wise guy Jim
Cagney will have *my* mouth
shut at the exact time
it don't mean a thing if it
ain't got that swing
then round out all the
things you could be by now
if you surrendered
to Mother *Vedas* and guru and Krishna

happy Lord Nityananda's Appearance
Day – He's crazy in love
of God and is God Himself
creates all universes – blow
your tiny mind.

*pp. 91–93,*

⁂

*It Never Entered My Mind*

Then we were sad, it never
entered my mind that you were
so enamored...of me
I never thought
well, it's true
I am aghast
plumb ironed out of ironic gest

my stooped shoulders are
a wishbone before you.
I bow down to Lord Hari.
In His temple

I didn't know...
I was so
absorbed in petty things.

Yeah, well...
Now I know better
I'm going home right now to
study and be good...

It's not too late, maybe I
can't dies with open in
*this* lifetime but there's
plenty more to come

Let my mind be fixed
on Thee.

*pp. 102–3*

⁂

*Body and Soul (Feb. 8 Take)*

Well, now that's a smooth sound
I did want to love Vrindavan on the trail
but body and soul have to come

he says only enough food (or sex)
or clothes – to keep body and
soul together

my body doesn't want to walk so far,
to be tired
my mind wants sweet
recompense, no I wonder I seek it
lying down to rest

soul's demands...I don't know who
he is *atmaji*
*atmavana*
*atma* body, soul and mind
I really want to be with you
you are my body and soul

the sentiment is on top the
beat best alternative
we know swift sayings of
*Bhagavad-gita*
but got to rearrange them
I mean got to find peak
moment to re-enter
body and soul
Krishna speaking to us

we cried and hugged two
old enemies standing before
Radha and Syama
at Vrinda-kunda
at Radha-kunda
he wrote me a note saying he's
writing his own book, God is now
his guru
take it man,
go free

pressed some leaves of *tulasis*
with old *candaka* caked
and in the envelope sitting now on my out basket

ship me out in a dream visa
from here to there and back
short trip
one spot life it's not
or why do you make
provisions (like ancient Egyptians)
to the next life
carry me on boat with cakes
and celibate intentions oh, next
life I fear the Death

the mind,
and the sweet moment of
life now
be it not *maya*
all under God
good men
playing us to sleep?
No,            tender
ballad true to
God and guru
he likes to say.

*pp. 103–5*

*It's Sunday, Ring the Bell*

Honey day
you'll have to hear some bad
news
contralto sigh...

on stage your bosom, hand to
the prima donna sings
Oh, Life...
and I joke back
here on the balcony
of life.

You ought to thank God
for this one and a half hours...
These things go across the lake. He said
"This is the *grhasthas*' (row) boat."
I said, "Leaky." He said, "And rocky."
I said, (meaning don't get so down
on married life), "It's crossing," and
I glanced at his fiancée in
rubber wellies her feet covered
in water in the boat

I can't tell a melody romp if
you don't give me a song I can
sing by. So, Etty says this *is*
the song, swing with it, find
Him here. *Ekatvam*. Everything belongs.

I say, yeah but I'm no *maha-*
*bhagavata*
song on Sunday
open mouth sing
no bell for crossing
God's feast awaits
that's song #1. Here's another:

So happy I could dance
on desk or tables
no is no, but yes is too
Go back to Godhead days

and hear the rhymed dance:
    I love you
    please be true,
    don't fall down
even if you frown
be true to those you love
the dance with love
I mean Krishna is going to
help us all and whatever good
that man did won't be
forgotten.
But he'll have to pay for
crimes, *they'll* see to that.

It's all a chance to be with God

in rhythm and poise you
remember Him. Use up
available fuel
rule of love is *bhakti*

it's Sunday, ring the bell
we are not in hell – a
feast awaits in the temple hall
and *kirtana* for the Lord.

*pp. 110–12*

❦ ❦ ❦

*The Take-Off and Flight of the Blue Heron*

You asked for this, the beauty of the world, the fear
they may be cinema song players, and you like Barhi be
sent down for it
your ear demands.
The beauty of a doodle in
ink, the joy of each moment
the Lord gives you...

don't milk it..."It's out of sight," we
used to say and "far out" isn't it was only
a trip to a moon they never made and
now a quaint or closed era

an error in myth, a stumble in
way to cast your error ass, punk...
you blaspheme the moment, you pollute
the same hand and mind that hears
the *sastra* and *sutras*...

No, I say it's just a fictive ploy for
me to write a life dedicated
over to Krishna
reminds me of a high school dance,
sagging crêpe paper, the fact that
you had no girl but were meant to
belong to God – and *that* too was
a make-believe romance
St. Francis
St. Teresa
Rupa Goswami
Please place me at my master's
feet, that romance took place on Second
Avenue, fading utopia...

we're still there and heard the worst
is yet to come but they can't take
away from us the right to chant

Hare Krishna. Flamingo flies and
from the marsh I scare unwittingly the
blue-gray heron into clumsy flight,
I didn't mean to...

swans rest and play in cold
water and I can see all this only with the
Lord's permission and this is only the
filthy minuscule suffering place, the
perverted energy.

You've got to listen with love that's true,
there's no objective place,
ridicule they will, and when are
you gonna lecture to them, "This should be
giving your love, it is not the twang of
a rubber band, it is beauty resonating
from the soul?"
And will you always hide in your
fictive detective stories? And will Krishna be
pleased by this dissembling art?
So, Shankacuda got his comeuppance
and even Mukhara embraced Krishna and praised
Him, although later she got back into the
*rasa* of chastising Him as
debauch of the girls

playful Krishna, greedy me to
have all the best sounds of love
even dripping sentiment of
calypso beat – all you said
you wanted to get rid of,
is now back in your life with little
speckle breasted birds
presages of spring – not yet
but it is not *that* far away when they're
seriously planning St. Paddy's Day Parade
mistakes...
count

Krishna doesn't make them
and you better, I know you
better watch out
But I'm serving with love
available not renouncing yet
        dovetail.

*pp. 151–53*

*Green Chimney*

Holy man, holy name, I am in my Church. I will worship straight, here is our service.

Ah, *hari-nama eva*
*kevalam.* Green Chimneys is the
name of this school, his daughter
gladly went to school there,
means he's a family man.
He's not Lon Chaney featured on the U.S. post stamps
with Frankenstein what
culture is this? Give us Srila Prabhupada on the stamp
of India.

I have a picture to show you of Boo Boo of Mt. Olive
and here's the album of
us twenty years ago when you were our leader.
Remember the time we locked Ju in the kitchen, Pie-face?

Sing a song
solo
old time
never forget
Oleo and God

so clear it is
O, you die

Nefertiti was Egyptian princess
God honors only glory
of loved offerings

serious face Saturday
on kneeler in Church
no good act of contrition is
God honors all never
mind but you really shouldn't
sin again

we were riding the train
do you remember

the good time? Oh, a swami and I
one time went door to door

sing the freedom for love and Krishna
the drum *mrdangas* only and a conga
in the park allowed early days
wooden flute, string guitar
incense fumes outdoors you
can't control elements but chant
in His (his) shelter Hare Krishna
mantras flowing East side up
to St. Bridget's tower

kids making fun in the school yard
at Green Chimneys, please hear me,
Krishna is your best friend, He's God,
I know you didn't hear this in
Sunday school. But we
offer our food to God
just chant Hare Krishna

World can't take away Hare Krishna's
very well even the reps
were falling apart

falling for it,
sad to say
oh, give us another song,

Stevie, Manu and Joe and Fran,
Oh, all became devotees at once
never mind...when they went to
Green Chimneys School before
they were devotees and went back there
again to preach

Green chin
Rear Admiral Frank
each one can become
efficient devotee
no one excluded

chimney chin and head of
the Deity is seen from
in close

My, the guru taught us right
now let's go home and tell
each Dad and Mom
your son's a devotee
now and must chant in real
believe time
oh, thanks for the song
and pray, yes you can
go from this school to
eternal romp. Krishna cons.

*pp. 159–61*

*Warm Up*

Now we sing a song:
well, I didn't
always feel this way chug
really meant to be a nice fella
my Mom and Dad
you know how it is
Prabhupada captured me like
Narada got to ten thousand

You put yourself on top / oh body, be
peaceful, drive me in a car
to Peace Lodge give a stack of
papers to write peace poems of
the nearby forest branches

say you've got to suffer a lot
dog's barks interrupt my melody
concentration. Please make
music sound scourge
the pot, the quick
this is the best thing he said

God on top, God everywhere
God in all knows that
Narada was acting He's
all pervasive so said, "I know..."

But I forget what He said
he (master) was telling a story
and I couldn't get it right
no Vaisnava heart

Why not tell of the clock
and the music a fairy tale
where books danced
with pen à la Hans?
Why not recall the

pain of Hamsaduta and
emergency meeting of GBC?

Your beads in hand you
chant your worth
sing a song
so long
oh, man
no time
God wills.

*pp. 176–77*

*Struggle Alone*

So, man, are you
on top of the humble
nowhere *neti-neti*
God consciousness?

Say when you have had enough
or will you wait for God
no that's what I call
going home the slow way.

He says the best thing he knows how to do.
Please realize I have no way to be true except to follow
what's been given by my...master and his books. The
songs are just for him in my...

Please I not am top
of moments I am a flop
each moment you need to pray
man proposes but God's the way

Oh boy, you're quite a poet we ought to hire you
in a band to play

percussion, and marimba, and bassoon
but a devotee can he wear a tux like a
penguin with a *tilaka* on? Don't expect
the public to buy this.

Parties of left and right scared
open the night of might
end tactics, can't be bluffed
maybe you'll learn it
and not be chuffed

forgetting all marshes and rains and planned
    energies he to go on his own
which means what?

Means I want a
man to carry me to my guru
in a little basket
like a Jagannatha dasa Babaji
but he said no walk yourself
that's the way Arjuna did it.
Fight.

Now, I'm going to pause in the wings and get this
    together in a Krishna
conscious way, you and me can make a team for
    *sravanam kirtanam.*

*pp. 180–82*

❦ ❦ ❦

*Quick Blues*

They give you only a little time and
no money, it's up to you to sing as you
can
    write while with the big boys
I say give me my time
    Krishna consciousness is the truth
I sing to the devotees only,
who else would listen?

*Tilaka* wearing hordes don't
dress right, Saint Paddy's Parade
Agha orange shirt the
cold I'm at home
not watching it
on TV

Sanjaya on TV
the war effort arrows in mid-
air Queen Kunti prays let calamities
fall

I pray what for Attention,
Awake,
Esgic lull me

here quick speak
into this recording what you want
your Dad's coming home from
Pacific
you don't know what –
your master is on high
the ISKCON picture
twerps
twist Agha Suhotra
Hotra Sue and you

no who Murphy case Robin
Patrick devils I caught you
brought you to trial in your
pajamas

he said I'm sober this isn't
written by me on wine
when I was in Navy we had
use of private storeroom
wineskin from Barcelona
now free and blood is free
of
God is Love
God is chant
mechanical is all. But I am giving it
never giving it up
save me.

*pp. 182–84*

(Part two numbering starts here)

*In Walked*

Krishna, the kids want to play Krishna
games, we have misled them in
so many ways, to be a teacher
while parents or guru or king is
no light thing
deliver them from death
or you die.

Snow White and the Seven Dwarfs
seven mothers, seven miseries,
four and threefold, threefold
bending form I am
so smart my Mama

and DNA and American
public ed. gave me all these
smarts and I read out of
the curriculum and learned
Kafka, O'Hearn, and Smyth and
drop names the bearded
bros...

then I learned to improvise
tap dance, chew gum
make sin in school yard
and scared and anxious and
in hiding all this
tell it, man, tell it –
"Okay, I will – " tell it
Let me, let me

Krishna Krishna Krishna Krishna Krishna
that's what you had to
know Krishna's name.
Where
did *that* come in I missed
part of the story, what
or how did it happen?

Ecstasy. Pain? Footloose.
You're not intoxicated are you except
for honey and holy names and sage's
advice opened your eyes.

Despite circumstances...
Krishna, I learned from my guru that's
where we take off, in walked
the Swami and then it happened
we got into something.
He played the *karatalas* in one-two-three
and said join us this way

I was a bit laid back at first
Yeah? Then?
Then I started in with the
others we thought it was a high
we could try...

Don't miss a beat. It's a terrible
thing to miss but we all make
mistakes. This audience is not going
to stand for much/short attention span
but still the end compromising,
controversialist

so, we got into this Krishna
conscious life
in walked 26th Second Avenue
and now I've told you
but not what happened next
something in the next epic.
I just hope we can
get it all out
remembering Him.

*pp. 3–6*

*Thanks for Pain Free*

He likes a beat, why is that?
Swami taught us you
will be with Krishna
and that will be best
Master. You are so mundane
and foolish recalling days that
never were
I...am here chanting

The truth is different. It's warm today, I'll go back in eager to read if I got a particularly bad mail, any money or news, and then put it aside.

Remember how much you wanted to be whole and free of pain? What's that? You say work but here's the work staring you in the face...Solo – tell the story of it, we're human too. We know what it's like but is this a pain to the anesthesia invented by scientists?

The desire of men to be free of great pain so he could pursue his sense grat. Get rid of Nazi soldiers' headaches so that they can kill better. Let us go to work like asses, enjoy like full sinners free of headache co-star. Thank you, God, angel of anesthesia.

A devotee is different. If he gets a dollar or a million dollars or a plane ticket it's not a bad thing. If there is a way a devotee can be free to pursue his studies and sing that's nice, and yes if he's stuck with pain he will see that too as a chance to serve the Lord. So, forgive me for preferring one to the other, and I hope I don't take sinful means to reach the end I enjoy.

Song this wasn't because
I had so much I wanted to say
Hello God, friends, mantras
my heart beats until
it bursts.

*pp. 16–17*

⁂

*Dear Mister*

I never thought I'd be here with the
water bottle hoping to review the letters.

1.
Let us hear from you, master
each letter you write is a help
tell me when to eat and walk, I'm
thinking of leaving the temple to go to Texas
and join the big bopper, whaddya
reason? Give me your blessings.
Sure, I say I never give them, so
why to you, dear Prabhu – no take out
"Dear Prabhu."

2.
Dear Mister Master you look fine today
prancing on the green thought I'd write you
from here say my family is okay but
I work like a horse to keep it going.
I reply What happened to your
plan to open a spa?

3.
What about the women I
mean shut my mouth. What
happened?
So, well so I hell I gotcha
on stage a tune for the Lord
nowhere no one else in the center
gad though, is bona fide? He
said so long he was anxious in his nerves and building
to resentment not knowing if his style was bona fide:
So few options were offered. I'm supposed to be an
exemplar, don't mock it but make it hear him.
Remember the time I was chanting *japa* and fell asleep
and you politely tapped me and then after four
attempts gave me your garland?

4.
I'm glad I came to see you before the war starts.
I am about to burst. I moved from X

Street to Y Street and I realized it doesn't help. I passed
my exams and my father. The boy kept it in him
for then years that...I am not at liberty to say in these
songs.

5.
In India, five percent speak English and they want to
drop it.
In Somalia...In the White
House they fear the scandal and concentrate on
Baghdad
bombings by February. "I'm a terrorist and proud of
it,"
he said and the judge sentenced
him to two hundred and forty years, "You
worship death and destruction."

6.
Relief I am not responsible for
what I say
just a news reporter on stage
singer of drums, my watch is on tight and
I speak of *Caitanya-caritamrta*
this is the worst
please give us the thing
the day in one shape or another
in God's insight and it I
really can't express, He's here in all
things
she wrote from the
mental ward. "I'm sick, they
call it – "

*You're doing okay, I replied*
*with words like that.*

*pp. 26–28*

*Not Mad or Sad*

Duck raising himself from the water, oh
dark imagination.
This is the duck of the spirit
the duck of the class of '57
Groucho's magic word duck
the Donald Duck
Dick
this is the way a man has to
spend his hard-earned dough.

"He talked to me the day before I
got married and gave me good advice."
"The other leader told me a story about you
which showed that you are a good servant of
Srila Prabhupada and I was proud."

I read this and think, yeah, well just
what happened to me
boat on island. I'm not afraid and
not mad or even sad
and I accept myself
Thanks for the advice.

God above, You see me foolin'
around and would like to reach You.
You'll frown at us fool-arounds
the breaking loose free. Come on get
out those towels orange, blue and pink
and the basin and hands, look out at lake
and turn him so he can see it
and then massage and pour the warm water...
please listen and don't carp. This is
what I wanted to say.
Gray and blue mix best in the water
Green-o
you got drafted-o
your Dad saved you – put you

in the Navy and the Swami said just
get out of the whole thing
worship Krishna.

*pp. 29–30*

*Open Valentine's Song*

Brisk, I saw a boat go by as
I approached the shed. What do you expect?
Lennie Lonny. So, I am in the way of the meteor.
  I am on the top show boat
wavering. Top knots and wood knots.
  Worldly

water and
old times
really makes no diff
Lord Krishna says.
Deciding factor is service
Let's say I did some
years ago

well, what about now?
Old times are now
Rama and Krishna are cute?
Stop the nonsense –
I need clean laundry and

I'm in a sixty-year-old category
want no shake up in welfare to dump me.
You'll be back next life in the best
possible hospital and get what you want in
terms of baby-fat and strong
bully boy and grow up a grown-up girl who
loves you to strut on the street with her
hand in your hand.
 But not in Goloka

Then, I say reconsider my request
give me a tutor / give me an
extension, my one guru to straighten
my head
I'll take the course hard, I'll
press the button for release from
the herd

so sang Sats on a sultry cool Feb
Open Valentine's Day.
Never mind how bad it sounds

God is Love, Loves me and I love Him
toot on my plastic horn
with eternal love for
Him, Acyuta, see Him
in the present senses and those
bye-a bye-bye
to blues wait I
see, you'll get yours
Hare Krishna Hare Krishna Krishna
  Krishna Hare Hare,
Hare Rama Hare Rama Rama
  Rama Hare Hare.

*pp. 32–34*

*Wake Up*

So sleepy over *gayatris* the Shropshire
lad said That's it I can't go
over it again
then to wake himself he played
a drum strummed a hum tapped a
toe

but didn't forget his Krishna, His names
are on our lips / make up for it
so much so that

Krishna shimmering, evolving world of *lila* you forget
please let us into those great
pastimes, Krishna what were they doing
we Western born and raised
are in a different camp
Prabhupada kindly

same some dig up from tin
oven alley, some new twist
now Yogendra instead of old
Govardhana, shoes, rocks, the
Vrajavasis who live there poor
naughty kids looking into the sun
shiny camera Indian faces
love we know for people and
moments so why not for God
transfer it
God-awful, God-lovely top
old and bottom

II
Wake up
toe and foot
you are fettered in the best way...

this is the marriage / he's the best man
in town, what do you know?
Krishna Hare, Krishna the names
mixed (like cereal and milk) are
also nectar, and He says you
can play with me but be ready
to work out, don't be a jerk
so, Tom you rascal boy and
Betty, you too better get
it together

I am with the hammer
happy to hear they insist on
making *EJW* in best format
I don't object

The bugle on the hill tells us
God's son is rising soon even
now a smudge of sun.

Rooster crows, barefoot prints
words of no account but
we must discipline ourselves to
get us over to the boat
and the temple floor, and sit up
*Pithecanthropus erectus*
and say, "Lord Caitanya." It won't stick in
your throat.

Playing in process every day is
more important than one solo's
worth. He was and is and will
be, and we admire
O, Vaisnavas
O, servants of Vraja

Hare Krishna keeps me awake and I mean that in
deepest sense. Awake to
love of God
don't be fooled.

*pp. 4548*

* * *

*Sunday Blues*

How did they like it?
I'm just drawing funny men with
spermy heads kiddy pies

abacus
let loose

on Sunday day go to island feast
I had mine
same riff same rut.
No say it's God. God omni-
potent
I pray to You please

don't even know what to say
I respect the boundary
wall

you know the way
to blow down the
chorus
wall
right on script wall the
automatic
soul
reveals
What do you expect
peace you want
piece you get

In Italy so many cars everywhere
tit for tat killings
in Belfast
Falls

this message is written on the
sly. The coming through message
You are the boundary wall
and you the reluctant self
in me
O Lord Unseen

Queen Kunti, my brother's
lecturing in faith, and I could
too. "So, here Queen Kunti is
saying..."
how amazing the
God who creates
is afraid of His Ma
after He gave butter to
monkeys
and maybe His tears were
faked

boy and Ma
I'm feeling better alone
Jive, let it go
with endorphin grunts
and sighs
relaxing morphine-like
*jiva* in bodies own
system

*jive jiva* is dead
comes back in another
chance
grunt on toilet
sing in shower
chant words on beads.

Pickin' away I am
hesitant to tell you I'm
jiving *jiva*

then tell the nursery story
push back cap and drive
down highway the radio
on your favorite Sunday
sermon.

Sats in the hall on Cc.

topics, Thanks for
lecturing on such nice sections
of the Beloved
Yeah, Yeah

good-bye, see you next
week
I'll do better when
I'm pure in future in Himalayas
I'll come down and be the *Maha-*
*bhagavata* who makes distinctions,
the best *gosthy*.

*pp. 51–54*

*Plain Talking*

This is an easy-going track. You are feeling good
because Srila Prabhupada supports you, dreamt you
were going to him to get straightened out.
But can you sing and convert the masses and
intelligentsia or anyone to Krishna consciousness?

Is that a secret?

So long we have waited
open the treasure, will you? No longer can I...oh, yes
God makes you wait until you
please Him sufficiently or whatever it
is He wants

or what *you* want as you
indicate by your lackluster

Don't call it a poem or song pretense. Just talk to us.

Okay, I open some letters but did not want to volt my imagination.

He's feeling different right now. Can't say where we're going. Hear the news of

devotees in Vrindavan who partake in a feast (eighty people) on a roof in honor of some guru's birthday? Which guru is that? It doesn't matter – it was a good feast.

Wail, Sats wail John calls of birds at dawn. Bye black bird gray hooded raven so big and fat dominates whole treetop.

Playing his dues candlelight nun. Write while you can. Spurts of devotion. Black on cotton bud. I asked her – she said, "Is there anything I can get you in Vrindavan?" I said, "Yes, a *simhasana* (throne) for my Radha-Govinda."

So, that's the way we go on a good morning. If pain comes we can counter it but always we want to please the Lord, if not with full price, please take whatever we give You and give us more *bhakti*.

*pp. 66–67*

*Ten Minutes After an Esgic*

My head, my pill
when will you learn?
what can you do for human- kind? This...talking and some
reader will be kind in turn.
When I face God – I cannot
but I think about Him, I resolve
never to leave this camp,
that much
and recovering from an ache I
go happily quiet to the woodshed
and sing, "The Creator has a master plan."

*pp. 71–72*

*Joy Broadcast from Shed*

The guy didn't want to record. He thought they were too far out, but liked it once it began. And now we hear it is "ordinary." I mean, nothing to be afraid of.

Normal sound with experience.
Oh shed, this is my parade day,
Memorial Day Great Kills or
Salvation Army on streets –
something you like
rock with it, sway
in holy embrace

wives of *brahmanas* took Krishna in
their hearts, He "couldn't" stop
them, you are free to do that socially,
take Him in your heart.

Troubles in Northern Ireland don't reach me
here right now, talk business with M.
in an hour or so, for now, see
gentle fill "the acorn of
your heart" wants to embrace
alone, strive up and down
through the days, yes you can leave
me alone with food under the
door and I'm happy as can be.

Harry, Harry, oh when you die
Mister, you will be sorry. Will I?
Krishna, let me love You
break down the walls 'tween us
and give me a solid wall of
affection easy way, Sat's Easy Way.
He said this is well and good
a kind of hype
I heard you read aloud to
yourself Krishna's words in a desert of

confusion and it felt better
like water in an oasis
He who thinks of Me...
who's not envious
who allows himself to write

all those men who wail, I
interpret it as divine I want to
be a Krishna conscious scribe
in emergency my brother went to
Singapore ISKCON to fight a schism
invasion taking over a temple,
and I stayed in a shed,
Didn't need...
I stayed in shed and say I
shed false notions. A victor over
a blue mood of self is
like a *sankirtana* win
is my good news like
money collection
breaking the fetters
winning.

Just a moment when I put the turban
on Krishna and it fits so nice without blue
tack, He's happy, no idol I
didn't want to mention and Her tiara
is golden like a teardrop
Krishna Krishna, You are my Lord
    Lord of Lords, be kind to us

row, row sunny now
sunny (not whole) day
but the oars flash
imagination to the bone
flies
late day, took pill to
reach you, I'm your man,

wasn't there for the fight in
rear of bus.
But I also have my fight –
want the right to be with the Lord's
Narada and company, monks who
pray
my turn coming up

Lord says, Don't be envious of
me and mine, and I'll tell you
confidential feelings of God
consciousness
you don't need to show off
but can learn to give to others
and not be displeased...

Hare Krishna Hare Krishna, Krishna Krishna, Hare
Hare Hare Rama Hare Rama, Rama Rama, Hare Hare.

*pp. 73–76*

⁂

*Mellow After Worship*

Boy, we was jumpin'
I was quiet on the floor

Where was Radha?
Where was the subdued horn?

I hear you lost an earring, is it in
the crack of the floor,

under a bag
hiding never to be found?

So many nice things came from Vrindavan.
One after another, the blanket, the

crown, turban, neck beads, Deity
thread, and words from devotees
wanting to help more...

Scream a little, "I want Krishna!"
Hear how great devotees act and
now your list of things to do:

1. Don't get cut by a razor on the path of devotion.
2. Be attentive.
3. Hear him sing.
4. Hide some things.
5. "He's crying," I thought but then I listened better and took it seriously. It's also not wrong for a man to cry. He was even in his youth on the quest.
6. Big tough guys are also needed to serve in this Movement.
7. Forget, link up – a *brahmana* doesn't want political power.

I'll meet with my secretary. He'll tell me he wants to go tomorrow in the van to work on our cottage in the south. There are so many good things, it's only offset by the fact that we have to leave the whole thing and we shouldn't be attached.

Lord gives and takes
it's all Him.
Sawing away, I'm just mellow to see
good in the yellow of a legal pad.

*pp. 85–87*

❧ ❧ ❧

*It Never Entered My Mind (Take Two)*

He's so sweet we're embarrassed

slow rising and falling, we heard
he was irascible but he's so tender
it never entered my mind
he was muted
and graceful
his friend too
we heard life was fights
in the back of the bus the
woman cursing out and
the cops with bludgeons

how delicate can it go...
measures stately we'll cry
for devotion attained – here
we were asking for more
complaining we got nothing and not
realizing the Lord of
Vrindavan was here
all the time...
our *anarthas*...
now I'll promise
yeah, so what if you are foolish
that happens
He understands, be human
with Him
dare to talk
and say I love You
but sober up too
sometimes I like this aloud...
it never entered.

*pp. 87–88*

⁂

*Naima*

Naima is a woman and I'm a man but
I'm not hers or she mine
I sing of thee
sister Sadi devotional muse...

I speak of freedom blues,
the happy quiet
me coming to terms
writer on writing
Naima make it "*Bhakti*"
*bhakti* the sky is made by
God so we can see it.

The tone is rich...He
coming though smiling, (no teeth)
    I'm okay for the day

I love I'm a puppy looking around
to love all wagging tail stub
I'm
Naima's dog

I'm my own man / solemn sober
Tell my medical how I
got through
but you too? You got what?
You got a cold, influenza?
But I thought I was the only...

Brahma with four heads in a joke shop they sold
black ink spill
turd rubber and
electric thing you put in your hand
give a partner a shock

O, Naima backwards
is amian I'm the happy
recoverer recluse
singing God's
story of
a poet, restless who just
wants a little fruit and yogurt
and everyone to say you are really
good

Lord, when you wore Your
white turban You sure looked
good, I didn't put Your
earrings on today and Radha's,
I was just so weak
and pained, you understand
I'm okay now, I'll rest some
time
When hell comes, who will
be spared? Those guys in charge and
the rebels and the counter
    blasphemers

I write for Thee
in myself
seeking God...
*Hare Krishna Hare Krishna,* tomorrow will be a better
day and today ends
fine. Naima...

*pp. 98–100*

*Down by the Riverside*

(In a dream I was waiting to use the bathroom in some community house. I began to sing, "Down by the Riverside" in different voices, high, low, medium. Then, in another room others took up singing in a loud celestial chorus.)

Then some person was asking
Srila Prabhupada, if we could sing this as a *bhajan*:
You see it rollicking
 riverside
people are gathered and they're
praising God
    what lyrics?

Well, I don't know, Sir, but
is it okay?
It's okay for you but not for me.
But if you put it into Krishna conscious lyrics then
okay?
Well, one time okay
one time, Balarama and
Krishna went down to
the riverside Yamuna and
there They met Baka
and killed him.

Is that okay?
If you like. Our master was
not so committal. He sat upright
on a small backlift *vyasasana* and
listened while this rough Aussie
explained why he wanted to
sing "Riverside."

Now, I don't know but Srila Prabhupada
will see me in a dream and in another
world where I'll have to explain this diving
in dreams and this riverside
proclivity. But, I wouldn't
dare play Ayler and Co. doing
their riverside thing. Nevertheless,
it's a happy tune and it's
spiritual in the context of boogie-woogie
black music or is it white
churchianity?

it's real the folks want to wash clothes and
body and sins in baptism – and
"Never sin again"?
Yes, Srila Prabhupada, never sin again and
always chant *Hare Krishna* to all tunes
you gave us, that comes first.

And so, they spoke and me
in my riverside singing in my dreams
of meeting the master – another was even
better when we served him and
he offered one of us incense and gave me
a block of wood to finish his
carving...

*pp. 111–13*

*Accept What Comes in the Life of a Devotee*

Smooth we want to be on top
clear head not too hot or cold
with equivalent of a girlfriend
for a celibate monk

means cheerful no non-
sense *prasadam* on time
things peaceful and quiet.

While the man plays his
horn blues too before
God, it's called *kirtana*
in the temple because he
likes it and has faith in his
Govinda and Radha.

But you can't always get
it so good, you know
sometimes it's down low
head pressure, some bad
story or letter in your
head some threat.

I know. But the prayer
beads do await you if

you pick them up
*pratyaksa* – direct perception
*avyayam* – always
and good *susukham* it's that way...

they're talking, all right
three men in God consciousness
don't bother them.

We do have *arati* on time
benign and beautiful forms
of Lords so well dressed
I only wish...

Get out and do some preaching feel the resist and that'll
clear your head
another way

See how they are suffering in illusion like
the books say. Oh,
do what you can
and don't complain

I'll take you in a wheelchair
if need be.
Try.

*pp. 118–20*

*Rough Soul*

A fellow is tired but writes anyway.
Song flute is Krishna / we are happy to do

the simple duties given us by our spiritual
master
Radha is a start

Always with Krishna
don't forget
Hare means Her
Always with Krishna
the duty I wanted to know was how
a rough person, even angry could be
Krishna conscious. Well it's so, he can do it.
He's *adhira* but his fingers stubby
turn the pages of the book
Krishna can accommodate
rough souls turn them
smooth in Krishna conscious form
now Nava Vrindavan shines
and brings us the Krishna melody
Srila Prabhupada was there in West Virginia and
brought Krishna consciousness to the land of phlox.
Taught of Narada teaching Vyasa and taught too
*Krishna Book* full of nectar of youth's pastimes.

man, I've seen hard times come, everyone
is suffering the mother said,
be he Iraqi or American – she
saw this in the care she was
giving her baby.

I said to my sister in 1965 –
actually, I wrote it in a letter
up all night sitting on a bench
in Central Park: "I too am
giving birth to a child, my
book, in writing." Thought
I was like follower poet
of Rainer Maria Rilke
Why recall it now

Because I want to be an artist
for the Lord *dhira* and *adhira*
can be brought to His lotus feet.
Literature and life and passion

the music soothes and brushes over
wow, what a horn is a trombone
it can roughen you and makes
you awe at sadness personified
the blazing, churning...
being on

so, I said this is an improper mixture
it's a joy of the self actually
hidden behind joy you feel for other things
like senses and family and muffins –
it's really the self.

The expert assistant of the person
on his knees before the altar
touches the Deities. Is someone
at my door or window is it the
raven, a break-in?
I trust it's just the fellows
exhorting me on

flute song be kind to me
a rough fool
Krishna consciousness odes are breaking
like surf, just want to be
allowed to enter the world
so, I answered them it's all Krishna conscious if
we connect the flowers in a garland
and give them to Krishna.

*pp. 130-33*

❖ ❖ ❖

*Offering*

Hurry, you've got to go to the
bathroom, hurry you can't refuse
you are going to live and die
you are the fastest Senator
the slowest old devotee

get off the seat Sats, let's hear
hairy Swami
scary leader
big GBC
he's got it...

now folks in my mind there danced
an old swing ballad I thought
is this fit for separation from
Vrindavan?

I then turned my head up to view the
mess that prevents the pigeons
and monkeys from entering down...

I was interrupted twice. Then I brought
my attention back to the girls and *gurukulis*...
this is serious. The speaker was saying
Pariksit Maharaja. He pronounced it
that way

I said I'm not important, I
will now surrender to Krishna so
I'm not one of those four persons in the
*Gita*
not a condemned rascal
I don't want to get caught
at death
blowing a mundane trumpet
Hayagriva's cornet is okay

and that Ekalavysand the Swami
in any context hang on to him

but don't expect to cheat
and gain Krishna's
shelter. *Bhagavad-gita* minus Krishna – no

now a friend said they didn't mean
to offer their song to Krishna but you
take it – like flowers and give it
to others that way

here Lord, I offer it to
You by offering it to my guru.
Seeker
of God finds Him sooner or later

and he who is serving Swami
Bhaktivedanta Prabhupada's ISKCON,
as I am, has to tow a certain
tune and law book but it's
pretty open in these days.

Rain blowin' sideways
strait clear
devotees in orange row hard
put in my order for a teardrop
shaped ornament to go on Radha
*murti.*

Put in my order for as many years and pain-free time
bow down.
You've got a little hunger and energy still... scrub a
floor,
smile in earnest
    song is for Him...

*pp. 135–37*

❖ ❖ ❖

*We Mortals Sing*

Right, little man, we is all mortal
you get into your prayerful groove
would like to receive God's word
in the inner mind
not needing intellectual challenge
just in the desert abiding

Each one does it his own way
I want to tell you mine –
I let the sunshine in
It does it anyway *mayam*
*idam...yoga isvara yam*
I'm preaching on behalf of the
Supreme Lord Acintya

the song I sing is laid down by
previous masters I repeat it
in my own way
natural
You can't expect me to invent
God or *sastra*
But I tell what I
actually go through to be a
rep of God

he's working out his classics
God is in all things but
aloof in His own
spiritual personhood
and acts
Don't expect Him
to come inside
the material world

Oh, you know what I mean to say.
I simply want to accompany Him
as He glances at the land

and sky. I want to say
Krishna, Krishna, I was there
with many mistakes but
was singing to the Supreme

the sky in this world is
a spark of His splendor my
song a spark of songs He
empowers them to sing
in the spiritual world.

*pp. 139–40*

✤ ✤ ✤

*During Mangala-arati*

This man with a stiff back of
neck is not the center of the universe.
O, Mr. Syms and Mrs. Smithson
you of all people in the world,
you don't know Krishna and Radha

I'm sorry for you, but I must listen in private to the pastimes of Radha and Krishna in the Vrindavan forest, because you are not qualified.

O Krishna and Radha, You are playing together. The song is You. Krishna wants to play, and I'm not qualified either. Leave it off then and say something appropriate to your audience.

You guys, the nights are tough, the police are on the lookout. I'm telling you let's chant Hare Krishna nicely. I know you can't pay attention so good, but at least try. Bring the mind to hear these things in the ear of the inner mind.

This fellow is not me, or I don't think he's the most important *atma*. God is the most important one and most attractive tricky friend, Supreme ruler. Those who make various library arts get the direction and strength from Him. They are reaching for Him whether they know it or not.

Hare Krishna for the masses, philosophy
for scholars and talks of Radha and Krishna with
Ramananda Raya. You can tune into
all those or none.

I'm writing at 4:55 a.m. which is when the *mangala-arati* time in the temple just ends, was never quite this lively, and I write to Bhakta Sam who has gone to the India festival, saying
to him, just worship Krishna and read and the guru is Krishna's rep. I spoke earnest with him.
Now, close it out/man, I will serve Lord Krishna with all I have and not despair don't be morose, I told him don't expect everything in one lifetime.

*pp. 153–55*

* * *

*Why Do You Go Back?*

Hurry fast. But I don't have to
run with them. I'm a monk who goes
his own way.
This is the thing I told you before
KC is smooth enough for me to enter
in the transparent media

there is no gold that way
you can't tell one brother from
another sometimes
a little angry a

little higher and sharper his brother
rolls over never played
dead they are the fastest
shaker

in *kirtana* they danced, "Rugby!"
he scoffed. I too didn't like
the rough stuff I
wanted to be pure
imagine I dropped out on
zonal guru red carpet
But I didn't

you said, "Stop." You didn't,
actually. You swallowed in
all tinsel smiles to girls let them
blink and look gorgeous all
devoted at you the giver
of blessing.

*pp. 159–61*

*Turning to Krishna*

Krishna, please let me praise You
a song is nice / we are about to embark
on a way day
The light will be there
remember Krishna at all times
whatever comes...

for example, if it is a flute, think
Krishna plays a flute
But some things may not seem
appropriate or spontaneous

The grass, the day, the men,

the small talk, the ISKCON-y
way you turn it around to Him –
"Krishna also had a pet deer
in Vrindavan and so did Radha –
He had a peacock..."

"Rangini"
the childish way you insert
the pastimes of the Lord into
your agenda.

"Yes, great *yogis* can go to
any planet they like."
Skipping back and forth it's
a trance you get lost...

"And so dear friends, brothers
and sisters...Let us get out
there and not persecute the
demons
but let them know
Who is Boss."

Don't deride just think of Him
forced march sometimes
the Lord of plenty creates
an atmosphere a way the devotees
turn to Him
but best atmosphere is in the
temple before the Deity or on
trips He sends us errands to
fetch wood, distribute a book...

Krishna, Krishna, I'm a little fool
hanging on all these years it will
seem so brief at the end,
what will I have done...

Krishna, here's a song, a flute,
a water glass, a
book, a look, and act
of repeating Your teachings
I did this for You
"If so, ah..."

*pp. 176–78*

⁂

*Jiv jago*

(Maybe tired of lines you write. Would you rather speak? No, I'm meant for words in ink too. I'll "talk" to you.)

You ring the doorbell, he's a
merry little fellow walking along.
I am that fellow following him.

We want it to go that way, you know.
Cripes, give us a list:
Jimmy Duncan, sour ball, hairy
loss, veering cross
censored ham, canned
eggs.

the clearest trumpet, clearest night
if my thumb couldn't write more
what would you say?
I'd preach
folks, please be kind to one
another, praise that brother and that
sister
appreciate their Good and
gather for a conference on how to
chant and read better...
Did you hear me?

I'm sinking and noticed the jet trails
and the clear winter
lakeside weeds, what a
beautiful day to drown...

Freddy is playing no phile no
clone...Yeah, but you gotta
follow previous masters and glad
for that...

He's talkin' the way
through I heard this
in Guyana. Is it
sentimental I now recall that
time and say hey, that was good
I was preaching, huh?
I was out there on a limb
me in tropes
me best sorts

Bee in beard and hat. No, I was
with shaved head a Hare
all these years
the orange skirt
not a cross dresser (dancer)
in India "all" men dress
in *lungis* or *dhotis*

Krishna, Krishna prompts me to
write this way
He's the Lord
on the fence
they play for real
and invent new ways to wake
up the parishioners who dough out with
the same old thing, it's their
fault
they ate too much, slept not enough
so, I pert them

and wish to only
be alive in art
O Krishna, all the aspects
of Krishna's beauty, the *gopis* know
laugh and joke and happy
turns in Rupa's drama for
pure devotees...

*pp. 182–84*

# CHAPTER FIVE – APPROACHING GAURA PURNIMA

February 23 – March 13, 1998

In Navadvipa seek sweet secret places
*sadhus* chant the main theme
is separation from Krishna as Krishna
felt in the mood of Radha.

*Approaching Gaura-purnima*
*Part Two, p. 130*

At the center of the Gaudiya Vaisnava tradition stands the towering figure of Sri Caitanya Mahaprabhu, himself an incarnation of Sri Krishna, the Supreme Personality of Godhead. With His appearance in Bengal, a new religious practice would be instituted, the congergational chanting of the holy names of the Lord (*sankirtana*) which would be the divine prescription for the spreading of the love of God in this present age. The celebration of Lord Caitanya's appearance is a joyous occasion for Vaisnavas as the faithful continue a joyful commitment to the *sankirtana* mission and its transforming power to awaken the love of God within human hearts. Gaura-purnima is the name of this holiday and inspires the name of this, the twenty-fourth volume of Satsvarupa dasa Goswami's literary series, *Every Day, Just Write*, a volume devoted to the weeks preceding this festive occasion.

While this volume is replete with inferences and reflections upon the significance of Lord Caitanya as both a religious figure and incarnation of the Supreme Person, there is an even deeper current that shapes this volume. The mood within these pages expresses a keen sense of loving separation from the Lord authentically inspired by the ecstasies and agonies embodied within the pastimes of Lord Caitanya. To appreciate this, one must consider what is most sublime regarding the spiritual identity of Sri Caitanya, that He is Krishna Himself possessing the inner mood of His eternal consort Radha. With his appearance in this world, in this manner, Krishna now experiences the madness of longing and transcendental love that Radha possesses for Him. It is this mood of separation which animates significant portions of Krishnadasa Kaviraja's monumental theological biography of Lord Caitanya, *Caitanya-caritamrta*, which serves as a touchstone for Satsvarupa Maharaja in this collection of writing.

Indeed, this mood of separation fills the pages of this volume of *Every Day, Just Write*. To begin, the author will reflect upon his physical separation from the land of Lord Caitanya's pastimes. This is literarily conveyed by Satsvarupa Maharaja's close reading of Srila Bhaktivinoda Thakura's definitive work on the holy *dhama, Sri Navadvipa Dhama Mahatmya*. In his meditations upon this text, Satsvarupa Maharaja does not merely reflect upon a geographical locale but opens the devotional character of Bhaktivinoda Thakura's text. This book is much more than a guide to the *dhama*, it offers a window upon the transcendental nature of this holy place. In this way, it is ultimately not a place to study but a place to enter with a heart opened by the power of devotion.

This mood of separation is further expressed by the author in the contrast that he presents between his unique experience of solitude in Ireland, and the enormous gathering of devotees who assemble in Bengal for the celebration of Gaura-purnima.

Satsvarupa Maharaja's ongoing soul-searching regarding his place within a preaching institution conveys a sense of separation, as the author charts his own path within the society established by his spiritual master, A. C. Bhaktivedanta Swami Prabhupada. As the author pursues the coordinates of his own existence, the reader is greeted, in both the prose and poetry of the volume, with flashes of insights into the ways in which Gaura-purnima may be celebrated with authenticity in a life of solitude.

Ultimately and most profoundly is the expression of spiritual separation in love, expressed by Satsvarupa Maharaja, which brings the reader to the very heart and nature of Lord Caitanya's existence. This is wonderfully conveyed by the author in his poem, "Blues and Puja" (*Part One*, pp. 71 ff.) in which the defining features of this musical genre is spiritualized, effectively capturing the nature of this sublime experience of separation. For, the Blues, as a genre, are celebrated for plaintive expression of the aching heart, moved by subterranean wells of both agony and anticipation. This spirit is precisely that which Satsvarupa Maharaja is able to express in this poem:

Well, all right I say
in KC *kirtana* is blues
we call it in our lingo
transcendental separation
or lament to purify the
heart's yearning.

*Part One, p. 72*

In a volume filled with reflections upon Lord Caitanya, memories of past Gaura-purnima celebrations, *sastric* commentary, and the poetry of separation, *Approaching Gaura-purnima* opens the heart of the reader to one's own dormant longings for love of God. This installation of *Every Day, Just Write* weaves concentric circles around this most merciful Lord Caitanya, with each moving the reader ever deeper into the mystery and wonder of devotional life, so that wherever the devotee may find him/herself there also is Navadvipa *dhama*.

> "And so, the night approaches, give us the full moon of Lord Caitanya but we can't see it here because it's covered with one thorough cloud. They're on the island hearing bhajanas and I'm here, you know why. I'll finish this work-play and get back to hearing Hare Krishna mantras for the last half-hour of the day that we waited for – Gaura-purnima."
>
> *Part Two,*
> *pp. 167-68*

*Cousin Mary*

I had a cousin Mary and that's all over, I was a bird and beast and that's not now. I was whatever anyone could imagine, and I could do it again.

Rough, victim and persecutor. No use
enumerating.
Sing while you can.
He's got a style he developed
it's his heart in code form,
developed.

Where'd he get the idea? Gravel voice,
sorry it happened this way.
O noble Purnamasi, the lines
of the best player in my mind. O slayer of demon
Madhu, O Dhananjaya, try to remember that.

So, we are right now perched in a devotee
mentality. Stand on the bandstand and read the verses.
If you get a chance tell the people something about
Krishna.
M. says you can just tell any good, real human
story, and they'll benefit knowing you are a devotee.
That's true too so just wear the *dhoti* straight, your
flaky bits of tasseled, untied *sikha*
and your crooked smile
(unfortunately, no one is perfect bodily,
it sags and falls with age).
So, this is what I want to say, Krishna is the
jewel most handsome man. But He's God.
The air we breathe and the suffocation.
Can't you see you're helpless?

So, forget the past and come pull the Ratha cart with us. Steve will stay home and write his term paper. He's still sassy with enough strength for three men, he says.

Now, I wanted to be on top to receive
any calls that come.
          Dry it sounds.

Something on her mind.
The director goes into the room with
a few prelim ideas and then improvises.
I just want to say
Krishna is the most glorious of all
persons, we have to be passionate about it
sometimes, not just dry,
or intellectual. He cries. He really...

Krishna, I'm coming home fast hope car doesn't crash
grasp my beads
tell folks about my cousin Mary and
pray for her. Mary Sessa did
I know her in Rosedale
and her brother and younger...

*pp. 6–8*

⁂

*Three Bird Songs*

I

This morning I was falling asleep and the
smooth Bird woke me from
gibberish
I turn to Krishna on the altar and
in the hearts and hands of
talented men.

So? So, I'm telling you walk with us,
be glad you're awake as for the fear of death
is certainly real but maybe you'll
get through, only once anyway and even
if you don't chant or if you bite

the dust and can't remember, Krishna
won't forget you.

The real thing will abide
happiness and take what the Creator
gave us and using it fully
yeah man, I say, "Krishna."

II

We can move along happily enough
banging our top hat a garage can
but I really want to be angelic, I mean
clean, free as a
working Vaisnava should
    should indeed.
He can work in any place as
Swami taught but trust him for help
for help and say I'll contribute to
your followers' well-being even
to the many living outside the
 temples,
I'll be good, ah
chastise me if you will
so, I cry again, sorry.
But do keep me
life after life
what it takes.

Can't stop from song, yeah, he
says but make it Hare Krishna.

When they played with the master
they were best, they knew
how to do it to please
the muse in his company.

Krishna is the bird in the tree
and fly in the sky.

Don't forget heart beat is to Him
and don't care about mockers.
III

When the fast boys race
Krishna is ahead of them
He lets them catch Him but
"I'll be the first!"
He married Radha
in *Lalita-madhava* that play but
actually
I don't know much and speak too much.

You got to sing alone
spirit, I'm not the best.
God gives the strength to bear
so you can take it
up among friends and give
it a workout
of Krishna conscious changes.

Who is the bird? It's God and
we work out in His company
for fun and keeps, and demons
fight us back, we sneak
in what we can before

death and leave it on record –
some guys got charmed, and changed
their bad ways to become
servants of Krishna and humanity.

*pp. 28–31*

*Ditties and Epigrams*

Maybe hearing someone who's not afraid
to play until death his music and thus it's
his dharma, offering to God,
maybe hearing him will give you
the idea
to worship out of the
thin stuff that you used.

Relaxing is one way and then jumping
up. The vines are hanging on bright green
all winter, but it's only Ireland
where I am.

I read how you should give your
life so others can be happy
as Dadhici did.

I wanted to be alone so someone
came up to me and said, "Why
are you sitting here alone?"
He had his trademark,
given by God.

Maybe I'll learn to know
profane from sacred...

II

All day keep at it
with breaks for merriment
until you have to shut down.
You sing and sit and walk and
trip and look for the holy
because you're supposed to
and you want to but
Oh, it's hard...

to go anywhere when you're lazy
or a self-condemning recluse
love people too much not
enough, tender as a twig
the whole world is mixtures
of moods and people

Cars and melons and windows and cops,
robbers, suicides, lawyers,
newspapers report it all
or none. You want to be
alone with your Maria
*Ave Maria*, Hare Krishna
turning off the mundane
you can't recall

when you were ecstatic
to love God as a monk
in a story book does turn on
the people who read
but can't do it
themselves.

III

epigrams. Uh, once a private
always a silkworm. Nonsense
hide kill afraid don't
invade me with your noises.

Once a jerk always –
once a black coal washed
Good habits are hard to
form and easy to break.

Be careful – *ahimsa* is the
*para-dharma* so don't kill
me spiritual drive *that's*
*ahimsa*.

*Blues and Puja*

I

KC Blues is a pun there
are no blues in Krishna consciousness the
*bhakta* said. Oh, no? What
about Hayagriva's "*Brahmacari Blues*" and
what you feel when you
don't want to serve on a
rainy day?

What about – do you know
what blues are? They are
a must for a sensitive living being.
"Will the blues ever leave?"
He wants them?
No, but he wants to sing
despite it, to express it.
Bluesman – who's that
on trumpet, it's your Godbrother –
when you hear he's got
the blues – chasing them,
with a music universal art
of it then you think different
maybe I can live.

Well, alright I say
in KC *kirtana* is blues
we call it in our lingo
transcendental separation
or lament to purify the heart's yearning.

The lyric bird is on the
branch even before dawn and
it'll be spring before winter
that's what St. Paddy's Day signals.

II

Star eyes, I saw Radha and Krishna
Their love...Oh, did you?
I saw my own devotion for Them
and tried believing that I am
I wanted to serve Them
day and night.

When you're tired
or after bathing
realize the need
six and seven and eight things
have to be done at once –
*puja* is like that.

He said I want to
play beside the master
assist him in picking out the
crowns and jewelry. Well, you
can do that by working in his *vani*
in his temple and knowing the Lord
in heart is helping you.

It'll be a good day when
you see the stars and think of
Krishna's eyes. You are so
ecstatic spewing out songs
hoping Krishna will
accept you into His band –
provided you do it
yearning and spewing for
Him.

III

I didn't know who she was,
some *gopi*? You fool, you're
not qualified to think
or talk like that. You lived
at Radha-Kunda a week, so
do monkeys. Those are not
ordinary Bronx Zoo monkeys.
But – the talk goes on
who bathed where
who's pure or not.

I just want to be with him
and assist in
preaching or *puja* where
I can pick a song sometimes
and feed the squirrel and cats and
say, "Here, come, chant Hare Krishna
and take *prasadam*." Just whatever

I do must be some kind of
Krishna consciousness I know.

I'm doing my rounds and
avoiding bad company if
you call that "blues" or
for Alice I don't know
but I'm open for improvement.

*pp. 71–74*

*Throwing Off Aparadhas*

I

Smile a little man and
hear old time music when
it was best by the master and
never equaled since –
you mean 1970s your
Srila Prabhupada, but I have hard time with
it, don't know I said I want
truth even if I didn't
like everything he did.

Oh, what is that truth?
Give me an example. Why not
just groove with the sound
of it pouring over rocks in
the creek? I said something
his English grammar or an
example I found a flaw in...
yeah, forget it at
least now.
            I credit you at least with
laboring and not giving up.
I just want a
drink of water offered to
Krishna by saying, "Thanks He is
the taste in water and
sound in ether."

Forgive me,
won't give up
working through *anarthas*
to hear master at
his best with

II

That song is you I said the
song is the metaphor you are
best when you don't argue,
but sing like a bird
the song is you
consumed in rhythm
and sweet conveying the
things that pop up
most wanting to say.
I love you.
Forgive me,
together look at morning fresh air, lake,
swans, God's consecration.
    The song is better for given by a master.

He said a cow walked here
see its foot
I said I see its dung
"Cow dung is your brain" he
said chastising like that.
So hard and harsh,
but they *are* all asses.

Don't get hung up –
the ass does work
for the washer man because
he has to
not because he wants to
in foolishness
as Swami says.

Be careful sing I say and
don't descend to guru
*aparadha*
I'm throwing it off
the poisons and turds

I want to be free
of it.
Best result.

III

Be true I will I don't
know anything else to do
true blue Swami in
socks
(two pairs) and
slippers got another
morning alone happy.

Did my *puja*, by sloppy
*gayatri*
who am *I* to find
fault with the best?

I will go to the kitchen and hear
him speak *Krishna Book*
while I cut up a small apple, pear
banana and juice
and offer it with
yogurt to the Lord of the
universe.
    Narottama dasa says don't even see
those who are averse
to hearing of the *rasa* dance.
The way of best
music is when the master
made it with us.

Relax, be yourself
true to me
this will be your
best date I say
smile with it.

*pp. 81–85*

*Traditional Lament*

O rainy day, let us sing to God
who is behind all things
and God – what's that racket?
II

I'm plumb out of luck.
Break my back on wrack no
I mean to say I've got it easy
and should not be decadent.
He writes, "I thought Prabhupada
said we shouldn't read
outside books" – he's a
punk rock star for ISKCON –
"so, I just want to understand
why in J&P three I find you
reading haiku and Emerson
Tufu and all. I'm just
interested in your answer."

My reply: "I was always a reader
and was strict to follow my master,
threw out all reading for 20
years and now started again.

I use it in his service as
a writer. But some are stricter.
If you don't like it go to one
who is strict as you
like. Go on a bike.
Don't look back to me
buried in a book a
look..."

The song is rife with the instruction
that Krishna consciousness must be taken by
all who join and plenty soon
they must give up four kinds of sin

and win the prize of a spiritual name
it's all the same
if some cheat and eat meat
it doesn't ruin it for those
sincere.

We toe the crooked Sanskrit
line and try to improve the
part in our hairs.
Amen. Sorry folks
for awry it's the world.
*C'est* Kali-yuga.

*pp. 88–90*

⁂

*Return to Song Bird*

Do you remember how to sing it's
between two days since you did
a magpie
a twisted cork
a piece of mirth and me.

Krishna consciousness you dig up from
innards but say here's the
truth we live by, wave a
favorable flag.

So fast he doesn't know what's
happening. Impeccable wavering.
He was grateful the man kept time.

Grunt of worker I like to hear
they like it.
We are approaching Gaura-Purnima
I have to get out there and see the
moon.

Jumping clock on my desk.
Stay away from me men entering
and slammed doors to disturb
my song.

II

I can't even turn my neck quick
without a crick. But the melody
must mean something.

He looks and hears just
as your words are arbitrarily
making yourself to write
liturgies, *slokas* and that sort
of thing. What would they say
about me approaching Gaura-Purnima
here in Inis Rath territory.

I have my drive to be alone and claim
something. It happened long ago and
right now I'm alive although in
last quarter, last eighth
home tired stretch.

III

He's a high-flying bird
Oh sure, he repeats himself don't
worry about that or count
them just fly with the
wild swans and quick darters
he's the bird of your ken
came to you, oh you
say I ask for him
but he came and God allowed
and said Let's see you direct
a Krishna conscious song

a godly person can do that
and this stuff leans to same
because it's pure song sound
now is the time
this year's Gaura-Purnima
this old man
get rid of self-pity.

IV

One more time we want to
confirm that you are a true disciple.
Yes! Of who?
Of Swami and song and birds
disciples and water and sky.

Ah, we thought so. You should
be...
wait friend, a disciple of
Srila Prabhupada is also a friend to the
others, don't dictate to me
what I can and can't be.
You can't change me.

Or rub out the songs and
the sky. He's so melodic
crazy, you can't understand
so I claimed and maybe was wrong
in a private world but chanced
it as we say
"On a wing and a prayer."

You better chant a little extra,
make up for your incompetence
deviant foray into the gutter...

*pp. 110–14*

⁂

*Memories of Gaura-purnima*

It's sad and loverly, lovely, the
boat is going across and he is in a
mind to celebrate.

The occasion is ten days before the Appearance of
  Lord Caitanya. I remember lots
of good times if I could single
them out
but they remain kind of mixed
in with the rough stuff.

You remember old Gaura-Purnimas?
I can't remember the first except we
were very glad to break the fast
and Rupanuga saw the moon from a
tenement roof and rushed into
the storefront to tell us.

I remember being in Mayapur, of course
and I was a boss?
I was on a roof torn?
I looked down at the masses
filing into ISKCON temple and felt
good and special in holy land.
*This* is the place to be on
Gaura-Purnima where it
originally happened and
happens still where people
know and love Gaura!

And other times. One time in snow
in Saranagati completely beside the point,
I didn't even want to give the class
and one guy showed off a little we
all do. And then I went back to writing
in the little cabin.

Another time and again and again, we were
in Mayapur – Allow someone else to
become a guru? Agree you are the eleven
best? Go see Sridhara Maharaja, fight
some schism? Rush back?

All in all, I'm glad to be alive
and this year it'll be quiet and
you could say inconsequential
tear drop
for all those times
that were great
and over and lost.

All get lost in river of time
not exactly Ganga
but coming back from there seeing
Hare Krishna mantra lit up in
many colored light bulbs
on top of ISKCON Mayapur building,
1976.

*pp. 118–20*

*Compulsory Japa*

Compulsory silent rounds
are just like the hounds.
What do you mean,
like a dream,
like a dream?
Aren't they *aparadha*
    or no more than cotton pods?

*p. 128*

*He Thought*

He thought he'd see a shrink
how he fell in the drink
ISKCON's loss to the world
his own loss to the pearl–
like idealism of youth, blah-blah.
No, it's really tragic pitiful
tears to fill a bucketful
at least it's worth to talk out
for 90 bucks an hour.

He thought he'd see a doc
to be psychoanalyzed
"You see I believe in our cause
and no, I didn't even pause to
think or feel, I'm like an eel
and the Movement is an itchy feel,
no more than that.

"Where are the friends I
joined to live with? Where
is the love to all who
serve him? I can't even talk
if I did they'd balk
so, I'll speak to a hole in the wall."

Get it off my chest, find what went wrong,
make it my true song.
"Oh, you'll never reach the root,
just spend a lot of loot."
You can say that, but listen,
this is serious stuff
and confinement's not enough.

*pp. 128–29*

*Approaching Hare Krishna*

Hare Krishna is for kids
old men would like it and so would squids
if they only knew their truth.

Hare Krishna is on the skids
in many countries
such as France
but give it a chance
it will rise again.

I know I'll be dead
before Hare Krishna fulfills its weight
temples in Kuwait
*Krishna Book* in every home
I'm bound to come upon it
and continue my progress in *bhakti*.

Hare Krishna, please forgive me
it's the pain behind my eyes
and the mind I can't control
I'm on a bad roll
I pray to you
and hope you find some good
in whatever I can do, Hare Krishna.

*pp. 130–31*

*A Headache Daze*

Daze of pain
like of days of rain
just pass by.
You seek relief
keep belief,

"soon it will clear."

How long
has it been
since I rose and read at midnight?
When will I return
to that routine?
I can't think it out
but lie and whimper
like a patient cat.

*p. 136*

*On Bird as Divinely Inspired*

There's plenty of ways to please
Lord Hari, your mind must be
on Him.

You hear Him and say
inside – O, Hari!
You're the one who lifted
Govardhana
and lifted the earth
on Your tusks and
sent Srila Prabhupada to lift me
and my generation.

You enabled singers to sing,
and we hide Your glory
as misfits – I hereby state
all are vibrations of the
Lord.

Concentrate to praise Him...
stumbling and pushing and trying their best to
make melodic song fast

Why fast? Why don't you ask
it's our desire to outrace
Maya and do a thing
like that dance on
the temple floor.
We are made to dance.

Keep the ruffians contained. It's a wild age!
Give them a *kirtana* that
cuts through and no compromise
Hare Krishna.
But Lord gave me
music too.

✤ ✤ ✤

*Don't Take for Granted*

Once upon a time, did they tell
the song all right?

Yes, I said, we survived the power
failure putting on our coat and hat
and chanting on beads fingering.

Once upon a time, did they conquer the jury and judge
in ISKCON
that you're a bona fide wig?

No! They said cut this
out, it's like a *sannyasi* playing
tennis and saying it's for his
health – we offered him
swimming is a Vaisnava sport.

O Lord, this little thing you
worry about. What to say?
If I met a man, I'd say

“Don’t take anything for granted
whatever we have is coming from
Krishna.” That wisdom of here
and now, so he’d be – or show
a little surprised. But I met
no one and got no chance and
now it’s too late.
Be romantic, if you can a
gray heron is calling:
Oh! Oh! Krishna -
inks and antics why
take stairs, go the elevator.

He’s ritual, herb, ink,
priest, mother, creator
*Vedas, omkara*, Camarillo,
tax, annoying
- all comes from
God –

He’s true one so go direct
the message through is
best taken.

Here’s to you and answer your question.
Don’t take it for granted.

*pp. 158–59*

(Page numbering for part two starts here)

*Smooth Birds*

Smooth rivets, maybe the rivets
they say sunk the Titanic
up and down the smoothest
beat wail scale.

The bird I saw was not in
the book. *C.c.* describes birds
flying home to Krishnaloka at
close of day. The cat...
the cat *camara*...the
man who can't pronounce the
birds
who yearn for moon
another for rain from
  cloud.

Peacocks make pure devotee
dizzy, and he faints in love
of Krishna. In dust of
Vrindavan. Those birds
don't do a few choruses and
sit down, but all day
and night.

In springtime they mate
and build, pure devotees
observe and remark, this is nature study.
  All honors to Krishna who has
subdued the *gopis* and Srila Prabhupada
tells us devotees just cry
for Krishna and say go wherever you
like, we will love you despite
you *lampat*
we will be chaste.

Nice as when thinking of
food or *rasas* or *japa* rounds
completed, the sun yet to rise
and we can go on a walk because
our heartbeat is still
strong for time being...

Bird, you sing and I say wake
to be serious and say birds

I say Hare Krishna Hare Krishna, Krishna Krishna
please trick me.

*pp. 7–8*

*There Was Once a Man*

He couldn't remember when he was supposed
to go home, he kept wailing and it wasn't just
business. It was love.
I flew the coop I came new

Free writing as we say so don't trouble me. I was with the Tots watching them from the wooden grandstand in the gymnasium waiting to get out like everyone else so afraid and playing games and wanting to be seen as good by the right guys in the crowd. You play your chances, be seen by girls, be cynical at all things, everyone covers their heart, doesn't even know who they are and this is supposed to be fun.

No one can help you, you need a guru and then you don't care for that crowd.

Do you, however, develop a similar pattern in more sophisticated ways within the ISKCON crowd?

Yes, to some degree but actually, your primary self-realization...you keep in mind on the pure instructions. Then you may get tired of official interaction but why quit your duties?

Once a man from Blast
had a seizure in Nast
and gave vent to Krishna
himself relieved of Pishna
I don't dig it, said the piano
man, and I told him in my country
piano means gas
oh, that's a laugh

he winked and we went to
the temple hall on time
the TP eyed us as we
bowed down and then I
blanked out.

He said would you like to lead the singing? I said yes, give me the mic:

There was once a man from Jizz
who lived on a fizz
then he met a Nama Hat
mad hatter and sat in
the hall of fame watching.

They asked him to leave
he said I'll shreve
and grieve the demise but
don't overdo that
it's not so bad
Don't be sad good times
are still here.
So, he beard his cheer on a
hand mic and said I better not chance
to sing *samsara* as you requested.
But remain quiet in respect
as a better man bellowed it out,
in Italy this was.

*pp. 8–10*

⁂

*Prayer to be a Devotee in Any Incarnation*

There was a man from Remus
There was me actually grateful to
the Lord in heart and sky and head to let
me write again with clear head and if

I'd be pinned down that'd be
okay too...

Old favorites don't decry their good go
under different names.
Reincarnations
  of bird.
I want to dedicate this number to my
loyal...to my cat and dog (he said)
Rainer was too young to go to
military school and a misfit there.

But you, Krishnaite. What?
You in the second row
bow
down to your Mighty.

Don't let no blasphemer blather
in here if possible kick him
out. While the ink lasts.

Krishna says I give you existence
I am the sustaining power
that you walk today and
I will meet you at death.

In sick and health on the
heath in a marsh an
advanced soul sees Krishna
everywhere. You'll be glad
to know...

That was me in the cameo shot
and one you, dear reader
coming up soon – see there
in the *kirtana* chorus so
sweet all swaying and singing

we are happy to be together
and happy alone sometimes
hip the words loose Krishna I
don't know much at all
have a ball
I'm not tall / in hall I
stood in shadow and
didn't know you but
now I know my master.

When I have to meet him next life
give me sense to quit
what I'm doing and become a
*cela* in uniform whatever
it takes
in reincarnation of a devotee
please be kind.

He just wants the truth
of Krishna covered lyrics
uncovered and surprise it's
Lord Krishna on the cake
take make
you better believe and
*sabda* is awaiting
come home to where
you don't have to be
born *gata*
          *agatam*
again after *soma* juice.

*pp. 16–18*

*The Little Attention*

This night come down and be with us star eyes. The man was alone and very happy to be doing *bhajana* alone. "No other path – I walk alone," take in the religious sense of *bhakti*.

Music modes the tune
and ancient hune
warlock the man
is woman too and sand
man is stopping us with
sleep.

Otherwise, we'd continue all day
to keep alive and well and read
the *Cc.* on *vaidhi* and *prema*
as R.R. said, "Food isn't
enjoyable unless you're hungry."
            Snap, snap the roll on
bop pretty bow-tie match
nature rain I don't want to
hear but can't avoid the
crowd of crimes pressed
right on you.

Admit a quiet life is good
to mine gems can help
busy people in jam.

Sketch, ruminate, keep on top
of the little bird called attention –
let him fly but lure him back
with nicest feed to your
bird stand.

It all comes back to a Krishna protection
    of things in sky.
When a man played on his comb
the sound amused only
and when he played on the harp
it was beauty but retired
however, when he said
here's a bird we spied

delight and didn't shake
the table
we listened and made
God conscious lyrics
to what was already
inclined to
Lord Krishna in forest
His play is most
concluded fun experiment.

*pp. 33–35*

❖ ❖ ❖

*Sages Sort It Out*

Tip, tip he was willing the chatter,
a foolish man wanted to take his time,
but when he turned to play,
his music his pleasure was "lost" –
absorbed in the work he was
made for. It's like that
when I get a pat on
the back and go lost in
a rip raft you
say I was soon made for this.
I never skipped school
happy
work towards
turds
happy make people
smile
don't see them in your
own little studio of eternity
ordering goodies by mail
distraction from the absolute
this is obviously a man unripe
in *bhakti* and his pains
prevent him.

Sing a sailor hat old days a
woman said she was a quark in
past life and now lives two at once I said
Oh, let go sister, let yourself
go detached...But how
can you talk if you don't do it yourself?
Bang, we're off at the gate
swimming how many, how did he do
blurts drip out blood
and black ink spurt, the pen
gets stuck and if it continues you
can't live, just flow
on the path you know
given you by a good God.

Man, you know a person looks
for a good time release from the
crowds and pressure of his day and he
who gives him fun and release is his
friend he'll pay for it.
Clap, clap. Sit down
clown friend, this is the original
genius of modern expression, giving us what
arises to you on the fresh attempt. You
say through God. I am pleased
why I have a body can't figure out
especially one so delicate it breaks down and
grows grotesque old can be put
into the most awkward condition
of howling pain and pleasure is from same
bones and nerves.

We really ought to hear from
sages who sort it out. They say the body
is given by wrong desires. God really
wants us to come back to a spiritual body as
the servant of God. And we better dance to
that. Don't ask why does He make
it so when we don't serve we ache?

I said whatever helps we'll accept. And that's the
    key
    Key West life best
    let's take off
        then he wrote.

*pp. 35–37*

*Saturday Sat Song*

You can't write so many songs you got to get
the exact right sound. I know
it can be done.
Please, please, stop clapping when I sing
you can't keep time so good.

I'm not a bank shooter or
so-cute mad artist you are bewildered
by where I'm coming from.

Separate the voices and find inside
a boy wan and worn and crapshooter
he pretends
he's a holy fad guru
pretends he cares, loves suicide,
loves word pretends he is
alone, that's it – I didn't mean
to write "suicide" but solitude.

You get mixed up sometimes.
I want things nice and polished, but
there are so many cartons and
belongings piling up in his room.

I want to be serious and God
conscious and be Krishna centered –
the one God immanent and
tell you so you get surprised I'm
so right on.

But here's the truth – cool air
coming in shed window, she
big fly, me covering up what I'm doing
not at Confession this Sat.
Because (*sat-sanga*) I
want to keep it a secret my privy.

One misty evening one clear day
the rhythms and blues of bright
sunshine square on this page.
Krishna is the residence,
country we live in,
and He meets us at death –
sustains us until then.

I say this but don't realize
it much. My receiving loyal.
This eon-long brief
to you a form of love
the K.C. of long ago is glad he got a clear
head enough to tell you.

clap, clap, you fools.
Now I retire so ladies and
gents can really applaud and
do whatever you want.

Amen
the heavens
are God's
open and beyond.

*pp. 42–44*

*Rushing to Get It Out Before We Get Cut Off*

Out of nowhere Krishna came they say
but He's never nowhere, He's
eternally situated you can't figure
it out.

Please regret, please be sweet
bring on the tiger the house of
dreams on the streetcar that
man, may mug us.
   The time eluded me all those
fools writing for a little gold but
the popular imagination is good too
to remember.

I was in good form
like a worm
am free of disease for awhile
you got a...and can't avoid
them
Then their eyes
you're sportin' and deliver
us pie and fresh berries
God in this life and the next
He's always best.

They can play at a moment's notice I
tell you we don't want to fight Lord
Hari in all things
ritual, butter, arm
chant – *sva-ha*!
Piano fingers.
He's the offering
and the object
I learned it in the *Gita*.

Take time, my Lord
I want to be there at the telegraph 1920s

style getting messages of icebergs and
Japs on the way to Pearl Harbor in
small planes with red sun on
wings.

FDR knew / Clinton too
they never went to moon
Krishnas believe don't tell
you sell the siren
time's up.

No man come in and act as *he*
is boss, he can play like that, but
we know he's another puppet
and God as Time really rules.

There, I said it
God is Krishna and sweet is the tale
of Rupa Gosvami to know Him you have to
be with regular devotees of His
*rupanugas, sanatanists,*
and Hare Krishna people come down the street with
Aghasura
open mouth children run in six
times while Madhu sings all
rehearsed

Sit theme fade.

*pp. 56–58*

⁂

Swami, contain yourself in six ways
when you do it eye pain can be
allowed or subdued and think
man, of Krishna and Hare Krishna
inside and out, you'll be okay.

*p. 59*

*A Secret or Two*

So, I tell you I'm coming on strong to
be with you all. The man said he got
a soul the *Bhagavad-gita* tells me so.

It's okay you got a way to go.
How long can you live? What does
the red hen of Maya mean?

I am not a rabbit dish. Do not like
at all when people are cruel to animals
but then who's to say I can be
truly a human sacrifice?

Stop, stop red cross you could
swim if you had to or drown
you too bowing before the Deity
have to rise and shine, man.

Asking questions, smiling at the verve
of the man asking questions He
wants to know and stands up and
asking God questions like talking
an animal talking and
crying, a horse crying like
in Chekhov story...

Sure, I want to go beyond myself
in the mirror. Cut off
a little toupee on the left
sorry, I nicked you, I do want to take care of you...

They're talking to God on high
in heart / I know a secret or
two, the clown wanted everyone
to laugh but they wanted to see
him hurt, see? I got the
epics too in paperback.

I could have been a good
student in English lit.

Why did you back out?
Where's your *danda*?
Won't you get bored and
lonely in Portsmouth?

You can tell in a moment
who's talking or singing. They die
well alright but Krishna, Krishna on the beads,
Lord we want to be a real person and
"dare You" dare them not
to be a rubber stamp make -
believe saintly person.

He said all this as usual: "Class
will be at noon and feast at 3 p.m."
Ekadasi potatoes and ringlets
and not good soppy apple
sweet sauce. I take what
they give.

Elevating man smiles
I told the man play a hot
I am not in charge I want
to pass the pen and taking turns
with men I love and be worker
in the line.

Bad, bad and sweet soul
the same thing blues they
are with him in tired tunes.
Be aware we want to be with you too.

But buddy, we need to be Krishna conscious
this tune doesn't suit us
*yukta-vairagya* doesn't compromise
pure *bhakti*.

You too, please bow down
to Bhagavan
be fleet foot
I mean, you read some
scripture I want to
can't go a minute without
it / you know
Krishna is the Supreme Personality of Godhead.

*pp. 62–65*

❧ ❧ ❧

*Heart is a Melody*

(Sing. I know you're not much with word music or
word choice but you can skat a little.
Krishna consciousness.)

The tiger loosed
the swan ran through the water.
He's really good with his song
he's a melody
heart is a melody.

Please release us from the bonds of
sleep if we don't need it.
I want to sing in my own
God-given tone, Krishna is the
one and only.

Give me a time on a radio show, and I'll
glorify Krishna neatly as I heard a
Christian do the other day, but
these countries think we are cultists
and we have to fight back. Madhu
does it cheerfully
and is satisfied to
win someone, just one person

in a talk. I can...
but tend to feel the burden
of it.

Trauma is on me of being a cultist / am so alienated...
alas, poor Rilke
we knew him well
Horatio

I like so much the dawn birds
the cold moon, the
yogurt and fruit
the ink flow
the stares of Michelangelo
the little books
the brook of Tusca
the alone melody of Time.

Spring cabbage spring to
the land birds fly up
from Spain.

Sing any melody and carry it back to
Krishna consciousness. You can be with
me and Krishna will forgive you...

*pp. 78–79*

*Haribol*

husky. Hurt. Winsome
released time for religion taught us
of Krishna in *Gita*
and in *Vidagdha-madhava*, I know
I'm not fit to hear
but you poured a little in
my ear and now I can't
stop.

Please don't release us from
the obligation to serve our master
in some country this happens
to be mine and you find
your own
everybody on beads same
chime when can I raise it to
actual call Hari
you teasing me,
you withholding
please, at least don't take
the beads from my
hands and mind.

*p. 80*

*Dig He's Audarya*

(My poor self, is wanting to be a friend. I got nothing to offer but my time and he don't know the art either.)

Mary was a lamb had
only three legs and sat down
somehow should be glad
he was alive man it was.

Tell me wiggle or wait the
forward move was so nice.
Sonny, you are the man we
want to be with.
If you could tell us one
thing only.

That would be chant Hare Krishna
less and less people write to me
I say hey kids you pretending
to be on a rowboat

wait'll you grow up.
Pup die, cat die
ramp daffodils I wanted
to say crack be sorry
me is alone melody
share Rilkean sad
for himself
perk
jerk
he resigned.

Bow down, son
it's the great
mountain
trumpet
erstwhile.

Bow down to emperor's young
wife and to stones on path
to all I am servant said
the guru as servant
beware the fat
  man.
Beware the irrelevant ditty
keep you in this world
all you need is time
to be a pure devotee

Goatey had three legs and
a cross-eyed stereotyped
look. Don't slaughter me.
Don't sell our hay to
farmers of slaughtered cows.
Tell them not to.
*You* tell them.
I got a Rilkean pass
rifle pass
pass the jive, please
pass the salt

Miss Malltine, you
have pretty eyes
supplied by God.

*Gopis* only for pure souls
clean yours of dirt
and chant Hare Krishna with a pain and brack
and pills in pocket.

Riff and roll knots in wood
pop out while I'm gone
rot paint and walls
ache for me to return?
No, nothing doing.

While power boats waste
time and fuel you'll
be in the South in new
venture for getting sorrow,
    tomorrow and four days more
it'll be another scene
no better than this you'll
have to work out smack
crash
the days go by
and curtain hesitating but
surely gets closer and
closed. Rambhoru
shows photo of
dead and cooks to heal
the dissension, the disciples
who never wrote say Now
we'll read the stiff's
Pokka Flat blues in
sixty-four volumes?! Where does
he get off? Two dogs in Switz bank
I bank on Swami
mercy home free
grab at rope of mercy.

Gaura-Purnima lecture – dig he's
*audarya*. Don't miss it
   do some *seva*
happily
sweet rice
no sand
understand?

*pp. 83–87*

*Swamis* worship Radha
with Krishna and serve in Their
amorous pastimes, soothe,
make sense control that way
in disciplined measure.

*p. 97*

*When Surrounded by the Influence of Kali-yuga*

I have to resist the bad guys
I have to make for the good
food, and hooded monk.

I am not going to be drowned by the fellows
who waste time in their grungy ways.
All this I declared.

Then you sing a song of March 10. We're
up and at 'em. The time we went to
the park with the Swami. Hare Krishna
Hare Krishna
Is that a Krishna? Yes, he wears
high socks so you may not notice him.
But I know these are

complicated postmodern times and
don't believe.

We won't even discuss it but just
give out *halava* and drink of orange juice
and yogurt and a lecture light and a
banjo player and a girl with lipstick
and eye make-up called Bharat
Natyam dance.
Here comes India
exotic at ya.

Plain oatmeal march of spirits
fighting against the sand of Kali-yuga
artists of this age are rockers
and cock pilots' pit.

The tuba marches on its own way.
Man do better than that, give me
another chance
Krishna chant you people ought to
be nonviolent / all is illusion
rise to truth
body is for service / I don't
care if you don't accept it.

#2

We had to put up with a judge and
merchant and long queues of cars' headlights
but unfortunately, there were young preachers
among us and they got out and went up to
each car and a crazy person with a book
and food for life
but some were too crazy and ridiculed
and saw devotees as prudes and fanatics
they wanted crushed
so, advisor said better go

to the temple. They insisted on dancing
a kind of two-step chanting to
appeal to the crowd.

Well, there is something in the music of
the *karmis*? No Bhakta Joe, come back
and don't listen. A black man preached
to a black Hare Krishna to give up the
company of the ofays in saffron. A
woman did the same with a sister.

A dog peed on?
A hydrant stayed.
A *swami*...the North versus the
South. They were dancing and strutting and calypso
Joe came out with a new song, "Harry
Krishna." The devotees got on radio
and said we don't ban the song but
the loose, sensuous bacchanal.

Now, on our own if we had no
outside influence what would you do?
I sing
Krishna is fun
Don't run away from Him
Become a happy
fellow of chant and dance
squeak a little in the right way.
Don't emit the bad forgetting of God
sound but – it isn't so bad
fury scurry of freedom from *maya*
turn on cold shower
we have our ways.

*pp. 100–3*

*Insist on God*
(As rain splashes, I hope I can find a voice, like getting into a railway car and finding a seat? Like what? Some words earnest through the covering. Words like rain.)

Hey, this dark theater is a good
place. The lonely woman or man
or dog or mouse. You can't say a
ball of dust is lonely but it may
look alone, personified, pitiful.

Sing out, Krishna I remember that God
the pod the hod carrier
thank God, I remember my self
is Krishna conscious soul stuff.
    I remembered in time that I
am a rep of God
"Always the missionary" even in
his fatal insular poems.

You go, get rid of you I'm
  for God conscious carrier those who believe in *sastra.*
We got to get it together better, setter or wetter
I'm using the borrowed energy.
If you can take it, steal it
it's still moral for the
Supreme Lord.
People don't care one way or
another and die out after best
efforts so eternal, *if* there
is – Socrates, Pascal, Descartes,
Thomas Aquinas,
James Joyce, Pirandello, the list
is aimless. Some believe,
so know, I know the
Vedic experts do agree
and science got
love of God is all
He'll accept.

#2

Ink finger let's roundelay
of your Lord
Bored? Room? Breakfast and
two-by-four

lie on a board to improve
your verses. Woman is
a broad. The broad
expanse
the plush border
Carl Bertsch of high school
my private garage.
Lord, Lord Ford
sword...I hesitate to tell
you he's talking of experience
of the Supreme Lord. He's fierce about
it.
Neighs and whinny the
Denuka got creamed
tell it!
Bala swung him Out!

Up to trees a panorama
of dead screeching asses.

God's smart bomb the
going alone to quote the
scripture of God say I
am honest and *still* I love
God.

Krishna pink, blue and yellow
any...God is brass and mind
and jewel and sand.
No atheists need apply.
Love required.

Atheist is okay too if he gets
to know if he dies and
sees Oh! Oh, death is
He I had to submit to.

I hear ya. I hear ya
Lord. I want God consciousness
themes.

They love and work together
this is the way
Krishna conscious melody *kirtana*
in shout or alone on
beads make clear
your intention
while alive.

*pp. 109–12*

*Descent of the Avatar*

(Kali-yuga influences include influence of the *sankirtana* movement on the world. Where else did they hear of the avatar, the holy names, Lord Caitanya?)

He came as Patita-Pavana
and the two brothers at Ramakeli said
there is no one as fallen
as we are.

I'm tired of insane people we are in the same place as the maniacs. "All Bozos on the same bus." Everyone is more or less crazy. That the conditioned souls, not the ISKCONites. But this too is a mad house of bewildered careers from early childhood abuse, chillun of alcoholics, dysfunctional scimitars came in the back door looking to be told what to do or to take over once they quail their worst shocks at hands of material nature.

The *avatara* of Lord Caitanya knows this craziness of many cults and cut and deals among the citizens of this repute.

Can I get relieved from the sad time? "*Avatara*," he said, "please give me Your mercy."

Shirtwaist  
waste time  
you have to stop blabbing  
be a straight disciple, and he'll  
change your name to Krishna dasa.

The *avatara* said, "You are My eternal  
servants and I accept you." Fortunate they  
were serious to actually follow.  
They didn't linger in bad noises  
and voids. Sooner or later I will too  
will have to leave all false or temp  
simulation as in my dream  
you'll go through tests of survival  
narrowed down (as in spelling bee)  
to fewer  
and finally killed  
so, there's no fittest who  
survives death.  
Please, Krishna *avatara*, give me  
mercy, intelligence to tell of Your glories.

*pp. 127–28*

*The Presence of the Friend*

Naima, I mean Krishna please be my
friend. There's no one but You and You are
all one needs. Each has You.
And all others are Yours.

Sure, we hear these things.
I want to burst out sometimes and that's
okay too but times we were sweet
like hand holding it's Your

hand, like a father's (sure like
lovers too when you qualify)
to assure me
you'll get through the death
camp disease.

Revolving births and deaths,
*I am here* and I'll protect you
  He says
        we don't always know what's
happening but can always turn to Him.

Krishna name private and personal
as well as shared by brave
soldiers sing Them
on the street.
I'm talking now about the quiet
touch and presence in any
mood conjuring appearing
Krishna.

#2

This you have promised us,
that if we surrender,
worship, *kirtana*,
offered to You,

You'll take us back where we belong.

Coming down as from stars and the
cool almost full moon I
spied this morning at 3 a.m.—
cold out there —his face
with O-mouth and eyes empty—
  he too.
Coming down the Milky Way
You, You to assure me
the knowledge we must accept and
don't trust your own intelligence
as Bhaktivinoda Thakura says...

In Navadvipa seek sweet secret places
*sadhus* chant the main theme
is separation from Krishna as Krishna
felt in the mood of Radha.
Share with those who can qualify.
It's the solitary lover of
Lord Krishna I aspire to know
from Him my own strength
and comfort - so I can
give the same to others.
Some day soon.
Hare Krishna chants from inner...
works fast but His.

*pp. 129–31*

❖ ❖ ❖

*Give Him Your Best*

Mr. Smith had a quirk
let it work we're not
gonna quit
on *yukta-vairagya*.

This is the way. Blow steam for
Krishna. Swan is way.

Don't give up earnest account
to worship in a church
especially the *mandir* of the
mind worst wurst.

I said Lord Krishna wants the free
and doing as He likes
on a bike or car
as far as I can
chasing the *sankirtana,*
but when you ask me "What do you want, how
do you want to serve Me?" and I look within for sense
of vocation –
that's the best I know –
give you mine.

Train sounds through the mind the head cleared for
action
in days when I was young
I was hampered,
stuff I'm free of now.

Krishna, You sure spin us around
but an earnest devotee gives his
very best for Your service.

Krishna plays as Catholic and
Zen and Muslim and Buddhist
and Cubist and Sartre-ist –
no, no atheists I don't
know
just Krishna is me
and my offering while
the earth world is too
big for me judge.

Don't be bewildered by them
out there cats and dogs and
big crows and tanks and guns
and newspapers
curlers for her hair...

I got a red pill on tap
just in case it gets rap
and then beyond that I'll
retire to a burrow.

Walking with Krishna be sure He is
with you be certain to
you're not topmost
but free to be happy.

Don't look in mirror at the fool
be true to the devotee he
made you said you
are eternally so
as Lord Gauranga said

in Ramakeli, "You two
are My eternal servants
you are now Rupa
and Sanatana," and we take it
and apply it
as you can.

Best foot, alone mostly this sweet
he gotta go and you gotta go and you
cough-cough not a perfect
film ending or choreographed.

But sweet Lord Krishna guaranteed
as His word in *Gita*
and guru backs Him up
you can't lose.

*pp. 135–38*

*Good Intentions of a Dull Clinker on Gaura-purnima*

On Gaura-purnima do your thing
for Lord Krishna don't mind how
crazy the world sounds.

You out there, cold stars and
night turning to morn, see the
devotees of Lord Caitanya coming
to worship and bless us with
some mercy to fulfill our duties
with *bhakti* pleasing to you.

The blessed words sometimes flow
too freely from us like glib
Don't wear a bib
be a real fibber if that's who
you are but let's look up
be special
today more.

Krishna Krishna Krishna *Haribol*
free me the influences even as
I surround myself with them.

Krishna living is nice, Radhanatha in
a jam but trying his best
Manu too and the kids and me
running out of ink and asking for
refills and paper...

So poor you don't even know
how the mercy of Navadvipa
moves over to Vrindavan you
are not among the...
Well, at least I'm with devotees
on this day and walking into an
ISKCON temple to give an authorized
initiation

Name: "You are now
Gauri-Hari dasa."

Looking ahead today I ask
not for extreme originality or
genius. We are meant to act
to please and that's by sincere
and simple chanting and serving.

So poor asking only that
clear "surma" vision so
I can see Syamasundara in
inner eye. Master says it
can't be done except by devotion
    starting with the ear.

Hare Krishna despite myself I'll
deliver goods I heard from
him and in his books I'll
be there on time if Krishna
allows me this day.

Hare Krishna chanting comes from Krishnaloka
even through me it's possible.
Hare Krishna Hare Krishna.

*pp. 152–54*

*You're Too Too*

I am going to my home in the head
I was there in Town Hall balcony,
not with Prabhupada in 1966 to see Burton
Green with Brahmananda.

I'm here in Inis Rath.
Yeah, well we're waiting don't take
too long in this

silent head
give us nectar.
You just give a little and we let you off
on surmised trust
your burst
head is your excuse
Don Foose wants to know. How come you read those
outside
 books?
Tell him I'm dainya
tell
him I was always a writer and
in Heaven (Goloka) I'll
write for Krishna or do the
dishes
Fishes don't fear me I'm
just a playful sort
ought a rabbit live free
on Govindadwipa?

Ought an author of *dainya*
be allowed free time
to rhyme released time for religion, Catholics down the
street and Hare Krishnas
Play, play loose in the puddles...

Tell it bro, white and saffron
surprise us please it's always
the same, more a game
and the GBC do something
now to furrow our brow
in worry over already
dead-head
ISKCON?

No, I want straight loyal speech
said Don Foose, he should talk,
a rocker from Austria, Cleve
cleave to your Lord and excuse

Lord Caitanya is merciful.
Lord Caitanya allows but no
nonsense.

Please don't expect too
much freedom in *maya* it's a
strict path He gave Jagai and Madhai
once they saw the light.

Coming home to this
rehearsed your band and give
us Krishna conscious nectar
to break our short fast
while it lasts, your life
to Krishna's
music of inner
and bow down to the
leaders
you're not one
you're two too too.

*pp. 160–63*

*Day After Gaura-purnima*

We wanted out, we wanted to be hearty fellows with
quirky whatever we are.

Rufus, he said a million times. The wear and tear of
Belfast, street lights overnight, guns and...Here we are
in temple with Radha-Madhava, here we are perfect,
purry cats. We are
making the most of it. It's fine, it's fine.

Hare Krishna toast and muffin and tea mint.
He says I'm urgent to talk with you. It's cute code
music back and forth
oh yes, now I'll talk. Give me
a little time on a typewriter or
personal pen ink.

Here he comes, the guy with husky voice. Here he
comes
Krishna walking in his bones
so, hold a meeting he tells us you may go
you may go home-free. The
worst time is not right now
so take advantage and be a hero,
I mean a sandwich
I mean, be happy
relax work the self your
poem doesn't have to rhyme but I
think it ought to divide lines
oh, harmonium Stevens
become a Hare Krishna and
play accordion outdoors
in Hare Krishna clothes the
expert standard musician said
"I accept him anyway."

Four, five, six, for who? For
God, it's all for Him. We want
that sort of thing
chant Hare Krishna
the music quieted down and we heard
heartbeats. We heard the Francis
Express
quiet you may be able to
   hear birds
day after Gaura-purnima –
   you didn't even look
for the moon. Where? Sky, stupid.
Up there. I forget it's cloudy usually.

Play *mrdanga*, smash khol outside guest
house Krishna-Balarama Mandir
an owl on the telephone wire,
   Germans, Russians,
      now they say you just sit
and here and now write an essay
Hare Krishna no time
take this kiss handshake.

*pp. 179–80*

# CHAPTER SIX - THE OCEAN AND THE DESERT

March 14 – April 2, 1998

*Nectar of Devotion* way, way up there. Beyond Geaglum clouds and rainbows. It's in the book – Krishna, eternity, *bhakti-rasa*, perpetual engagement...

*Part One,*
*pp. 24-25*

Nectar ocean
and desert heart
the hare riots
the pheasant also pecks
and I offer my devotion
*dandavats* hundreds
of times a day.

*Part Two,*
*pp. 63-64*

Standing at the very center of this second volume of Satsvarupa dasa Goswami's collection of *Every Day, Just Write* poems is the remarkable volume entitled, *The Ocean and the Desert,* itself the twenty-fifth volume of this unfolding literary project. With this title, *The Ocean and the Desert* employs the symbolic richness of these two contrasting features of the earth to depict the depths of the love of God and the spiritual poverty of the human heart. This is effectively accomplished through both prose and poetry, conjoined in the series within this volume, "Preaching and Poems" which is both serious and playful. Central to the literary shape and spiritual aesthetic is Satsvarupa Maharaja's extended meditations upon A.C. Bhaktivedanta Swami Prabhupada's *The Nectar of Devotion,* which is a presentation and study of Rupa Goswami's incomparable introduction to devotional life, *Bhakti-rasamrta-sindhu.* Satsvarupa Maharaja announces his reading plan at the beginning of the volume in which he describes the particular way in which he will engage *The Nectar of Devotion.* He writes, "Do it with love. Bring your love. You're not a critic, not an outsider to this book. It's written by your spiritual master for you. It is the best way to be with him" (Part One, p.2). While this text is typically read as a guide book to devotional life, the author does not intend to read it analytically or dogmatically but rather with a contemplative mood. This reading will be prolonged and will span the several weeks that comprise this volume of *Every Day, Just Write.* So, throughout the pages of *The Ocean and the Desert,* references to *The Nectar of Devotion* will abound. For this text will be Satsvarupa Maharaja's companion on this journey to the ocean of the love of God even while standing on the barren shores of the heart's desert wilderness. In this regard, consider this passage:

I thought of a title for this volume, *The Ocean and the Desert*. Both. *The Nectar of Devotion* is the ocean I am approaching three times a day. But I experience the desert

when I do so. *Bhakti* is the ocean and my heart is the desert. Maybe the title is too much "both," but I like it. I go from one to the other. They both exist. There is some dynamic between them. The desert forges the disciple. He goes with the desert and finds the ocean within it? Anyway, something. *Nectar of Devotion*, please take me, dry as I am. Sprinkle...

*Part One, p. 112*

As a stylistic counterpoint to the contemplative mood of this volume's prose, Satsvarupa Maharaja introduces two poetic series in which he ranges freely from one theme to another in a manner characteristic to this series. To begin, the reader encounters "Preaching and Poems", which addresses a variety of topics within the preaching life. Consider this stanza from the series' third installment, which translates a prayerful mood into explicitly poetic form:

Krishna, I remember You in the
temple beside Radha, I
remember my days and nights
and fears. Krishna, please let
me remember You as I go
down, You wearing Your
outfit of the day and me
serving You – new
and next.

*Part One, pp. 33-34*

The reader is further introduced to "Sampler's Poetry Hall", a series which begins with an imaginary poetry class taught by a Mrs. Sampler, who offers her students a theme for a poetry, which then becomes a springboard for creative writing. In poetry both weighty and light-hearted, Satsvarupa Maharaja gives his creative spirit full reign. In this instance the prevalent theme of the *ars poetica* is addressed:

> Praise God with eloquent speech.
> Wish I could. Is that what Father Manley
> Hopkins did? Praise God with
> homely metaphors with lotus
> *lilas* great skill in Sanskrit,
> now English, American, Siberian.

*Part One, pp. 233-34*

Creating prose that is simultaneously poetic, Satsvarupa Maharaja leads the reader to the very inner realms of his heart. Ocean and desert create a complimentary topography of the human heart: yearning for the living waters that issue from the Lord while simultaneously confessing the poverty of one's depths, this is the terrain upon which the devotee marks his steps. Like the Christian desert monks of the second and third centuries, who struggled upon this terrain before God, so Satsvarupa Maharaja chronicles his own participation in that primeval wrestling as he chants, reads, and writes within the solitude of his home in Geaglum, Northern Ireland. The reader should not consider a place of solitude to be merely a setting for peace and rest. This hardly the case. In this volume, the author maps territory that is of the greatest risk: the complete baring of oneself before Krishna while yearning for a drop of His life-giving ocean. This is a voyage that this is not for the faint of heart for it demands radical honesty and a spiritual humility that is born aloft by a confidence that the

Lord is eager to bring the soul to that boundless ocean of the love of God.

Throughout this journey, *The Nectar of Devotion* and the process of prayerful reading heighten that sense of separation which marks life in the desert. However, following his meditations upon Gaura-purnima in the previous volume of *Every Day, Just* Write, Satsvarupa Maharaja pursues the sublime insight that this desert experience of separation from the love of God is ultimately the experience of the ocean's *bhava*. Satsvarupa Maharaja, in this critical volume of the *Every Day, Just Write* series, transcends the polarities of ocean and desert, and opens to the reader a vision of the greatest manifestation of love, that of transcendental separation.

Rupa and his brother
("Oh, don't bother!" says the grem)
were ministers
(ha ha)
and they rhymed in Sanskrit and
I'm not fit or not for renewal
on the avenue of doubt be
aware you can deploy
various tricks to read worthy.

I will bother, I will care
("So he says. But I'll trip him up
familiarity has bred boredom, the
guy is half-dead.")

Effortless step on his head, tread
softly. Any attempt is good
food for the spirit
("Oh, cliché!"). *Touché*!

*pp. 2–3*

⁂

Static convention
Krishna Krishna Krishna
just rock with it (lullaby)
crib rock not electric guitar
rock, cradle rock
Just say Krishna Krishna Krishna
sway and rock
get it?

*p. 6*

⁂

Poems are like homes geodesic domes you
live in without a wife.
Strife for all what do you
expect – to lie as God?
The hod carrier,
potato-eater.
No meter. Krishna consciousness
on the way.

*pp. 10–11*

❖ ❖ ❖

Poem is a way to preach
to outreach
(in reach)
to college students and pots
give him hell in tots
music. Poems preach *like*
they say like a red rose
like a fire hose a pose
of poesy. They like
peanut butter and regular butter.

They are Frank Sinatra and
Beethoven coming to Krishna consciousness
by grace of guru, you
the poet. Shot. Give 'em hell and Goloka.

*pp. 11–12*

❖ ❖ ❖

Swami reads the book
with reverence stick to it (fly paper)
always the same? No, it's new
my, my I don't believe you.
I think you're a fraud.
(Swami replies – Goose to you.
I'm reading a little at a time.)

*p. 26*

Swami be patient
we tell ourselves
attraction for food
M. brings it on a plate for Deities
in a minute. Seek relief.
No more theme. The body has its own
endorphins but they don't work on call.

*p. 28*

Man, you was okay in your day
Fay wrote a poem hey
Nonney Day Shake's songs
fools and Caliban and teacher
watch out your shoes
are showing.

Was okay in his day burnt
noble candle until and
cold light Yeats they
said did it and Matisse.
I said everything and then
he stopped.

Krishna consciousness for boys and girls
Good Humor truck
collected their money and gave
it back to change maker
on his belt and opened the
door to refrigerated truck for
popsicle, fudge, purple ice rocket
latest junk to suck and
bite on young teeth.
Good-bye to that.

Krishna, I remember You in the
temple beside Radha, I
remember my days and night
and fears. Krishna, please let
me remember You as I go
down, You wearing Your
outfit of the day and me
serving You – new
and next.

*pp. 32–34*

⁂

I...bought a preacher's kit
and lived with them
learned a lot and now
I say one preacher is worth
a birth, he'll save the world
and I'm just saying he ought to
be the best and full of love
to which our master replied

Miss Lynn Ludwig, they're trying
their best and what about *you*?

*pp. 35–36*

⁂

Pray *swami*
realize your needs
and say Hare Krishna mantras and hear
You can do it?

Swami Balmy

wants medicine
and peace
mimics saints
inside out
in a jiff –
he's a whiff of real

*pp. 36–37*

*Mangala-arati Offering*

Let's be pleasant, you know that
*susukam*?
Yeah, is it true of me too?
Why not?

Be quiet a little. We don't want people
to hear you waltzing on the ceiling.
Don't want to them to hear you playing.
Gin rummy with a priest (you lost
eighteen dollars.)

Hoarse romance singer of blues.
She's the girl from Ipanema. The
priest was watching pro-football on
TV when the scholar entered the
room, pushing door open with his
suitcase.

Krishna songs, Srila Prabhupada said, not ordinary.
Sing but *in* Krishna consciousness.
Okay, but what later (now) when you find the
official Krishna songs as your friends
make them are rather limited
too ethnic or too rock

I mean, can you go to
world music and find
Krishna there?
Huh? By inserting the lyrics?
yes, and by...

The man was like a bear the
bear was like a man
the Krishna conscious element was strong – at
*mangala-arati,* I wanted to tell my friend
about Jacob Needleman's book and
why I wanted
to go to Vrindavan and roll in the
dust, sand
but there was a
problem.

I wanted to send out police of spirit
in search...I mean, I may go
to talk to you of something I like but
you're not in the mood for it.

He's talkin' I do appreciate it
so urgent. He said, "Sometimes, when
things get rough I disappear. So,
where am I at? I can't claim to
be religious if I turn to nothingness."
We said, maybe you're losing your
faith.
He said, that's not the answer
neither is that mysticism crap
so, they said this is the
missing link in Christianity.

Sing a song of sixpence
pockets with raisins
and nuts and I am here
no beer
just milk hot and

cows protected on our
farm we work hard.
This is the end of
a song
with not much
pretty form.

Please accept it is an
offering to Sri Krishna – He gives all
we should return the gift
and this comes from my life
right now in Wicklow
where I bathed and slept and
intend to walk where I did
fourteen rounds *japa* already.

*pp. 44–47*

❧ ❧ ❧

*Talking to Mr. Mulligan*

Listen Mr. Mulligan, is that your name?
Foley? Listen...
He replies, "What is there to say?"

There's this – How come you talk on a telephone right under me, my heart's in a quandary. How come I have to empty my own urine bottle? And why do I have to be alone and white-haired?

Be glad, he says, you don't have a headache (heart ache) right now, do you?

Yes. You know. I wish I did have a sort of heartache. I wish they could talk to me. East

coast says West coast is too sweet but sometimes...I *do* have a sweet tooth and don't mind being cool. I'd like to fall in love and stay in a mellow sort of mood perpetually with perks and original work.

So, Mr. Mulligan, I guess my complaints have petered out but more will come. When they come, I can either bitch or boil to myself or just let it go. It's hard. I do accept your reasons and your own desire to please. You told me a story yesterday of a devotee who cut himself and pumped blood on his way to hospital. You added, "It all turned out all right." Thank you.

*pp. 51–52*

Once there was a man from Ants
who wore Sansabelt pants
he hurried to lead a crowd
out of a fire and was praised
this made the news and
he said I cruised into danger
because I knew God, Krishna
would protect His devotee or
if I perished it would be
service and the soul doesn't die.

*p. 60*

Spriggle wiggle – the owl lost its
prey right out his talons from
a strong wind. And prey ran away.
The buds, I told you, got blighted
and what can you expect?
It's the world.

Fast here is much munching.
Nappies, I thought he was old enough...
gruff bare dwarf dreamer
stalker. Peed pants hive sakes
the parade crowd pressed forward
the *Garda* said, "Look at this"

and Aghasura twenty yards long
and fifteen feet high, a boy of
Krishna proportions saved them.

I stayed home and *kichari*.
Am I a preacher? 'Shebang whiz fat
I much in springtime warm water
*sac-cid-ananda's* beard
Rama-Krishna's foist
God in hoist ladder
the Vaisnava's kitchen ordeal
beads around your neck
you strangle I'll be happy
free and not listen to doubters.

I'll fight back, that's a preacher
that a boy
get 'em
go fight scratch
it's for Krishna
we win! We smashed you.
You smashed us.
God is truth.

You Yamas, go to hell. We
gotta win at day's end
somehow, I think the revenge motive
isn't appropriate, but we are ready
to run and fight too
blast bash
Arjuna and Hanuman loved it.

As for me, chops ain't strong the reviewer
said, but I got my licks in before clock ran out.
Mincemeat

love preach love
truth of Krishna I sent
the message scrambled for the prize

and just quote *Gita* as
he speaks. Krishna is highest and His
name's in this age the Sola Via
take it friend, I wish you would
and some juice and carob balls and book, money?

*pp. 60–62*

❖ ❖ ❖

*Japa* rounds
always go well but
Prabhupada chants better
aspire for that
rhythm and awake.

Real saints know
open heart universal
Krishna *Nama*
devotion does work
so good so good
*madhuram*
*madhuram.*

*p. 68*

❖ ❖ ❖

*Asleep Awake*

So, you are now awake now in a bop
measure but what is illusion all
the energy following?

Some guys (devotees) want to be always
active at least they won't fall asleep which they do
with beads or book.

So, master says don't do that *babaji*.
Work hard. But I'm saying...
Racing in a car to get to *sankirtana*,
fighting the crowds at Ratha-yatra and
St. Paddy's Day...keeps you awake.

I'm not moralizing...just saying
gruff fellow sings bugs out of the grain
in the wood...
sins do that too, regret you
can't sleep.

He just runs on from momentum. I
want to see a guy calm awake from
something deep,
be glad you're sad.

"You were hypnotized by Krishna"
Srila Prabhupada chuckled and thought it over and
chuckled again, "Yes." Hypnotized
by Krishna so instead of earning bucks
they worked for Krishna in New
Vrindavan or Boston.

Heated pressure. And when you confront the
nondevotees there's
plenty of that. That steam you
could cook by.

Singers in the night, traffic flashing, when they robbed
us outside the Brooklyn temple and we had to drive
with windows broken and knowing the passports were
stolen and it was my secretary's fault. Asleep at the
switch.

awake at the alert. Then there's
deeper level of awake to the system it
hurts you.
Sleepy farm ISKCON

in the way we like it, don't want a
big tourist attraction that demands
constant Caterpillar tractors and
everyone running around in marathons.

Awake or asleep in the deep
snows he died, blessed rest
request embrace me and give me a dream
I can act out.
Awake! Christ said you
disciples couldn't stay awake with me
when I needed you (emphasizing he
was alone and would have died that
way) Awake he told them
*it* could come at any moment for
you too.

Awake to wrongs and then right them.
So, this here bugs out the system
has required reading in the school of
free devotional service we started in Wicklow with
a classroom of one while
everyone else is awake downtown.

*pp. 76–78*

Two flags crossed / pics of alarm / a pen that writes
through all hesitancy / No more rhymes intentional /
no rules for fools /.

The style sideways / I want to
be with you as friend. Don't be sick of me.
Those sheep are dopes but mind
their own business right up until you kill
them. Virtue in that? Let go.
This place.

Miss Match / Tom Mix / Mix patches.

Krishna consciousness is the paramount place,
and we shall go there and stay there.
I never wanted out. I was only testing the waters to embrace all things in Krishna consciousness that's what I wanted to do.

Relieve the memory / peel back some layers where he screams but never gives up God- given love talents.

Those were bad times when they persecuted innocent people with mob mentality. And it still goes on.

*p. 83*

⁂

*My Symphony*

Out west where I boldly reside in a
cottage a poem appeared in symphony.

Miss Planner Sample is a dictator and
I am not.

Oh, plans and fingers, may I sleep on time
stop on time. May I dream an interesting story which asserts itself into prose and
poem.

Never mind. The wishful thinking. The day is
like a ship sinking but we don't drown
dead although we do drown in a
certain sense.

Each one. Thank you, Ms. Sampler for
giving us a cue. I don't know what
a symphony is except it uses a big
orchestra and is composed in advance – an
ambitious affair.

Toyota trucks, let them pass.
Let them all pass and leave me here
writing. Krishna consciousness lyrics we need if
all songs on radio were like that, if
everyone carried bead bags like people
wear shoes and carry wallets and
purses, it would be a different world.

New World Symphony – I address this to you –
time of devotees in good standing,
lovers, humble workers, followers of
the rules. A devotee is not a fool,
yet I like simple days.

As the sheep clip grass and I pray for peace
(my own and the world's) this ineffectual
person at least doesn't regret or aspire
but just want his poem published
or not. Get it out. Sym. Phony.
Simple. Funny. Miss Sampler, go
home and leave us to our own ideas –
in Krishna consciousness study hall.

*pp. 88–89*

*A Little Revival*

Hurry, squeeze in something. Before they
come in and take away your time
your sweet will
this is the way I requested it.

Yeah, okay, I'm awake and digging the
groovy sounds. What? I mean I'm
Kana's fan, son, merry-maker
you'd better make Krishna conscious sense,

son.
He says I'm here for you.

He depends on Krishna loving him but I'm not sure it works out that way.
Hare Hare.

Once, a fellow had fun
to stay awake and play
he invented a game
it's all the same he
mentioned Krishna in fifty-two contexts
and said, "Think of Krishna in the
rain"
even in pain
Don't forget loving service
to Lord Hari.

So, was He pleased?
I never know, but at least
I kept His name on my lips, and the devotees I live with are stalwarts.

Tell me more.
I don't want to bore you, but
here's the scoop – Krishna played with
cows and ran off in interludes
when He wasn't with the *gopis*
in love.

Here comes the male Kakkhata
here comes Karala and Jatila
the fierce old women.
Wow, I think that will be fun indeed
now I know your time is brief

but
Krishna said I never forget but you do and

know why I come to this world
and you'll come to Me.
I'm topmost, your soul
is My eternal part and parcel.
The *bhakta* is the best of all,
have a ball.

No, you mix stuff I
can't always know why you do this.
Please be friend to
the master by serving the dust
of his feet.

We said I am sad not
I just want two friends to
walk and talk and *krsna-katha*
exchange devotional thoughts
that help them and help
the Movement.

Friends not in sense grat
and we others can hear them
in reverie and be inspired for
our own service. Thank you,
now I feel a little revived.

Thank you, I will return the favor
and do a nice offering to Him for
you to see.

*pp. 96–98*

❖ ❖ ❖

Twinge, twinge little star
behind the eye how far
I wonder will you go?
Shall I pop an Esgic now
or wait and see?

Twinge, twinge and yet I read,
you hold you back I
cannot write or hold my beads.
Is it right you do this?

Twinge, twinge what's your signal?
Do you want me to be sad?
Is this a way to surrender to Him
which I forgot in my onward
work to make the poem
and read the book and up the
quota of rounds?

Twinge, twinge go away I'd
like to say as in the song
Rain, rain go away
little Johnny wants to play –
but if you must then I
will try to stop you and if
I can't – surrender
abide in Him.

*pp. 103–4*

Improviser Jim was afraid
he'd be seen as an impostor and
not as good as others his
brothers. So, he got out his
set definitive Lewis Carroll
Alice and looked up Rabbit.

Improviser Jim was afraid of the
subway and stayed at home
didn't roam, even loam
made his ankle hurt. And
he was afraid of Burt.

Then how can he expect to

join in with the pioneers
of raw wisdom new emerging
forces? He can't. He only
wants to not be thought of
as...Milquetoast – he
prefers yogurt and apples and
austere talks and walks and
juicy *krsna-katha* to
redeem his self.

Now, I will play taps and lights
out. I'll get away from...

I'll pray to God in secret and
wish you all goodnight and
chant, Hare Krishna Hare Krishna, Krishna Krishna
Hare Hare,
Hare Rama Hare Rama Rama Rama...

*pp. 110–11*

O Lord, a Ford's got to be sold
M. is so bold as to ask a price
they can afford but they never
go for it because they want to cheat
him down, thinking he's a bereft
slob or why would he try to
sell such a pretty white one-man
RV that could take a preacher
to France?

*p. 116*

*Veering to Krishna*

Tad, I want to ask you can I go
to Vaikuntha? Why ask me? Ask
yourself. I want to sing a song for
Radha-Krishna, may I?
Yes, you may. You may take
one giant step.

Permission granted. Krishna was wearing
Brownish, copper clothes with a peacock
feather. He was standing with Radha and
I offered Them cups of water in

the forest of Vrindavan they played the
excellent trick on Abhimanyu and Jatila
with Krishna masquerading as the goddess
Gauri.

Excellent day ahead I say without aide
of any hearing aid or electric timpany but
I must say that the seagulls are going over
well and we'll be happy Wheeling, West
Virginia not withstanding and the
downfall of practically everybody.

Millennium and can't save us but
Krishna will. He will evince simply
by a fragment of a prayer say,
the full Ganges, leaning tower
700 wonders of the world.

I'm not here to make it accessible
or to drink whiskey and don't allow and
cigarette smoke.

Clear air draft on tap let
it be smoky pure sky of clouds.

I intend to remember Krishna Lord of Yadus,
who was such
a close friend of Arjuna and all Pandavas, yet they suffered.

So, what is this? What is this "hypnotism" that their love increases despite the bad luck?

It's the nature of love of Krishna like drinking
hot cane juice
tap, tap don't wake anyone
in this house
you just mixed everything like
a granola trail mix the
saintly expert abode and
your own mulling lane
and avenue.

Yeah, I was hoarse and happy
from singing Hare Krishna in the
parade, just a happy day
to tell you Lord
Krishna loves His best devotees
and gives love even to the neophyte tigers.
We do wish them the best,
tell people, cows, camels, dogs, and asses
to take to Krishna consciousness a.s.a.p. and
be relieved of gallbladders
and stones in next life
or think of Krishna when it happens
and say, Lord Hare Krishna Hare Krishna
you do this
I don't know why.

*pp. 121–23*

❈ ❈ ❈

Oh, I'm dovetailing it.
Tailgating it, hitching my
writer's thumb onto the back
of Swamiji's speeding truck.

But how is my bicycle?
Where is my wild patience and
fearlessness
compassion
love of fellows and so on?

*pp. 128–29*

On the roof of the...
Preaching, preaching, man, don't
forget you got a message.
Your time is running on
the stopwatch don't
botch your valuable human...

*pp. 133–34*

Walking strutting on a stage, entertaining people
with beat and smile like
they tappin' their feet and we
get in some message or distribute *halava*.

Don't just stand alone before the Deity
he said but bring someone there
and he looked at me as a *babaji*
culprit staying too long in Vrindavan.
But he *lives* there!
Dada da dee da-da dee
dee dee.
Preaching is reaching
for the man's heart and mind
if you find it hard I
say don't quit keep it up

in good company of
fellows
preachers, reachers, teachers
rockers and sockers.
  You'll reach the goal, won't be in
a hole...
this is the target
just getting it out for you.

So, he told and I was too tired and
dull to say otherwise.
I thought this may not
be the most inspired but at least by the
clock I'm keeping a preach and poem.

Oh man, lovely were the
forms of the Lord and
I used to be fired-up
and here we have the champion
Synderji Mahatma gonna
talk to you of his lectures
in Russia where he combated
the snows and Orthodox,
and even the KGB
resurgence, Mahatma...

the preacher of the year
no fear I'll study be strong
in faith and knowledge
of the *sastra* which is basis of
all preaching and *vaidhi*.

Get rid of the humanizing which
could lead to womanizing or
at least deviance. Listen, I'll be
glad enough if we get one from
all this to be a devotee. That's all he asked.
Just one person.

*pp. 134–36*

⁂ ⁂ ⁂

Sometimes, you have to speak
when someone else
is speaking his heavy thing
telling of how "we" were murdered.
And he's gonna get revenge.

*p. 136*

⁂ ⁂ ⁂

Krishna! Save us.
Krishna chant and wait He'll
tell you what to do. He is with
all of us always.

*p. 137*

⁂ ⁂ ⁂

Stevie Study Hall prepared for
his exam in *Bhakti-sastri*.
He didn't have to rhyme ham-bone.
He would be expected to regurgitate
some Sanskrit *slokas*.

I passed *Bhakti-sastri* in 1969,
why do I have to take it again?
They have no records of that.
Take it again. It's an updated
harder test than when Prabhupada
himself gave it.

In the study hall, the beautiful blonde...
Why I should be here? I should

be in an ISKCON teepee
or at least alone. Yes,
I will arise and go now to a
thatched-roofed cottage and practice
*nirjana-bhajana* while my disciples
stay active at the Kmarts.
I will...I hereby...who cares?
I will not do it for cheap adoration.
Even Prabhupada wanted to it
(see Sixth Canto, Daksa
curses Narada.) The alone *sannyasi*
is not condemned provided he does it
at the right time and place.
Well, I thought, this is a productive
session. In the future, I'll just think
of the light green auditorium without
having to come here and leave my room with
the altar and the shelter of silence
and wind and Srila Prabhupada's books nearby.

And I'll preach the *dharma* of
the Six Goswamis. As taught
by His Divine Grace.

*pp. 137–38*

*The Promise*

The promise I made to the Swami
I will not abrogate
the gate is open
freedom is ours
regulated principles of freedom.

Obey orders is ours to serve
I promised I love to be with
the Lord.

He is the Promise Keeper.

Yeah, this way please you have to be with
us. I promise but can't keep it with
my own strength. I can only wish to be
with Lord...

And great *ksatriyas* like Arjuna and Bhima
when they promise – watch out –
it's death until they keep it.

But Lord Krishna broke His promise
to save His devotees – the
greater of His two promises.

My little wish to die
in good grace but
more than that to
master I said you I promised I

could leave your service so don't renege. Ah! Sore point
the demanding kid
the demanding reneger
the eternal servant Govinda who
copped out after six months.

I promise not I surrender not
I don't do a damn
the world isn't false.

Krishna – He says what can you
renounce? Nothing. Only the
illusion that you are the Lord.

The Lord is the master. Krishna
You are promise
You promise You'll take us
to You

and that is the promise I live
for in the back of my mind
the bet is staked
the ground is sure
Krishna will take to Him
the best devotees.

Anyone can come in and stop me
writing but you can't stop
Krishna in His promise.
If you chant My name
offer Me *prasadam* – I'll
    accept it.

He says think of Me. Read the book
Swamiji says He'll bring us.
But it's not a business deal.
On me is the burden
  I said I'd stay a *sannyasi,* I said
I won't go back to illicit sex or
gamble or intox
so, let's

sing freedom and love of God, which is waiting for us
to reach.
Yeah, the Lord won't renege
neither will His servant
pure sky, rainy sky, doesn't matter
the chant will break the bones of
death / the Lord won't fail
singing it for those who take it...

*pp. 148–50*

⁂

Heifer and Fifer pulled the load
as long as they lived,
two oxen. But when they grew old
they roamed and ate and
remembered the days when
"Whoa!" and "Gee!" governed
them and they pulled the plow and
once they pulled a wooden
sleigh carrying the mayor of
Cambridge on his way to a
Krishna consciousness Slide festival where
Heif and Fife ate some kind
of *luglu*-looking oxball -
sweet which could deliver
them *sukrti* enough to take
birth a tough *bhakta* human
on Chicago's South Side –
their hides went for *mrdangas.*
And Rajarsi passed away.

*p. 151*

*Letter*

This is just a short note to say hi I'm fine in Wicklow
hope you're good up there in the sky with Norton
Wilder and company.
I saw egrets you sent
Krishna is here as well. I know He's everything! I just
read that devotees of Krishna in Vrindavan are
topmost and if we can't live there physically we should
think of it.

So, I'm thinking...well, I said the sky is Northern
Ireland but you know

I'm in failing position
faces grow older
they sag and we can't blame them for that. The soul
"dies" seven months at physical death and
    rises in next body in painful condition. You've
heard this. I wonder what we are doing
about it.

Srila Prabhupada told us how to tell people what to do.

I'm sorry if we fall down
crestfallen
lust anger with one another's trips.
You better say hello to the plants and creatures for me.
Absolve me, make me happy be in Krishna
consciousness wish we could
chant a garland of beads in
ecstatic states.

I say work at *sadhana*
slow or medium
just do your best I found
it works don't give up
see you at Easter and
each day in the heart of Vrindavan
we're all included
he says
I believe him
trying it out,
Yours,

*pp. 154–55*

⁂

*Sampler's Poetry #4*

All right, for today now or never
you'd like to write a Krishna conscious
poem under light in view of the clock
in the view of the Supersoul in the heart.
But there are mixtures...

Write sideways. Scratching alone.
Krishna. I feel some reassurance of my
spiritual master. Someone wrote me from
India, Mumbai, said he was happy
writing a book on falldown and recovery
until someone told him that Srila Prabhupada
said he'd been poisoned, so
he asked me, "Tell me in one word
'yes' or 'no,' was Srila Prabhupada
poisoned?"

I replied "To the best of my
knowledge, Prabhupada was not poisoned."

Can't be ironic or sardonic about that.
I don't believe he was poisoned,
we disciples are not that low. At least
I didn't.

You didn't. What an understatement,
what a small virtue. What did
you do positively? In the larger sense
did you poison his Movement? Did you
add virulence or sweetness?
Did you...

These issues mar the attempt, or they
are the attempt. Chant and be with him
and leave humor mongers and accusations
and even your own lackings. Fill up
hours, look for sleep to rise refreshed

for more time with him in
*The Nectar of Devotion.*

*pp. 162–63*

⁂

*Dancing Hari*

Well, nice time for all including
we went to Mass, had hot cross buns
on the way home, it's Lent right?
The Passion of Christ
is outside of our scope.
We dance with Krishna. Not with Durga or
the Devil or Kali or Kali-yuga
puppets. We dance *kirtana* of the Lord
Krishna.

Don't be sassy or fool around with us. I got
a secret indulgence. But in private I practice
the nine principles of devotional service, in public,
*kirtana*. I got a book how to exit
from a rigid religious upbringing and make
decisions for yourself. I'm gonna be all
right, Alright, all I need is a little
money so I can buy my CDs, videos,
blaster, TV special, dinners out, car,
jeep, take Sal out for the night –
work your ass off to pay light bills
and heating in these Northern parts it's
no good.

I don't see how repressing will help
I don't even own a horse
although I watch the neighbors from
my window.
Hail Mary, Liguori, Black Madonna
Hail, full of grace, every creature has
soul, save the flowers, offer to God

give up your renunciation and possessing
your *lobha* and greed,
take the Lift up by *bhakti* so
swift.

Hey, I'm Hari, a Hari in debate
why bad things happen to good people
I can explain, give me two minutes,
I can recommend chanting God's name
any bona fide name of God.

I can run the government
write the poem
cook, nook,
I can refrain from sex
and money I can beg and
I can read a *sastra*.

So, why not hire me for your next bar mitzvah
seriously, I'll do it now
and let you know how I do at
death, stick around and you can
have my corpse and legacy I'll
tell you what happens after
death and if mine is a success well,
celebrate.

*pp. 172–74*

❖ ❖ ❖

Quote the great *acaryas*
give their evidences,
what Rupa Gosvami quoted from
    *Srimad-Bhagavatam*
play, pluck the strings of the same
instrument they played in days of old...

*p. 183*

Preach – ye Krishna heralds, go proclaim, go door-to-door with a lotus of Goloka. We know you are inclined to serve His mission.
Go door-to-door
and when the labors are over
we will part no more...
the Lord, Caitanya, will be pleased
to take us.

O Krishna, lover of my soul
bring me to Your chest.
While the tempest rages of
mad modes. Please bring me close,
I'll be fearless in the storm.
You can do it, and not just me
receive my soul at last
let me give relief to all
let Your healing stream of love
enter all with purity and strength.

*pp. 183–84*

Bring us to You
our song shall bring us to Thee
sweet Lord, cut through all
crippling majesty
and all sin gone
arm and arm with Your eternal
playmates, far away from crocodile of doubt,
Lord, make me.

*p. 184*

*Sampler's Poetry Hall #5*

Whew, you expect me to step into that?
Motorcyclist passes hunched forward, some
kind of colorful embroidery on back of jacket.
They used to wear them from the war with
a map of Guam or Guadalcanal
and Iwo Jima and the name of their
infantry division. See them at an airport,
startling.

While you wore your frock,
a flat-bed truck rolls by. You think it
may be someone to stop at this
house and interrupt me. This is usually
a quiet road. It's Saturday, 5 p.m.

Foxgloves, not yet. First gorse
appearing. No dandelions even. A little
animal turd. Gray gradually lighter
when you leave house at 6 a.m., into the
pine lanes. But I won't go there to -
morrow. Stay in this garret shaped room.

#2

Hare Krishna road show. Bored stiff? No,
but only mild interest. I plough through the
*sastra* gradually. I toast to the all world's
*acaryas* and go to sleep on a mattress on the
floor. Collapse for a few hours, wearing
earplugs, you usually fall asleep for
only a few hours and surface like a small
whale, say, with a dream that needs
to be recorded.

And so...creatures didn't enter through the hole.
I did not have to make a tourniquet. Pressure
points. Panic. I don't know first-aid. Irony,

jests, failing heart. Failing wit. Depend on
the process and the liberal master and the power
of words. I made it alone and
not interrupted. Now, I'm ready...

*pp. 186–87*

❦ ❦ ❦

*To Hold Their Attention*

(Sleepy-eyed, music keeps you awake. Intelligence makes it a Krishna conscious shape in words.)

Mr. Smith, I'm awake at the top of
the ladder in the shoe store looking for that
size 8, Hush Puppy, in gray alligator.
Don't be ashamed. You can
improve any circumstance by being
Krishna conscious in your own way.

So, he came down the ladder it was
John Climacus' ascent in steps up
to God,

was Charlie Chaplin, the ladder falling.
The latter former
the farmer of cows we
don't want to sell him silage
don't patronize slaughter
don't even hurt any living being.

So, these Krishna conscious persons put on hats and marched around the town. In the hall the lecturer tried holding their attention but it was hard with just one soloist and he had a British accent proceeding from one analogy to another in transcendental science. They wanted something more variety.

But this was a low-budget thing.
Dear people, chant with us.
Happy's science.
"I wouldn't want to lecture," said M. who sings.
And the lecturer didn't sing. And
I, for example, am best writing.

#2

Boy, I wanted more relief than this brought.
What do you want?
To be awake empty stomach use it in
Krishna conscious thoughts to share.
Then honor a breakfast,
then talk with the secretary
then rest, maybe dream but
somehow all these in Krishna's service.

When I die it will be likely
I'll have some kind of Krishna conscious
thought and can
go on to be with Him, I don't
say back to Goloka right away (I
realize it takes tremendous *laulyam*)
but next a life where I can
yearn intimately for it.

At least serve again in Krishna consciousness
in some capacity and be open to *Mahabharata,*
*Ramayana, Srimad-Bhagavatam, Bhagavad-gita.*
Maybe born into that culture, but
Kali-yuga is getting so bad. Lord, what
will You do to protect Your
servant of servants? I'm
sure You know and will do it all right.

One twilight / one morning
a solo, he asked the people
to chant Hare Krishna with him

and he gave them breaks.
That's all, just singing and walked
home barefoot
dust raising from cows.

*pp. 195–97*

⁂

*Link*

Now, the fast movers know I'd
like to go with them and inject Krishna
  consciousness in
whatever we do
yeah, but when you were back
in Navy (dream) you didn't.
Ah, forgive me.

Now, I'm awake and riding
Krishna danced by the moonlight shape
until dawn and then He
went home. The doe-
eyed *gopis* danced,
the does and bucks
the trees and water –
is this all right?
 he heard the flute
the flute / the flute
the fruit of ascetic
the wrangle man
get free...

Go forward, it's coming from God
man, I like it but in the
subway how can you think of
rare Krishna pastimes?

It's possible they're doing
the technique isn't all
it's true the Bird played
at dawn and even during
the night when spring came
we heard it.

Our job to link things to their
natural link with Lord Hari.
He's meant that way.
Link/trade fours
men and women all are souls
all for free rent
put floor in
stay in room and chant
ask asylum quiet
depend on Lord no matter what
write your silent notes.

Now, I say there has to be a driving beat
make it sound "Hare Krishna" tune
or I'll add it.

The simple stuff can be omitted and
the harder. I just want to be
alone with Thee and pray and
meditative notes to You and me on
the swing ride home
denying God is no good.
I'll deny taking part in
crap games, shoot-outs barbecue
fast, do-nothing *karmis*.
The
way...

*pp. 197–99*

* * *

*Sampler's Poetry Hall #6*

Holy night I hold back.
There may be a message for me in
the hallway which could make me
forget I had a headache.

But probably the air is all I'll get. Just lie down. We will
nurse you. Sing soft in your blood:
O, 'twas once a stranger
who came to know the Lord.

That's nice. I hear you were one
of the first disciples. Let me hold
your hand. No? You're a *sannyasi*?
Did you ever think of why you
might get these headaches and what
their secondary benefit might be?

He rolled toward the wall, said Hare
Krishna, said Sri Caitanya, and Mahaprabhu.

Said Vrindavan, especially in Karttika is
good for you. I'll move there when I
go to Heaven. Oh, I wish

I had an *adhikar*. Master, master.
This way the day went gliding to dusk, and
he was glad to be left alone under
a comforter. Close eyes and expect to
wake two hours later, all of a sudden
you are semi-conscious, here a bump,
turn over and go back to sleep, back to
wake, it's never (the present) quite
what you think it will be. Always
hard and He is always kind.

*pp. 208–9*

*Practicing Alone*

Do you remember when you used to
be able to dance? I remember I couldn't
dance with girls, so afraid of stepping on their feet
but alone I can dance and now in
*kirtanas* we dance
exquisite rumble.

We are the ones who come in out of the
cold. Hare Krishna Hare Krishna. From nine days
on nine islands in Navadvipa to Govindadwipa
to house...in Wicklow.
Alone upstairs, we'll hear his music.

Ah, you have to take responsibility,
it's your show human being.
He said to Arjuna, "Now do as you
like." Go to hell or Goloka,
it's up to you.
I choose Swami Bhaktivedanta's way.

Plain porridge with honey
red beads to chant with fingers
in company and alone
with our Swami, his
order is hard to follow.

#2

I remember you could work nicely
with a group, you could do it
all alone – I don't mean
vice like self-abuse
self-liberation
not love – but a *bhakta* has to
have time to pray to
Lord Hari

and quiet cave is a good
place.

Fastest man on *mrdanga*...
go ahead, express yourself fast and slow.
We want to be naturally
happy Krishna conscious persons – is that possible in
this degraded
age...

Yes, I think so. You have to be a worker
in a niche. I've heard it's good to
do something you don't like to do –
but that's hard for me.
Give me something I can do.

I was recalling the expert yo-
yo playing – not that,
but today, writing a letter to
a devotee
not very expert I just want
to try to be

#3

the first guy on my block
to meet prose standards
rose growing in mud
daff.

They come over the wall
I fight them back
kick and punch
you'll get no quarter
kick and fight.

Oh, in a dream we fight
and love and dissolve
enmity, I'm no longer

afraid of any board judgment
I'm going to practice this alone
but if He
pushes me somewhere else

I'll write the story of it
or if I can't even write
so tight my Lord then
I'll be relieved of that and
chant names – You
won't take that away
You promise
we're eternal souls, Yours.

*pp. 219–22*

⁂

Damn, I'm not in desert –
every man sees for himself

Sats is *cela* can write God-given
hurry and wait
I don't preach to you –
got to do it myself.

*p. 226*

⁂

A poem came down from Go-
loka written by God or a
pure devotee like Rupa.
Now people want to write from
their neophyte attitudes and that's
good too, provided they don't
jump over.

I chanted in the temple.
We-we. I brought my mind
back to the higher Self or
wished I did.
Bob did 40 books, Josha
dasa in Berlin, Bob did
25 *maha*-books each
we gave them a peach
as a reward. They smiled
knowing something
tastier than that.

The remnants in the Deity room
assume you ate them and
gave some to friends.
People. Be. Faithful.

#2

Jumping up / I'm ashamed in
such goofy beat mood
to look at my master
He sees me
I'm preachin'
I preach this way in the sway
we're going in pajamas
Where are those guys who are
talking about sound?
Here's the pound for dogs
Let me out.

To preach and stretch
I am the
no way fellow got a
message.
                Massage me not
just celebrate a clear day
"You deserve one"
head open I sweat.

Crisscross
man with pen drawing "Krishna"
word and "*bhakti*"
listen to this.

Sound, I am silence, Krishna says
as well as stone dropped
into well
frog and mate
neigh mare
goat spit llama
drum-drum
the sound of standing
the starts clinker
the boof of woof.

He is all sound but transcendental
sound that changes your heart and
life is preaching
stands you hairs
on end you on
chair edge.

The sound compound or
unheard of an *acarya*, no recording
available of Rupa Gosvami or Lord Caitanya
in sixteenth century, just as well,
Creator wanted it that way.

Go home! Sounds that hurt.
The altercation when a man told
the mother her baby son could not play
the drum in the temple. The sound
of a hurt. Car brake. On ice.
The splash
crash
    the quiet of peace when pain
when
    pain stops

smelly stuffy odor
oh, give us release – where do
we go.
Swami says I am 77 when
I "die" I take another body. Hear sounds if you are
lover
of Krishna sounds
or else you don't know.
There is preaching for everybody star, sun, moon
Gaura-Nitai to all.

*pp. 228–31*

*Sampler's Poetry Hall #7*

Well, I wasn't really serious but tired of guys
who are atheistic dogmatists and say
"Stories we've concocted from random clusters
of stars in the skies." Do they threaten me?
I just don't like to hear smug atheism.

God. God. A poem should be in His
service. I don't care so much for vowels,
consonants. They come and go naturally
with any speech, why make a big deal?
Ars poetica.

Praise God with eloquent speech.
Wish I could. Is that what Fr. Gerard Manley
Hopkins did? Praise God with
homely metaphors with lotus
*lilas*, great skill in Sanskrit
now English, American, Siberian.

Ars poetica, a man's got to be a real
person and a devotee (woman can too)

and write strong, honest God consciousness.

Be against the atheist or "allow" him to
have his space but when it's your turn
praise God. I admit it is expertly
when you slant it, implicit, when it's
not spouting divine rhetoric but some
daily experience.

This green study hall is a good place.
I'm too timid and aware to stand up on stage
and give a KC lecture to these louts and eggheads
about *bhakti* and surrender. Wouldn't work.
They would hoot and holler. So, write your own:
God gives ability. If you are interested
there's a process to reach Him. If not, sad
shmoo, you'll die and not know
how you may fall and waste.
Don't mean to scare you, but –

*pp. 233–34*

(Part two numbering starts here)

*Pure Devotee? Not Me*

But not me, yes, me too I'm in
on it, I'll be there with the others.
I'd like you to know that.

I don't want to miss the boat. Intensity is
required I've heard but how and
what kind can I apply?
Searching? Or calm?

He became expert and wanted to pay
no price except be better

Krishna left Mathura
I mean, Vrindavan but didn't
really He remain in the *bhava* of
separation?

I can ride a pen on a page.
I can eat a small meal voraciously I can draw
a crude three people in colors chant sixteen rounds a
day
can be satisfied to be left alone
can answer your letter in several
pages, can lift a small
bundle, endure my own
headaches at this rate
be a Krishna conscious respectful person
if I'm not mistreated much.
I don't know how I'd if it got
rougher, that I don't know.

You? You can? Oh, we can drive
a car, rent a car, avoid a swerve,
go into the city and run a restaurant,
pay a phone bill, sell a painting.
And can you remember Krishna
the Lord of the *gopis*?
Can you go to India and be welcome?

Who here can obey Srila Prabhupada? We!
I mean in all particulars and hard essence? We!
Who here will go back to Godhead at the end of life?
    They are singing songs of liberation
but not for me.

"Strictly commercial" to tide us
over, make people happy, sweep it under
the rug, didn't hear about the missing leader
and Sats keeps silent in the rain.

Get it together, the disparate elements
might just look good later.

He says, don't disparage any devotee
trying to go through the usual changes
we may be small-timers but we
won't be like the *karmis* ever
it's hard work to remember Krishna
but his guru and chant silently
and you might
and give your pay and time.

He said, but what about himself? I think
he'll be a next saint in forty births from now
if a pure devotee gives him
*suddha-sattva* – glance and wish and
words
    But not on his own
strength-controlled ecstasy.

He can finish, but that doesn't mean
he finishes in first place.
He's trying and I know, but there
has to be complete exhaustion of material
desire, and I just don't see it right now.

So, if you want to be optimistic,
go ahead and shout
I say, keep at it sure
    and we'll see
Hare Krishna Hare Krishna oaf Olaf
I'm just letting off steam.
Pure devotee?
      Not me.

*pp. 9–12*

❖ ❖ ❖

You have to risk
the lawyer risks, the big preacher –
he hopes he's not undoing his *sadhana*,
hopes Krishna will give him strength to
visit and manage sixty cities of temples and
a guy like me risks that it's best to
shrink the field to one desk, one house,
and not even a daily walk.

*p. 20*

Not night he can't write that sort of
assonance. Golden guilders, paid-for
receipts. A box of crayons. Fall back
on some old riff. Don't waste a moment
is a sign of *bhava*.

Improve your time. Rhyme is a game.
He doesn't stop, half-sleep walks
asleep over frozen tundra about
to die if you stop. I've got it easy.

Krishna conscious man seeks to advance
by constant ardent efforts
which he hopes will attract
Krishna's mercy. You've got to
set it right in *siddhanta*.

It's all right if others don't understand
as long as I love and try and say Krishna,
Krishna. Take a moment to
feel – where am I?
Think of chanting, of prayer.
Is it possible?

Krishna Krishna staying on his course he continues
round the globe sea voyage in smallish

boat, radio to her husband every
night, "I may not survive this storm."
Memorable woman – she did it!

And I will cross and so will you.
Pray to remember Krishna at crashing
end. He is there, we have
mistaken ourselves as important, as God. Now, please
turn to Him (I said).

*pp. 22–23*

⁂

*Just Reform*

Glad to be here free I wanted to until they stop me.
Krishna, I want to be Your man
but my man expressing
whatever pockets I have.

There's no hardware in heaven.
They say he was a guru but then
he has to behave in a certain way
his spiritual children
This is the stalwart standard
"More *sastric* content in his
speech and writing."
We want to see him
more at our picnics.

I like *sankirtana* you don't
I give Krishna conscious hats out
on Mad Hatter table you
know...

He's an ex-English major
has to take a dip bath and
be good on his birthday.

#2

KC KC KC
get a banner and T-shirt
we'll be happy to detox you
and be with us
we'll bring you as prodigal son
give you Imitrex
deep breath therapy but
you're old Sats
one of the original.

But it's different now get
in line if you want to be
a devotee. We'll give you
meals and refreshments we
big guys have
we don't want you so much
alone.

This sort of tax wax has to
stop if you want to play ball
with us. This Movement is
rigorous and you'll (wink) still
find time for fun for
example get into a *gamcha*
and frolic with us on Ganges
bank, dive in we
happy, we rub out
enemies by parliamentary
forensic proof and
the junior ones will
look up to us.

A guy like you could have
lots of *sisyas* just reform, and you'll have work
harder and renounce.

No, no, I must swing he said
upon a star
I won't renounce the spirit I
found to sing with music given
by friends who try to
be devotees when I apply
my ecumenical touch to their
rough, sophisticated offerings.

So, the dialogue is underway
and the best one will play stakes
high for me I just want
to please Swami but I
can't jump through quite so
many hoops joops
to you
in my own mind I'll
find a pen to sing
the thing is black and
white written in secret
can't take it back.
   Be careful.

*pp. 33–36*

Yeah, we'd seen before a man
juggling some wooden pens but
didn't know you could row a boat
for Krishna and be a clown too.
Didn't know a dog could dance, it's
a little disgusting and we want the
traditional...

*p. 43*

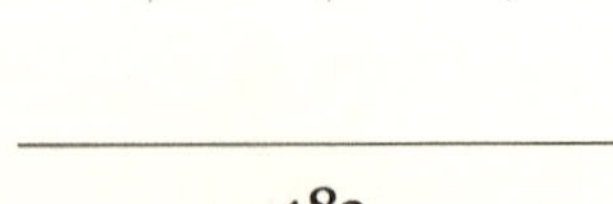

We chant and change the world
to white, blue throat and
Balarama's dress went white
on sound of the purity of
Lord Hari's *venu* played
on a moonlight.

*p. 44*

❖ ❖ ❖

*Sampler's Poetry Hall #9*

*om* rain, he made a record *Om*
but you can be sure he didn't know Krishna is
the source of *pranava. Om* is Blank to
them. God's sound *omkara.* As if
I know something they don't.

All day he was straining to read a certain
number of pages. Forgot what poems are
or rubbage. An old pineapple slice on a
wet piece of *sandesa*-like sweet. Don't
feed this gerbil too much.

His friend worked construction on a house.

Another friend said, "Why don't you give your
house a name?" I thought and said, "How about
My Old Flame?" Or frame over the
door: Pittsburgh Pirates.
No, really it could be called *Nirjana
Bhajana Retreat Center* for one.
No admittance if you don't love me.

Pro-actively, pro-retroactive the committee said
for the first time in history a woman elected
in charge. The sensitive issue of child abuse...
has to be dealt with. Earth shakes. The

guy who insists on writing verses scattered
has to ask whether it's the responsible thing to do.
He says, "Yes, even more so."

He's into finding himself. So, he called his own house
My Krishna Place, the place I'd like to
live in. But it's up to Krishna what happens.
A streetcar named desire, *laulyam*.
Oh, I'm sorry I asked. I was thinking you could
call it Om or Okefenokee. Krishna Krishna at
any rate we'll chant in there Hare Krishna Hare
Krishna, Krishna Krishna Hare Hare
Hare Rama Hare Rama, Rama Rama Hare Hare
and write every day. And this too.
This is important. I could call it Poetry Hall, K.C.

*pp. 48–49*

❖ ❖ ❖

*Can You Offer This?*

(Can you write fast at least stay awake
I'm aware I'm talking to others not just the wall.)

I say hello folks sweet talk this is
here ministry of justice wants to say to you
hello
hello God is love you
ought to pray to Him and give your money
you can give it to me and
I'll give it to Him.

Scratch – there is no room for me here
but you and I together
Krishna is a swinger these cats
are so good.

Wow, you're a guru?

Shut up and listen to this
don't tap your toe here, bite your lip.

Oh, I see through it now it's just an art
a deception they are ordinary people
not Krishna lifting up Govardhana
(How do you know *He* did that?)

You can hardly tell one brother
from another. I can tell
because they're happy individuals.

We were talking of Krishna in our car
and he said, yeah, I like that and I see
it this way. Then he liked it my
way. We exchanged inner
thoughts
    and got to work
     a duet – a
    Krishna science gay sad no more Nietzsche *Gay*
    *Science,*
can't use them words anymore. The synch is gone.

Too worldly to use in His service.
It was rejected by the board of
censors. I said wait. I want
to use it in *yukta-vairagya*. They
said no if you were an ordinary
person maybe but you're a guru and
can't, we can't allow.

I appealed, but in the meantime
composed two hundred songs the real
thing is if Krishna likes it and
he was silent while the drummer flared
    I hoped.

*pp. 60–61*

*Click, Click Dandavats*

Well, it was a sunny rainy day
the big speaker on the radio
was booming softly in my
alone-boy's room, 1950s.

Click click, little did I
know (not at all) that I'd become a *sadhu.*
Okay, an aspirant *sadhu*
he's resolved.

Didn't know the DeBoer
brothers would drown. Didn't
know I'd be lifted out.

Again, I tell you fascinatin'
rhythm don't tap your foot.
Piece by piece they laid
the boards, built the altar,
and I was happy to wait.

Don't interrupt, I said. Let me
sing my refrain.
Providence, I said
go to bed sleepyhead
I'm alert in the science
of God you need emotions
a hard heart won't do.

The jubilant one is fine one after
another they asserted what sounds
to me like devotion in the max
and control as an art.

Is it dated and signed? Yeah, they are
each a spirit soul. You can know
when Krishna is fresh never
tires, above modes, nectar,

Rupa wrote ecstatic from
God-vision.

They never tire, they never
quit, they are considerate and
can get angry for Krishna I'm
talking of *sadhus* with qualities
in part what God has
in full and even God lacks
four qualities unique to Krishna.

And Krishna is subordinate to Radha write this on your
subway car
graffiti, it's in your
*own* master's book a
summary study.

Nectar ocean
and desert heart
the hare riots
the pheasant also pecks
and I offer my devotion
*dandavats* hundreds
of times a day.

*pp. 62–64*

Friends...close friends
no fiends, no storks
on muddy bank. Oh,
what's in the mail?
Ah hell, my fingernails ain't
bitten at. I'm a good
reformed peacemaker.
Tell stories of no malice,

got genuine concern for the
mind at time of death and
yet an active use of *yukta*
*vairagya*.

Tell him – no more golf
indoors or out no more
Jean Shepherd in print or
audio and – we haven't completed
our investigation yet – if you
are indulging in improvising –
either in music-inspired poem
or prose (I think that covers it
all past and present, night or
day, by no man-made or *deva*-
made weapons or recording
devices) – cease it!

Report to us in three months what
you did to comply.
We mean business,
signed in computer scan group
signature,
The Highest and Wisest
Ecclesiastical Body (including one
woman).

*pp. 62–64*

Dovetailed his preaching with income
selling trinkets. Don't put him down.
What are you doing? To preach.
Don't ask me,

I feel pain, and still I am writing this
so, I deserve a medal or two. Got finished, got
delayed and worse, each one,
no one had it easy.
Hare Krishna on tap.

*p. 71*

Top hat and spats – haven't heard from
my friend in awhile. I live on
friends' donations. And, that's another
reason you got to sweat it out
and be careful how you spend
money and time – you belong to
others.

*p. 73*

Now mama, now papa,
now wife and kids and house
pepper garden and hut
and car, we are all things that
come and go. So, be with Krishna in
eternal – your soul belongs to Him.

Be happy in His service and say
look for mail, for hail, for
praise you'll get blamed and life
will deal you four and three-fold blows.
Christ the body aches and people
want to torture you because they're so twisted so,
God consciousness is a way you'll serve
and can best go on with this. This is the best.

I'm worn out and hurt.

Be true to your Swami sing a song to hear later I'm giving
up to preaching...take a rest and come back
strong enough later.

With a little pain a guy cries out
I too want to preach bitch not
take an educational course on how to
preach mannerly.
I just don't got guts for it
but certain things I did
and as a bystander I cheered
and got envious toward champs
and their excesses.

*pp. 73–74*

The sad part is all we want to be devotees and the
world needs devotees
where will they come from?
They have to be dug up by the compassionate
preacher who writes to them and knocks on
their doors in embarrassed hour
so, I sing a crippled note
preach to a chicken and toad
my money to help the cause.

Some outright film, show feast
beast I'm repeating it takes the
firm of a book for a new
week's entertainment. Hot club
do this instead of wasting time.
We hereby won't give up, I
won't be a leader in that but
there are more roads than one
tired of saying this but can't stop.

*pp. 74–75*

Swami, you rush so thoughtlessly
when you pray *gayatris* you'll
be asked about that at death.
May I mention it now. Don't give up
in hopelessness. Revive, find a
way to sweet remembrances of guru, Gaura and
Gopinatha.

*p. 84*

❖ ❖ ❖

*Progresso*

Well, I said I don't want to be sorry
I missed the boat in KC to Goloka. This
was said by me on March 27.

They didn't kill any of my friends yesterday,
that I know of. I looked out the window
at night when I couldn't sleep from my
darkened room. Saw the lights on in several
houses in the valley, 9 p.m.
didn't know that before.

Krishna is real He interrupted the wrong marriage
saved Rukmini and accepted Her as His wife.
Grand Canyon
my old aunty you are what you
seem.

The people in my life that count, are dear
to me, I love to write them notes
and say, let's do this and that progressive
flow of production.
My eyeglasses falling down the front of
the nose herald old age shrinking.

No shrink required by me to figure
why I died and fried in

ISKCON in the 1970-80-90s.
It's just the nature of the animal
that we wee-weed and forget.

But don't forget Krishna. If I were
a member of a band I'd
keep quoting Krishna lyrics and
message
*katha, avatara, sastras*
gurus, karma, *bhakti*, *prema*
*bhakti* and the new arsenal to me –
  *vyabhicaris, sutas*,
Suta Goswami until they'd get
sick of me if they didn't like
members of our community.

They say, No Krishna is allowed.
Well, I'd say, that's to you.
I'd keep making Krishna antics
they satisfy
those friends
and new congregation.

Dragnet by BTG and *prasadam*
leftovers, Govinda restaurants someone
who saw us, got a book –
I'll not give up.

Two nights in a row I
played the way I like.

God, it gets maddening they work
out hard and don't quit
building a chimney in the
recluse's house – Don't
chicken out, we tell him
keep working it out for
Krishna
you mix

your pure devotion to Lord Hari
your fortress. I
will love Thee always.
Don't matter how long or short
I am. Be Your devotee in anguish...

*pp. 85–88*

❈ ❈ ❈

*He Can't Wait*

Dragging you out there to sing in the streets.
You don't wanna? "Golden Nuggets" the
top band in Ghana (with congas) allowed
Hare Krishna to share the stage with them and this is
what we do, jam "Hare Krishna"
whenever we can.

But you dream ace just let go
I do I say gooo goo
God is nice too I am who I
am brave in your own
two-piece suit *dhoti* and *kurta* and
don't shave but twice a week.

But to do that you have to be very
strict and rigid and stalwart.
You need to be so centered on
Krishna that you can't think of
something else
you need a Krishna guide
to inspire you to kick out all else.

He said he fantasized he had met me in
1971. (Don't come in right now
I'm writing) – yeah, he enters, unclasp
the door. Don't bug me, I say.
You...

The man in the moon is too
soon a tune for me to break up,
"I'm lonely," she wrote to me,
maybe she will get a roommate.
I'm lonely – how bare and
inadequate to say that I prefer to be
alone with just some back-
up team I see briefly who can
mostly just leave me alone to
range around in trust.

Lennie Tristano, Lenny Silverberg,
good-bye, I hardly knew ya –
I'm saying good-bye to all of
you in time to go to Goloka
where you want me
to go, I know.

He can't wait. He left to do his
work. Well, I can't wait either.
I'm eager beaver chanting on clock
time fast as hell
go to Krishna science
Ralston cereal
he left out notes / under
stars / under the attic roof he writes poems
as happy devotee.

*pp. 108–10*

⁂

Preaching is witnessing
declaring, "Oh yeah, I know!"
and such. And to say beautiful is the day, she walks in
beauty as the night, literature

classes, getting an "A" to impress someone, get a better job –

is not preaching per se
oh yeah, yeah, shout is
not either pure chanting
waaiill of train
whistle. But then when was I ever able to do it
that way?

*pp. 115–16*

⁂

Ireland is mostly gray skies. Now: Krishna science is excellent. You have to sit down and study the books and chant beads. But when you meet devotees it gets particularly difficult as they demand give more and more and you want them to like you. "Prabhu, can you cut these flowers, can you give?"

Words, the poet went alone and took of his shoes. Ah. He gave up all aesthetics and creeds (but kept his sneaky faithful intention to glorify God, simply waiting for the right moment) – here it is.

Krishna science is emotions of release for God who is our Light, a person with Radha and *gopas* not to be repeated to you faithless poetry experts. You slobs. You great people. Keep it a secret but tell them –
We have to die, and life is a tiny moment in eternity. Please help yourself to a better next life. Please.

They said we wanted poems like Rilke and Ginsberg and Yeats. I said this one too: the beeswax

crayon is happy to get smaller in the service of free
drawings that liberate the spirit but all gets
tested at death. Uddhava...

He said, You keep talking of death and
    Krishna, I'm sorry
we want a poetry session. I got disappointed then
and figured whatever I did is for now and it's
getting dark enough to wind down and sleep, first
night of daylight savings time. Krishna consciousness
good you say and water drinking,
presence and safety
I feel His divine presence.

*pp. 120–21*

*Little Melonae, Lord Krishna's Servants*

Man, I want release I want to serve
you, I want to be a boy who is happy
with his porridge *prasadam*
although he knows it's temporary.

Little Melonae characters in fiction with
a Krishna conscious grace. You know how
it goes
you are an old-timer don't give up
reading master's books, Krishna looks on
you that way. Again, again First Canto,
*Bhagavad-gita*, it's always fresh, I'll find that.

Every art and discipline is repeating
themes and new things are old soon as
bringing out traditions.

Sing a freedom song
O Krishna, my secret is love felt in
cold breast without lust a
man for a woman, a cat for a dog,
the ancient mariners for creatures
in the sea,
an alligator for its eggs
perverted lust mirrored
in creek.
But we get the *prema*
focus by gradual
work. We'll get there.
Krishna Krishna chant. The way a
man plays his best. The way he's searching
as March is going into April
I'm not out there hunting flowers
I'm mostly at a desk with papers
and transcendental books searching with
last days of good eyesight.

Getting the beat up. He said give me ten
minutes, and I'll produce an image for you.
Give me a hundred dollars, and I'll analyze
your malady and prescribe.

Give me love, give me your writings and please
take mine. Be polite and loving and don't
get a speeding ticket, don't crash,
stay awake.

Heavens, be no the red alert
for your own death sudden
be ready to jettison all
that may have helped you, but was
just office temporary.

Go dive for the eternal
Bhaktivedanta accepted you
and gave you your name

that means you will be saved at
death. At least good next life
for pursuing Krishna
little Melonae, Lord's servants.

*pp. 130-32*

⁂

Swami, control senses
women keep afar
and don't read nondevotee books
make your life striving
in earnest for service
to Krishna, and your master
will be pleased.

Swami, you jerk your lurching
mind is carrying you
pampered fellow I like you
want you to write and rest
but don't ask, "Was I good?"
Just write in process
and don't look back.

*pp. 135-36*

⁂

*Can You Ride a Bike Free?*

A poet sings along and is happy he doesn't
forget what he's supposed to do.
Don't make fun of serious workers in
that art.

Oh boy, Radha and Krishna
me on Earth street biting my fingernails
"Earth Angel"
Allen...no, no, no, leave me alone

I didn't know / no one told me
what to do
Swami, swami I follow.

You are proud *svatantra avadhuta*
*hamsaduta* – went through loyal meetings of
concern for ISKCON to kick out the
bad element and uphold the Body, the
club, the right rulers who should
not be misunderstood.
Now, give me a pole walking stick
I'll go where there are no stars
sky covered in low clouds
low mountains out back.
Give me recluse recourse reprieve
Krishna science is fact you can
study. He rips off a long snort.

My Lord wants to be the fair person
do-dee-doo. Be quiet and let the
men tell the story that has to be
told. You can hum along, but don't
wrench me loose.

Quick, before anyone comes,
before your finger's all black
sing the song for the pen then
got downstairs and cut up apple and pear
and think, "It's for Krishna."

Boy's teacher writes me how I can answer
a student who said that he feels joy riding his bicycle
without thinking it's a Krishna task?
I'll say, yes be happy for Him.

Can he draw a red clown a black
pine a story hood, free a fish from
the net? Don't destroy leaves.
Can I be rivet-free?

Don't sulk, be a fellow of
devotees and if possible, wear Vaisnava *tilaka*
even in Navadvipa keep your faith.

Them squeaks so happy so free
as boys. School days they were
full of frolic. Krishna devotees are real
people too happy saints who pray
absolute science sounds to God Krishna
cowherd boy of great beauty
*gopis* know
be careful
   hoist up the flag.

*pp. 151–53*

⁂

*Sampler's Poetry Hall #12*

I'm in my room, and people are in theirs,
or because it's spring they may be outside
the new calves of the cows stay
close to Mommy. Show your friend.

I had a good idea, and it flew away.
Oh – put something Krishna conscious
   in the copy on the
back of the book. Don't just say
I'm homely, I drew these pictures.
Take the opportunity to preach.
Spring green pastures if I didn't
notice. Today was the (grand) opening
of the Govinda's Restaurant in Dublin. Wish
them well. Don't be unnecessarily
   clever
what caught your attention?
What was *worth* catching your attention?

If you fly a kite, if you get too many books
to read. I think you are doing all right in
your own way. They wrote me a
letter, "We are thinking of moving to
Florida." I was surprised. I found
today the grand opening of a tape
journal by me. Now, that's a cause
for celebration.

Through the swinging doors of the
   auditorium enter
and leave the poets. We had no assignment
ad cashews and a banana and a nice
peach. Don't forget Radha-Govinda -
you do forget Them but at night now
remember. And remember to read
in his books. Remember - at the time of
death all will be tested. It's called -
not *prayascitta* as you thought,
but test. Do you love,
What do you love?
See next life.

*pp. 164–65*

*Whirling Along*

Now, we give you time to breathe and be
yourself. I wanted to go under the light
hear music and write to it. To it?
You can be assured. I will give you
assistance.
Madhava and Rukmini
those eligible
going to Africa, to Panama, to hell,
Purgatory, to Easter week vacation,

Death, next life, Dublin,
a mother's womb.

Not going to whore house, streets,
*kirtana*, temple, woman's wiles,
lessons, classes, labor camps, place
in my mind forbidden for devotees.

You do things not deeply, say, "It's okay,
I'm not giving my heart to this. I just
need a little relief from my main
services." Do you say that?

Memories forty years ago pop up, but
I don't think to mention it. Maybe you
can put it in your talk-journal – that
nice stylish thin brown suit you had
even while you were living almost penniless.
God-awful, how you got through this life.
No, I can't follow all those fragments of
memories, worms, snails out after
sun-rain (with no shells) stuff rushing
down the drain.

The music whirls that way
and whirl it, we get whirled around together.
They are trying something they never tried.
Hare Krishna Hare Krishna, chant
on your head. Sit in a bed or shed and chant
he said, we are planning on big
things to improve. I said, Don't forget
mere survival. Be outer, talk with
secretary about dynamics of the temple.

This is no poem or song or *katha*, just quick notes
while a man is
bowing and bowing his viola,
while art demands you make up

Visvakarma told it made
ornaments, buildings.

Krishna science, bricks build up chimney,
Lord God, I must at least
hear what You have to say and write
better – since I'm not risking You
look inside yourself
try to improve your devotion
so, you'll be able to help others...chant.

*pp. 174–75*

❖ ❖ ❖

*Sampler's Poetry Hall #13*

I drink water, one warm slug. At the
first sign of pain, I don't catastrophize.
I'm following Dr. Marcus' orders.
Oh, but the pain! No, he says, don't
feel it, don't give in. Stand up straight.

So, I tried to watch a movie, thirty minutes of
"Jesus of Nazareth" and then go to bed early.
Think I'll make it. Each one alone. The
little children in this house don't have the
aches. But they ache as children who
don't what to make of life.

Hare Krishna. Twelve days before Easter.
The pain enters the cortex of the brain
it says – sorry about that. I say,
help yourself; I'm gonna be detached.

No, truly I'm not following Dr. Marcus
anymore. I've got my own idea how to
deal with this. Don't try to cure it,
but endure it and wait for it to go.

I'll be peaceful and active on the morrow.
The poem is a crow. A cow in the
pasture and a sheep. Beep, beep the car
goes in town but out here it's quiet
and if you can't say your *gayatris* nice
at least you can say Krishna twice
and lie down and figure it will leave in 20 hours
at most and you'll be fine, meantime
you are meant to be a soul and so don't
forget it.

*pp. 184–85*

⁂

*April Fool*

So, the man came out of the woods in his
April voice. I just want to be myself and
reach original sound. Ach!
I want to go back to Radha and Krishna
but we keep this dross.

April fool, here's a mismatch.
Get up your twisted hand. Whatever
happiness you feel will vaporize.
If you miss this chance, Srila Prabhupada said,
to ten thousand people or at least to one thousand
in Golden Gate Park and the followers,
the immediate cheering worshiping disciples,
withered down to ten percent or less
remaining – but whatever you do is
good for...

Breaking clichés I just want to room
with my mommy. In Vrindavan under quilt
they put two young children into one
bed in the heatless January room and
everyone could hear the banging and voices of
the guest house, dim lights, brown-out,
but at least they're in Vrindavan, in the

fortress and as householders if they don't get
up for *mangala-arati,* no one will
come after them – as long as
they pay their bill for the room.

Sorry, I couldn't make a song I long for a day
when I'll be qualified
to sing good stuff with you all.
I'll be with the guru then
just keeping awake with you now
a kind of fire watch
in case there's a blaze
Krishna conscious poet pots
plants and waters and remembers
holy master and notes – *hidalgo,*
means a mayor of God.

*pp. 193–94*

*Why No One Writes Me from Mayapur*

We beat a drum, geez a fellow's got to
run he was happy with me eating a
muffin with honey on it
I said, "I'll say good *gayatris,*"
but I never do.

Due dew on grass the cow's
quiet tragedy. I get to
live near them it's
doom, doom...that's
the world in the West,
not in India?
    Not as bad. I want to be that
way. Tell people here is where
Krishna stole the butter, here
is where I got initiated, Swami received
the toilet paper from bum

I didn't let Eliot into the storefront
Mukunda came and went to California
Hayagriva in beard and finger cymbal.
Broken window and
broken promises.

Here's the original brick, here in this
box we keep Swami's things, a mosquito
coil, it's all dispersed now. You
were given *vani* that is not lost.
Now, here's the best group,
here are the faithful *pujaris*.

No one writes me from Mayapur anymore
now, I am mundane splayed
out in my own head whereas
they are holy saints living with Gaura
Mahaprabhu as their best friend the
contrast to me
reading Rilke they're reading skies
and Ekacakra and holy *nama* why
write to a pooper like me?

It's got to be utilized properly
hop on a song and you
won't forget your worshipable
worship pop dad
plaid pants
break open old truths
until one day your "madness"
will be Krishna-centered, until then
the morning happens and I see
and the day goes on
not forever can you play.

*pp. 195--96*

❖ ❖ ❖

April 2,
Le Nectar, Nectaire
 Le Nectaro
The Drink of Devotion
the Ocean of Doubt
Dob
The Dob of Delight
By Srila Rupa Goswami
The Nectarino Ocean The true *Sindhu* of *Bhakti*.

*pp. 199–200*

Swami's lunch hard veggies.
Want something else? No, I take
as they give. I believe in
my master's direction – *sastra*
in my life.

*p. 201*

*Sampler's Poetry Hall #14*

April fool. Three pieces of mail hit the
floor from the chute at 2:45 p.m., right
on time, just as I was coming out of the bathroom
from my afternoon bowel movement.

It was mail for me. None of your business. One
man with the M.E. said he must
come to Eire to speak with me even if I
said, "No time." That's what I will say.
I have to write poems,
dry Srila Prabhupada's clothes on the radiator and
*gamcha*, hot and nice...

Therefore, I can't see anyone. I'm embarked

on a talking journal, and think I'll reread
*The Cloud of Unknowing.*

I have to keep quiet in the house as
I'm only a guest and never know when
someone is home or about to enter just
when I'm stomping San-pan blues
upstairs.

There are reasons why you shouldn't come
to see me: I'm not on my knees in prayer all
day, when I'm not in the half-lotus
chanting *japa*, or breathing from diaphragm or
watching movies to distract myself from
pain.

I am reading my master's books. I don't see
others in the tradition of Zen hermits. "Don't
try for it, madam," said Samuel Johnson –
an author isn't worth seeing; just read
his books if you like him.

So, to the Hall inmates, I say adieu now
in case there's no time later. May you
each discover happiness in God, serve Him
and know the soul's eternal dharma.

That's not a poem but a wish and
could be the best thing you ever get.
Sorry, I'm puffed-up. The green hall,
the stiff chairs, the nondevotee rhyme,
life, God in all, forget or not –
we will. And one act for Krishna is worth
a million not.

*pp. 208–9*

*Cowherd Boys Break Loose*

You can make mistakes, you know. You are not so above all that. "You're impertinent," a brother told me when I mailed out *Guru Reform Notebook*.

Please sir, we expected a song not
these wrongs. We expected a song...
So, K.C. people are good, bright faces.
We expected.
Keep writing what comes. I eschewed a
dream. I offered the porridge even if
salty to the Lord and didn't know for
sure what was what.
Krishna and Madhu-mangala. Krishna the
parents. I sing in those words. I am a
person of flesh and body and I in gas and
electric neurons. Oh, please be
true, he said, I am the priest

I sport with the boys
crazy loony without
the parents and *brahmanas* we
are somersaulting making fun
of girls' purity and all
strictures – cowherd boy
stuff mock the day is long.

Krishna, clear of nescience. My favorite T.P. stands
to make stately announcement –
No *sannyasis* can park
their RVs under the trees near the church,
the neighbors object. No more please
the day is short enough and we have to meet

no meat sense enjoy
God of *isvara* is fact
Don't imitate
or pollute

be who you are, follow your
guru and your own way and serve Krishna
 purify what you've got. I love
Krishna and ask His help.

*pp. 220–21*

⁂

*Little Song Before Dawn*

Lay me down, get up and serve swerve the
man, don't depend on the fellows who can
be your guides.

The Lord of all is not a crazy man or limited in any
way. He is pure. You can be relaxed and loping free.
Sure, why not? But I want to see your muscles flexed
and working out.

Before dawn devotees gather and
sing together and offer the best they can.
Let it be direct holy in Vaisnava *parampara*.
The moon is a Vaisnava.

The best person is the original person Brahma,
and he is not the ultimate best. He wants to
be born as grass outside Vrindavan so
the Vrajavasis will step on him.

I am wishing to serve my friends
make the magazine better
don't try to crash my gate
just be a good fellow and write
according to what you have learned
do *lectio divina*
ruminate your cereal
be holy this week and don't
disgrace us / I will die in

medium *rasa*, the time will drop
away, everyone here will vanish.

And only a few books will help
people in the future. Or many?
Chant Hare Krishna.

*pp. 221–22*

⁂

The counter of the bar
the man wild playing the cymbals
*kirtana* beat is for fired up
devotees who can stomp
God's glory isn't for quiet
meditation but a blast get together
crashing down rhythms of conch
and cymbals and lots of heavy drums
expert Bengali and rock beat
from Poland and hand clap they
smile and sweat in the group inner and
women and children and cooled down
sort of people got to the edges of the
crowd and peter out after ten minutes...

Get a little spark in your soul
before it's too late. Rev it hype it
up some say, it's just an outer thing of energy
and jumping they had to do in their blood

Well, that might be but let me see
your spirit of courage and virtue in another
way and don't put down this front-line
row of charge and shout...

Religion is good dancin' for God in the
road we're on the bus to Mathura, we are
walking around Govardhana, we're going down
the street with a big *kirtana* party and

no one is complaining and it's India or
it's Poland, New York and no
one is dropping out if the people police
and hooligans come
we're the ones and Lord Caitanya
is glad.

#2

But there is also time for reflection
and mood of quiet soul, just as after
you went in to see your spiritual master
and he was alone with only a small
desk lamp at night or pre-dawn and
that's only a memory now
and not even that...
you've got something way inside to
keep you going, but it doesn't seem like
much...

Sad call it,
wanting that essence that brought
you as one person to his storefront,
to his feet, not wanting to lose it,
but as you look back over the decades
and mistakes – couldn't not make them
you are not exactly sure where you
are now or what will happen –
and how you lost the thing, the essential
"good devotee" tag they gave you and
why you are cynical now
and alone.

What have you got? Where is Swamiji
and his men? Why separate him from his
leading followers and his mission in
the institutional form? Is it *I* who
separated? Did it happen? If
they say, "it doesn't happen in

true men" are they always right?
And the troublemaker schisms and the
lawyers and the whole crunch
a little person (each) gets a lost-
feeling and *that* too is another
way to be with you,
turning to you
in whatever slow music we can
find that links us to divine message
presence – tell *that* and you are
preaching too.

*pp. 227–30*

*Sampler's Poetry Hall #15*

Wind messages. A poet. The spurt of ink from
the peaceful pen – *santa-rasa*. So, I finished
my reading of *NOD* and finished my attendance at
the Poetry Hall and the series called
"Preachers I Have Known." I am satisfied
to start new.

If God will allow it. In the Jesus film
by Zeffirelli, the Zealots want violent
rebellion but Joseph and the rabbi said
the Messiah will bring peace and he points to
eternal salvation. That's all right.
Jagannatha Swami is also a peaceful Lord and
Lord Caitanya, who is Jagannatha Himself,
teaches a peaceful revolution by
*sankirtana*.

Thank you, Mrs. Sampler and poets in the green
hall for allowing a devotee of Krishna and
Prabhupada to join you. I wish I could
have sung wonderful songs of Krishna *bhakti*

to sweep you into the current of
love of God. No metaphysical argument or
asking you to join a movement – but to
give you *The Nectar of Devotion*.

I could not in a way that would over-
whelm your poetry-hungry hearts and
minds. I'm not a skilled man. But the
word "Krishna" has appeared in the
hall. And from you I gained the
enthusiasm of those who want to write.
Why are we doing this? What love? Who
is the Lord? No one? Your self?
Wherever you go,
may God's name come to you at the end.

*pp. 231–33*

❦ ❦ ❦

# BIBLIOGRAPHY

**Poems, Volume One**

*Every Day, Just Write* – Volume Four, *Our Group at Nilacala*. Port Royal, PA, Gita-nagari Press, 1997.

*EJW* – Volume Five, *Room 42*. Port Royal, Gita-nagari Press, 1997.

*EJW* – Volume Six, *A Writer of Pieces*. Port Royal, Gita-nagari Press, 1997.

*EJW* – Volume Seven, *Simplicity in Irish Spring*. Port Royal, Gita-nagari Press, 1997.

*EJW* – Volume Eight, *The Primrose Path*. Port Royal, Gita-nagari Press, 1997.

*EJW* – Volume Nine, *Something Reading or Writing, Something Reading or Writing*. Port Royal, Gita-nagari Press, 1997.

*EJW* – Volume Ten, *Choosing to be Alone*. Port Royal, Gita-nagari Press, 1997.

*EJW* – Volume Eleven, *Sacrifice for the Bhagavatam*. Port Royal, Gita-nagari Press, 1997.

*EJW* – Volume Twelve, *My Secret Life*. Port Royal, Gita-nagari Press, 1997.

*EJW* – Volume Thirteen, *Accepting My Limits*. Port Royal, Gita-nagari Press, 1997.

*EJW* – Volume Fourteen, *The Diary as Devotion*. Port Roral, Gita-nagari Press, 1997.

*EJW* – Volume Fifteen, *Econoline Preacher*. Port Royal, Gita-nagari Press, 1997.

*EJW* – Volume Sixteen, *Put Yourself Out*. Port Royal, Gita-nagari Press, 1997.

*EJW* – Volume Seventeen, *Blackberries*. Port Royal, Gita-nagari Press, 1998.

*EJW* – Volume Eighteen, *Free Kartikka*. Port Royal, Gita-nagari Press, 1998.

*EJW* – Volume Nineteen, *Radha-Govinda, We Hardly Knew Ya*. Port Royal, Gita-nagari Press, 1998.

**Poems, Volume Two**

*Every Day, Just Write* – Volume Twenty, *The Lord Reigneth*. Port Royal, PA, Gita-nagari Press, 1998.

*EJW* – Volume Twenty-One, *Getting Through*. Port Royal, Gita-nagari Press, 1998.

*EJW* – Volume Twenty-Two, *Return to Quiet Heroics*. Port Royal, Gita-nagari Press, 1998.

*EJW* – Volume Twenty-Three, *The Best Gostyhanandi*. Port Royal, Gita-nagari Press, 1998.

*EJW* – Volume Twenty-Four, *Approaching Gaura-purnima*. Port Royal, Gita-nagari Press, 1998.

*EJW* – Volume Twenty-Five, *The Ocean and the Desert*. Port Royal, Gita-nagari Press, 1998.

## ABOUT THE AUTHORS

**Satsvarupa dasa Goswami** is a writer, poet, and artist. He is also the author of Srila Prabhupada's authorized biography, *Srila Prabhupada-lilamrta*. While previously traveling, lecturing and instructing disciples worldwide, he has published many books including poems, memoirs, essays and novels.

**Rev. John F. Endler** is a senior Baptist minister who serves a congregation in Hartford, Connecticut.

www.ingramcontent.com/pod-product-compliance
Lightning Source LLC
Chambersburg PA
CBHW030844030726
47495CB00005B/1360
*9781942770978*